Creating and Digitizing Language Corpora
Volume 2: Diachronic Databases

Also by the editors

CREATING AND DIGITIZING LANGUAGE CORPORA
Volume 1: Synchronic Databases

Creating and Digitizing Language Corpora

Volume 2: Diachronic Databases

Edited by

Joan C. Beal
University of Sheffield

Karen P. Corrigan and Hermann L. Moisl
Newcastle University

Foreword by Shana Poplack
University of Ottawa

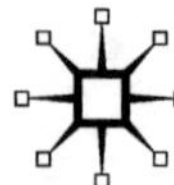

First published 2007 by
PALGRAVE MACMILLAN
Houndmills, Basingstoke, Hampshire RG21 6XS and
175 Fifth Avenue, New York, N. Y. 10010
Companies and representatives throughout the world

PALGRAVE MACMILLAN is the global academic imprint of the Palgrave Macmillan division of St. Martin's Press, LLC and of Palgrave Macmillan Ltd. Macmillan® is a registered trademark in the United States, United Kingdom and other countries. Palgrave is a registered trademark in the European Union and other countries.

ISBN-13: 978–1–4039–4367–5
ISBN-10: 1–4039–4367–2

This book is printed on paper suitable for recycling and made from fully managed and sustained forest sources.

A catalogue record for this book is available from the British Library.

A catalogue record for this book is available from the Library of Congress.

10 9 8 7 6 5 4 3 2 1
16 15 14 13 12 11 10 09 08 07

Printed and bound in Great Britain by
Antony Rowe Ltd, Chippenham and Eastbourne

Contents

List of Tables

List of Figures

Foreword

Only two or three decades ago, those of us who had the patience and the wherewithal to construct a computerized corpus of recorded speech, however clunky, were the envy of our colleagues. In those days, linguists interested in quantitative analysis simply slogged through their audio-tapes, extracting unfathomable quantities of data by hand. Cedergren, to name but one notable example, analyzed 53,038(!) tokens of phonological variables, culled individually from her tapes, in her 1973 analysis of Panamanian Spanish.

The gold standard for transcribed corpora at the time was the concordance, possessed by a fortunate few, and coveted by all who were doomed to manual extraction. Of course the vintage concordance was largely limited to lexically-based retrieval, but at least it was searchable. The papers that Joan Beal, Karen Corrigan and Hermann Moisl have assembled in these companion volumes are eloquent testimony to how far the field of corpus linguistics – now rife with electronic corpora – has come in so short a time.

Building a corpus arguably involves a greater investment in time, resources and energy than any other type of linguistic activity. Decisions are legion at every stage of the process: sampling, ensuring representativeness, collecting data, transcribing them, correcting, standardizing the transcription, correcting, tagging and markup, correcting, and facilitating retrieval. Adding to the challenge is the fact that at the outset of the project the researcher is often not even familiar enough with the materials to make the best decisions, and changing midstream is costly and time-consuming. What could possibly make such a huge front-end investment worthwhile? Dealing with corpora at every stage of development, from fledgling endeavours to large-scale, heavily exploited enterprises, these reports offer a state-of-the-art synthesis of the problems researchers have encountered and the solutions they have adopted to deal with them.

The focus of these volumes is on *unconventional* corpora, like the non-standard, regional and dialectal varieties of speech, creole texts, child language, and the correspondence, business transactions, prose and plays of past centuries discussed here. Each poses problems hardly imaginable to the early builders of more orthodox corpora based on written or standard materials. The unifying question is how to 'tame' them, in the editors' terminology. Taming, as understood here, is largely a question of representation: How to represent forms for which there is no standard orthography, what to represent, how much to annotate, how much analysis to impose on the materials, how to represent ambiguities and indeterminacies, how to represent the finished product to the end-user. Noting the diversity, not only in the models underlying different corpora but also in their methods of encoding and analysis, the editors, themselves seasoned corpus builders, question whether it is reasonable or even feasible to aim for standardized protocols of the kind employed in traditional corpora for the collection, transcription, annotation and preservation of their less conventional counterparts.

Perhaps the first to grapple with the problem of taming unconventional data were the Sankoff-Cedergren team, whose *Montreal French Corpus* (Sankoff and Sankoff 1973) was built to elucidate a stigmatized variety previously widely believed to be an incorrect version of European French. Their goal was to show that the 'deviant' forms were part of a complex sociolinguistic structure, by tapping into different sources of speech variation: inter-individual, intra-individual and intra-linguistic. Chief among the problems inherent in such an endeavour was the issue of representativeness: How to guarantee representativeness of all the possible diversity in speech, while maintaining randomness in the selection of informants? They achieved this by implementing a detailed sampling frame, which, in contrast to their material procedures, has not yet been superseded. Their problems and solutions hark back to a simpler time, especially as compared with those corpus linguists face today. The transcription protocol – standard orthography – was dictated by the number of symbols on the punch keyboard for the IBM computer cards they used. Correction was effected by removing the card containing the error and inserting a correctly punched card in its place. The 100,000 cards containing the transcriptions then had to be converted into reams of computer printouts – and all without dropping a single card! In an era in which an entire corpus can be carried around on a memory stick or an iPod, it is worth noting that the print concordance of the 3.5 million-word *Ottawa-Hull French Corpus* (Poplack 1989), for example, occupies an entire wall – floor to ceiling – of the Ottawa Sociolinguistics Lab. The technology was primitive.

Since then, striking advances, not only in terms of hardware, but also in the area of annotation systems, have revolutionized corpus linguistics. No protocol has yet emerged as standard, though – as observed by the editors in initiating this project. So it's no surprise that the issue of annotation enjoys pride of place in these volumes, with researchers weighing in on what to annotate, how much detail to include, and whether it is preferable to replicate markup schemes of other corpora or tailor them to one's own. It is clear that the old problem of finding the right balance of quantity, recoverability and faithfulness is still with us. Faithfulness at every linguistic level to data with much inherent variability (i.e. all speech, and many older and/or nonstandard written texts) inevitably results in diminished recoverability and less quantity. Without sufficient quantity, statistical significance is impossible to establish and full cross-cutting conditioning yields mostly empty cells. Optimum recoverability comes at the expense of less faithfulness to the many variant realizations of what is underlyingly a single form.

Each of the contributors to these volumes grapples with these problems in their own way. Some prefer to abandon one or more of the principles, others respond with complicated interfaces. As a result, the corpora described in this collection illustrate the full gamut of possibilities, from an annotation system so rich and complex that it already incorporates a good deal of the linguistic analysis, at one extreme, to virtually no markup whatsoever at the other. Linkage of transcripts to (audio and video) recordings and syntactic parsing will no doubt the wave of the future.

The projected use of the corpus, as *end-product or tool,* is clearly the determining factor. Those for whom the corpus is a tool tend to advocate minimal annotation. These researchers are able to tolerate more indeterminacy and ambiguity, either because they have determined that it will not affect what they're looking for (e.g. a number of the corpora described here provide no detail on phonetic form or discourse processes), or because the sheer volume of data available allows them to omit the ambiguous cases or neutralize errors through large-scale quantitative analysis. Others, for whom the corpus is the end-product, tend to aim for consistency with guidelines for existing corpora, even if these do not seem immediately relevant to the proposed research. So what is the best annotation system? The amalgamated wisdom to be gleaned from these contributions: the one that works for you. At the moment, then, the answer to the editors' query regarding the feasibility of standardizing transcription protocols seems to be a qualified 'no'.

Comparatively less emphasis is placed on the issue of *representativeness*, the extent to which the sample of observations drawn from the corpus corresponds to the parent population. Achieving representativeness for (socio)linguistic purposes involves identifying the major sources of variation in the population (of speakers and utterances) and taking them into account while constructing the sample. Few corpora in these volumes, by necessity or design, claim to be representative in the sense of Sankoff (1988). Rather, in most of these contributions, (as in much social science research more generally), the sample is opportunistic. This is an issue that every corpus must come to terms with, since even large numbers of observations cannot compensate for a sample frame from which the major sources of variation are missing. To the extent that the sample does not span the variant answers to the research question, pursuit of that question via that corpus can only be spurious.

Whether representativeness or annotation is more fundamental to the eventual utility of the corpus is a moot point. It is worth noting, however, that the awkward, and for some, simplistic, transcription protocols of early unconventional corpora did nothing to diminish their interest, value and current relevance. Hundreds of studies have been, and continue to be, based on them, perhaps because the research questions they were constructed to answer are still burning ones. The same is of course true of a number of the established corpora described in these volumes, and no doubt will be of the many more incipient ones as well. The good news is that these repositories have an enduring value that far transcends our automated treatment and handling of them.

I end this foreword by returning to the question I posed at the beginning. What could possibly make the huge front-end investment required to build a corpus worthwhile? Obvious answers include the enormously enhanced speed of data collection, enabling consideration of ever greater quantities of data with relatively little extra effort. This in turn increases the chances of locating rare tokens, achieving statistical significance and determining which factors condition the choice between alternating forms. All of these are inestimable boons for quantitative analysis, but they pale in comparison to what for me remains the most exciting aspect of corpus work: the opportunity it affords to serendipitously discover what one wasn't looking for, to characterize the patterned nature of linguistic heterogeneity, and in particular the hidden, unsuspected or 'irrational' constraints that are simply inaccessible to introspection or casual perusal.

How much closer are we to the goal of agreeing on a standardized annotation? Well, we aren't there yet, though only time will tell. In the interim, anyone who has ever considered building a corpus or is engaged in doing so now will want to have a copy of this book close at hand. The wide variety of contributions convey much of the excitement of this burgeoning field. Despite inevitable differences in methods and projected end uses, the common thread is the shared goal of finding and implementing the best practices in corpus construction and preservation. These companion volumes, examining both synchronic and diachronic corpara, serve as a model for how to achieve them. For this, we can only be grateful to the editors, who encouraged such stimulating dialogue.

SHANA POPLACK

References

Cedergren, Henrietta. 1973. 'Interplay of social and linguistic factors in Panama'. PhD dissertation, Cornell University.

Poplack, Shana. 1989. 'The care and handling of a mega-corpus'. *Language Variation and Change* (Current Issues in Linguistic Theory, 52), ed. by R. Fasold and D. Schiffrin, pp. 411–451. Philadelphia: John Benjamins.

Sankoff, David. 1988. 'Problems of representativeness'. *Sociolinguistics. An International Handbook of the Science of Language and Society*, Vol. 2, ed. by U. Ammon, N. Dittmar and K. J. Mattheier, pp. 899–903. Berlin: Walter de Gruyter.

Sankoff, David and Sankoff, Gillian. 1973. 'Sample survey methods and computer-assisted analysis in the study of grammatical variation'. *Canadian Languages in their Social Context*, ed. by R. Darnell, pp. 7–63. Edmonton: Linguistic Research Inc.

Notes on the Contributors

Will Allen worked from 2001 to 2005 as a Research Associate on the AHRC-funded Newcastle Electronic Corpus of Tyneside English (NECTE) project in the School of English Literature, Language and Linguistics at Newcastle University. Since then he has been working as a Consultant Trainer for Netskills, Newcastle University, delivering and developing internet-related training.

Joan C. Beal was a Senior Lecturer in English Language at Newcastle University until moving to the University of Sheffield in 2001. She was Co-investigator on the NECTE project at Newcastle and is currently Professor of English Language and Director of the National Centre for English Cultural Tradition. Recent publications include *English in Modern Times* (2004) and *Language and Region* (2006).

Karen P. Corrigan has held lectureships at University College Dublin and the Universities of Edinburgh and York (UK). She was Principal Investigator on the NECTE project and is currently a Reader in Linguistics and English Language at Newcastle University. She was awarded a Leverhulme Trust Research Fellowship (2000–02) and has recently published *Syntax and Variation* (2005) (with Leonie Cornips).

David Denison is Professor of English Linguistics at the University of Manchester and has held visiting posts in Amsterdam, Vancouver, Santiago de Compostela and Paris. Recent jointly edited publications include *Fuzzy Grammar* (2004) and *A History of the English Language* (2006). He is a founding editor of the journal *English Language and Linguistics*.

Susan Fitzmaurice has held academic posts at the Universities of Cape Town, Cambridge and Northern Arizona. She is currently Professor of English Language at the University of Sheffield. She publishes widely on socio-historical linguistics and pragmatics using the Network of Eighteenth Century English Texts as a major data source.

Elizabeth Gordon taught at the University of Canterbury from 1967 until she retired in 2003 as an Associate Professor. She is co-leader of the University of Canterbury research team on Origins of New Zealand English (ONZE) and one of the authors of *New Zealand English: Its Origins and Evolution* (2004).

Jennifer Hay is a Senior Lecturer in the Department of Linguistics at the University of Canterbury and is also a member of the ONZE team. Recent publications include *Causes and Consequences of Word Structure* (2003), *New Zealand English: Its Origins and Evolution* (co-author, 2004) and *Probabilistic Linguistics* (co-editor, 2003).

Raymond Hickey studied for postgraduate degrees at Trinity College, Dublin and at Kiel, Germany. He completed his German Habilitation in Bonn in 1985 and has held professorial appointments at the universities of Bonn, Munich, Bayreuth and, currently, Essen. His recent publications include *A Source Book for Irish English* (2002), *Corpus Presenter* (2003) and *Legacies of Colonial English* (2005).

Francis Jones is a literary translator and Senior Lecturer in Applied Linguistics at Newcastle University. His recent book *Prevoditeljev put* (2004) examines ideology, identity and literary translation studies against the break-up of Yugoslavia. Aided by a British Academy grant, he is currently researching poetry translation processes.

Margaret Maclagan is a Senior Lecturer in Communication Disorders at the University of Canterbury, NZ. She is another member of the ONZE research team and was one of the authors of *New Zealand English: Its Origins and Evolution* (2004).

Warren Maguire is in the final stages of his PhD research on vocalic mergers in Tyneside English at Newcastle University and was formerly a Research Associate on the NECTE project. He currently works as a Research Associate on another AHRC-funded project, namely, 'Sound Comparisons: Dialect and Language Comparison and Classification by Phonetic Similarity' at Edinburgh University.

Anneli Meurman-Solin is a Lecturer in English Philology at Helsinki University. She has published widely in the fields of historical dialectology/stylistics and corpus linguistics. She is currently a Fellow of the Helsinki Collegium for Advanced Studies and acts as a domain leader for a research strand at the Research Unit for Variation, Contacts and Change in English.

Hermann L. Moisl is a Senior Lecturer in Computational Linguistics at Newcastle University and he was Co-investigator on the NECTE project. His interests and publications are in natural language processing, neural modelling of language, and multivariate analysis of corpora.

Terttu Nevalainen is Professor of English Philology at the University of Helsinki and the Director of the Research Unit for Variation, Contacts and Change in English. Her publications include: 'Early Modern English lexis and semantics', in *The Cambridge History of the English Language* (1999), *Historical Sociolinguistics* (2003, with H. Raumolin-Brunberg) and *An Introduction to Early Modern English* (2006).

Helena Raumolin-Brunberg is a Senior Scholar in the Research Unit for the Study of Variation, Contacts and Change in English at Helsinki University. Her interests include historical sociolinguistics, language change and corpus linguistics. She has recently published *Historical Sociolinguistics* (2003, with Terttu Nevalainen).

Naomi Standen has been Lecturer in Chinese History at the University of Newcastle since 2000, having previously worked at the University of Wisconsin-Superior and St John's College, Oxford. She is co-editor of *Frontiers in Question: Eurasian Borderlands, 700–1700* (1999), and author of *Unbounded Loyalty: Frontier Crossing in Liao China* (forthcoming 2007).

Ann Taylor is currently a Research Fellow at the University of York. In cooperation with colleagues at the Universities of York, Pennsylvania and Helsinki, she has been instrumental in creating syntactically annotated corpora for Old, Middle, and Early Modern English, as well as publishing on historical variation in English and Greek.

Linda van Bergen obtained her PhD from the University of Manchester in 2000 and subsequently held a British Academy Postdoctoral Fellowship at the University of York. She is now a lecturer in English Language at the University of Edinburgh. Her publications include *Pronouns and Word Order in Old English* (2003).

List of Abbreviations

AHDS	Arts and Humanities Data Service
AHRB	Arts and Humanities Research Board
AHRC	Arts and Humanities Research Council
ASCII	American National Standard Code for Information Exchange
ASP	Active Server Pages
BNC	British National Corpus
CC	Canterbury Corpus
CEEC	Corpus of Early English Correspondence
CEECE	Corpus of Early English Correspondence Extension
CEECS	Corpus of Early English Correspondence Sampler
CELEX	Centre for Lexical Information
CLAWS	Constituent Likelihood Automatic Word-tagging System
CLEP	Corpus of Late Eighteenth-Century Prose
CONCE	Corpus of Nineteenth-century English
CS	Code-switching
CSC	Corpus of Scottish Correspondence
DAT	Digital audio tape
DOE	*Dictionary of Old English*
DTD	Document Type Definition
ECOS	Edinburgh Corpus of Older Scots
ESRC	Economic and Social Research Council
FTP	File Transfer Protocol
HC	Helsinki Corpus of English Texts
HTML	HyperText Markup Language
IA	Intermediate Archive
ICAME	International Computer Archive of Modern and Medieval English
ICLAVE	International Conference on Language Variation in Europe
IHD	Institute for Historical Dialectology
IPA	International Phonetic Alphabet
LAEME	Linguistic Atlas of Early Middle English
LALME	Linguistic Atlas of Late Medieval English
LAOS	Linguistic Atlas of Older Scots
LIDES	Language Interaction Data Exchange System

MU	Mobile Unit
NAS	National Archives of Scotland
NECTE	Newcastle Electronic Corpus of Tyneside English
NEET	Network of Eighteenth-Century English Texts
OED	*Oxford English Dictionary*
ONZE	Origins of New Zealand English
OTA	Oxford Text Archive
OTP	Orthographic Transcription Protocol
OU	Overall Unit
PCEEC	Parsed Corpus of Early English Correspondence
PDV	Putative Diasystemic Variable
PPCME2	Penn–Helsinki Parsed Corpus of Middle English II
PVC	Phonological Variation and Change in Contemporary English
SCOTS	Scottish Corpus of Texts and Speech
SGML	Standard Generalized Mark-up Language
SPSS	Statistical Package for the Social Sciences
SQL	Structured Query Language
SS15	Fifteenth Sociolinguistics Symposium
SSRC	Social Science Research Council
TACT	Text Analysis Computing Tools
TEI	Text Encoding Initiative
TLS	Tyneside Linguistic Survey
UCREL	University Centre for Corpus Research on Language
UKLVC	UK Language Variation and Change Conference
VARIENG	Research Unit for Variation and Change in English
XHTML	Extensible HyperText Markup Language
XML	Extensible Markup Language
XSLT	Extensible Stylesheet Language Transformations
YCOE	York–Toronto–Helsinki Parsed Corpus of Old English Prose

1
Taming Digital Voices and Texts: Models and Methods for Handling Unconventional Diachronic Corpora

Joan C. Beal, Karen P. Corrigan and Hermann L. Moisl

1 Stimulus for the volume and its overarching aim

Four of the contributions to Volume 2 (Allen, Beal, Corrigan, Maguire and Moisl; Standen and Jones; Meurman-Solin; and Raumolin-Brunberg and Nevalainen) arose from invited presentations at the workshop on 'Models and Methods in the Handling of Unconventional Digital Corpora' organized by the editors of the present volume that was held in April 2004 during the Fifteenth Sociolinguistics Symposium (SS15) at Newcastle University. The book project then evolved by inviting further contributions from key corpus creators so that the companion volumes would contain treatments outlining the models and methods underpinning a variety of digitized diachronic and synchronic corpora with a view to highlighting synergies and points of contrast between them. The overarching aim of the project is to establish whether or not annotation standards and guidelines of the kind already employed in the creation of more conventional corpora on standard spoken and written Englishes, such as the British National Corpus (http://info.ox.ac.uk/bnc) and the Bank of English (http://titania.cobuild.collins.co.uk/boe_info.html), should be extended to less conventional corpora so that they too might be 'tamed' in similar ways.

Since the development of the Brown corpus in the 1960s (see Francis and Kučera, 1964), the variety of electronic corpora now available to the linguistics community and the analytical tools developed to successfully mine these data have gone hand in hand with improvements in standards and guidelines for corpus creation and encoding. Historical and vernacular electronic corpora of the kinds described in Volume 2 pose an array of additional problems as regards standards, since the creation of such databases often requires the encoder to come to the task *ab initio*. As such, while the resultant corpora are clearly high quality resources in their own right (and extremely valuable research tools within the discipline to which they relate), there is considerable variation in the models and methods used in the collection of these digital corpora and in their subsequent encoding and analysis, largely because the underlying theoretical goals and assumptions of the researchers are quite distinctive (cf. Ochs, 1999; McEnery and Wilson, 2001; Milroy and Gordon, 2003, p. 143; section 2.2). There are marked differences, for instance, in the nature of the data contained therein and they also vary in: (i) the levels of phonetic, lexical, grammatical and semantic annotation that they encode; (ii) the means by which information is accessed/retrieved by the end-user and the manner in which it is displayed (whether or not the written/spoken word or multilingual texts are aligned, for example).

Advances in technology, from the ability to digitize historical manuscript materials and field recordings to the dramatic improvements in computer hardware, software, storage facilities and analytical tools, have enabled the collection and organization of such data sets into a growing number of user-friendly electronic corpora. The latter have the potential to offer new insights into linguistic universals, for instance, since they allow, for the first time, rapid, systematic and efficient comparisons to be made between languages across both time (real/apparent) and space (geographical). In addition, these corpora should be utilizable by researchers from a range of disciplines so that they are potentially as accessible to the socio-phonetician as they are to the discourse analyst or historical linguist in keeping with the aspirations of the Linguistic Data Consortium and Oxford Text Archive, inter alia.

These companion volumes are unique, since public output to date has primarily concentrated on describing and assessing the models and methods which underpin conventional corpora and the annotation standards/analytical tools developed specifically for them.[1]

2 Outline of contributions and their methodologies

Will Allen, Joan Beal, Karen Corrigan, Warren Maguire and Hermann Moisl in their chapter discuss the issues which arose in the compilation of the Newcastle Electronic Corpus of Tyneside English (NECTE). This corpus differs from all the others described in these volumes in various ways, not least of which is that the primary data from which it is compiled consist of spoken rather than written material. As a corpus of twentieth-century English, consisting of data recorded in 1969 and 1994, but including speakers born as early as 1889, it covers a period which has only very recently come to the attention of historical linguists (Mair, forthcoming). Like the corpora described in the chapters by Tagliamonte and by Anderwald and Wagner (both Volume 1), the NECTE corpus consists of data from a non-standard variety of (English) English. However, the NECTE corpus is more complex in that it makes available to researchers data in a number of formats: orthographic transcription, phonetic transcription and sound files, as well as providing TEI headers which include detailed social information about the speakers and the circumstances in which they were recorded. The team compiling the NECTE corpus set out both to preserve and make available data from two sociolinguistic surveys of Tyneside, both groundbreaking in their own ways: the *Tyneside Linguistic Survey* (Strang, 1968) and *Phonological Variation and Change in Contemporary Spoken English* (Milroy *et al.*, 1997). The methodologies of these two surveys, and the difficulties encountered in attempting to trace and preserve all materials from the former, are described here.

Other chapters in this volume discuss the challenges posed by attempts to provide 'diplomatic' editions of early texts, in which spelling and punctuation are highly variable. The transcription of spoken, regional data throws up similar problems, since dialect words often have no fixed spelling: indeed, some have never been encountered in print before. This chapter outlines the procedures which were followed by the NECTE team in reaching decisions about transcription and in creating a glossary.

Another challenge faced by the NECTE team was that of tagging the orthographic transcription files: at the outset they were pessimistic about the suitability of automatic tagging programmes designed for use with Standard English texts. However, it did prove possible to adapt CLAWS4 for this purpose.

The NECTE corpus is a Text Encoding Initiative (TEI)-conformant XML document, the standard recommended by the Arts and Humanities Data Service. As van Bergen & Denison (this volume) also point out, potential end-users are not all familiar with these standards, so the next phase of NECTE will involve the creation of style sheets which will convert the NECTE corpus into HTML and plain text versions for ease of visualization.

Susan Fitzmaurice's chapter describes a diachronic corpus designed not to be representative of the language of the period covered (1653–1762), but rather to provide a sample of the written repertoire of a network of individuals living between 1631 and 1762, with letters from a number of contemporary writers unconnected with this network included as a control. As such, it demonstrates, alongside Raumolin-Brunberg and Nevalainen (this volume) the ways in which diachronic corpora can be used for investigations in the emerging discipline of historical sociolinguistics (Nevalainen and Raumolin-Brunberg, 2003). In particular, the Network of Eighteenth-Century English Texts (NEET) is designed to address issues raised by the application of social network theory (Milroy, 1987) to historical (socio) linguistics (Tieken-Boon van Ostade, 1996, 2000a, 2000b), and a number of sample analyses are provided in this chapter. Texts included in this corpus come from four genres: letters, essays, fiction and drama, but it is the letters which pose the greatest challenges with regard to methods of corpus creation and annotation. Although searchable text cannot preserve the visual character of autograph manuscripts, the corpus preserves as far as possible the spellings, abbreviations, deletions and insertions found in the originals. However, this faithfulness to the original is at the expense of accessibility, so, in order to enable tagging, parallel, modernized text files had to be produced for some of the texts in the corpus. This need for parallel versions of texts when these are to be subjected to different levels of analysis is also a feature of the NECTE corpus and the LIDES project (Allen *et al.*, this volume, and Gardner-Chloros *et al.*, Volume 1). Even with modernized text as input, Fitzmaurice found that the automatic tagger designed for use with modern American English had to be substantially adapted in order to facilitate analysis of eighteenth-century texts. Once again, there is a parallel here with the way in which the CLAWS tagger had to be adapted in order to work with a regional variety of twentieth-century English (Allen *et al.*, this volume). Like the other corpora discussed in this volume, the NEET corpus holds potential interest for scholars from a range of disciplines, including historical and literary studies. Fitzmaurice points out here the importance of including as much historical, textual and bibliographical information as possible in the header, in order to facilitate access. Like Raumolin-Brunberg and Nevalainen (this Volume), she notes that, when creating headers for diachronic corpora, matters such as social classification are not straightforward, since any such categorization depends on knowledge of the ranks and strata of society in the eighteenth century.

Elizabeth Gordon, Margaret Maclagan and Jen Hay describe the Origins of New Zealand English (ONZE) corpus, which contains recordings of people born in New Zealand from the 1850s to the 1980s, that is, from shortly after the official start of the European settlement of New Zealand in 1840. It consists of three separate collections: (i) the Mobile Unit (MU) archive of speakers born between 1851 and 1910, (ii) the Intermediate Archive (IA) of speakers born between 1890 and 1930, and (iii) the Canterbury Corpus (CC) of speakers born between 1930 and 1984, which began in 1994 and has been added to each year since. The ONZE project was originally set up to study the process of new dialect development in New Zealand using the MU corpus, but is now also using the other two as well for both diachronic and synchronic study of New Zealand English.

The chapter is in four main parts. As its title indicates, the first part, 'Format and purpose of the archives', gives a detailed account of the above component parts of the ONZE corpus, and raises methodological issues specific to each: for MU reorganization of spoken material and identification of speakers, for IA dealing with different types of recordings, and for CC confidentiality with respect to still-living speakers. The second part, 'Preparation of the data', describes the reworking of MU, IA and CC by the ONZE project via re-recording onto modern media and orthographic transcription of the recordings. It also gives details of how information about speakers is held in databases, and refers to work which is under way to integrate this information with relevant analytical results. The third part, 'Making the data available to researchers', first deals with copyright issues, and then outlines several measures 'towards a digital interactive format for the corpus' (p. 94): time-alignment of audio and associated transcriptions using the Transcriber application, conversion to Praat-compatible format to enable acoustic analysis, and development of a web-based application for viewing, filtering and searching the time-aligned corpus. Further developments are projected for streamlining the current technicalities of accessing the desired part of the corpus and to go beyond orthographic to phonological search functionality. The fourth and final part, 'Use of the corpus', outlines the types of analysis that have been carried out on the corpus to date. Since the original aim of the ONZE project was to trace the development of the New Zealand accent, the initial analyses were phonetic/phonological and, more specifically, were of three types, each of which is briefly described: auditory perceptual, auditory quantitative and acoustic. The authors note that the digital formatting of the material will enable 'a much broader perspective on sound change than has so far been possible' (p. 101): grammatical analyses beyond the phonological level, as well as extraction of information of interest to non-linguistic researchers like historians. A conclusion summarizes the discussion.

Raymond Hickey's chapter describes a diachronic textual corpus of Irish English spanning 600 years from the early fourteenth century to the twentieth. As such, it provides a useful historical overview for the variety tackled from a purely synchronic perspective by Kallen and Kirk in their contribution to Volume 1. The Hickey corpus also relates to other atlas-type projects such as the Syntactic Atlas of Dutch discussed in Volume 1 by Barbiers *et al.*

A Corpus of Irish English (originally published as Hickey, 2003) aimed to collect a sample of Irish English texts that could be analysed so as to further our understanding of the genetic development of Irish English (Filppula, 1999) and to assess the impact that this variety has had on extraterritorial Englishes (Tagliamonte, 2000–03; Hickey, 2004).

As with many corpus creators in these volumes, Hickey addresses issues of representativeness, which, in his particular case, revolved around selecting texts from a range of periods and concentrating on those that were 'linguistically representative of Irish English' irrespective of whether or not they had 'literary merit' (p. 106). There was also an attempt to favour dramatic texts over other kinds, since there is an argument that these may well approximate speech patterns more readily and thus be less constrained by what Milroy (2001, p. 535) has termed 'the standard language culture' more often associated with written materials.

This chapter additionally offers preliminary analyses of the corpus, addressing the critical question in historical (socio-) linguistic research of how to make the best use of problematic data containing lacunae of various sorts (see Labov, 1994, p. 11) and the extent to which these limitations can be overcome by taking a 'careful and objective' (p. 123) approach to analysing such data.

Anneli Meurman-Solin describes the Corpus of Scottish Correspondence (CSC), whose creation was primarily motivated by the realization that 'royal, official, and family letters were a data source with unique properties in research seeking the reconstruction of both past language use and social as well as cultural practices ... Correspondence is a unique source in the sense that it offers both linguists and historians a wide range of informants representing different degrees of linguistic and stylistic literacy and different social ranks and mobility' (p. 127). Since the Corpus of Early English Correspondence, described in this volume, covers East Anglia, London and the North of England, 'the focus on Scotland seemed very relevant' (p. 127).

CSC is based on diplomatic transcripts of the original manuscripts and is continually being expanded as transcription, digitization and tagging proceed. Revised and expanded versions will be distributed annually; the first distribution will comprise about 500,000 words of running text. The description of CSC is in four main parts. The first, 'Representativeness', outlines the criteria for the selection of texts to include in the corpus: (i) to ensure diachronic and diatopic representativeness, 'so that the corpus will permit the creation of a diachronic linguistic atlas and provide data for historical dialectology' (p. 128), (ii) positioning of texts on a continuum in accordance with their validity as evidence for particular research questions, and (iii) inclusion of 'variables relevant in the framework of historical sociolinguistics and historical stylistics and pragmatics' (p. 128). These criteria are discussed in detail. The second part, 'Digitization principles', notes that the principles used in digitizing the diplomatic transcripts of the archival materials will be described in the forthcoming corpus manual, but provides a brief summary of general practices with regard to such things as change of hand, folio number, paragraph structure, and so on. The third part, 'Basic and elaborated tagging', gives an account both of the principles governing the tagging of the CSC and of their implementation. The tagging is, first, 'designed to reflect a profoundly variationist perspective. The shape of Scots over time, place and social milieu is assumed to reflect continued variation and variability, resulting in a high degree of language-internal heterogeneity' (p. 135); an essential of the tagging system is that it should enable identification and analysis of complex patterns of variation and tracing of multidirectional processes of change. Second, the tagging system 'has been tailored to meet the challenge of tracing developments over a long time span' (p. 135). Third, the system must accommodate 'the inherent fuzziness and polyfunctionality recorded in language use when examined drawing on representative large-scale corpora' (p. 136). Fourth, the system must allow for the full range of zero realizations of grammatical features included in variationist paradigms. And, finally, the tagging system must 'provide information about the non-linguistic features of the original manuscripts whenever such information may affect analysis and interpretation of linguistic features' (pp. 136–7). The tagging software that implements these criteria and used by CSC is agnostic with respect to 'modern formal syntactic theory' (p. 137), and provides annotation both at the level of word and morpheme and at higher-level syntactic and discourse units. There follows a very detailed account of the tagging scheme. The fourth and final part of the discussion, 'Work in progress', gives a brief indication of what its title suggests.

Helena Raumolin-Brunberg and Terttu Nevalainen's chapter describes another corpus, or, rather, suite of corpora, designed for a very specific purpose, in this case, as with the NEET corpus, to test the methodology of historical sociolinguistics. The time span of the material included in these corpora is from 1410 to 1681, thus overlapping with the earlier part of the NEET corpus. The Corpus of Early English Correspondence (CEEC) corpora consist of the original 1998 corpus of 2.7 million words; the CEEC Sampler, a more accessible subcorpus of the 450,000 words not subject to copyright restrictions; the CEEC Supplement, consisting of material either not available in 1998, or only available in modernized spelling; the CEEC Extension, consisting of later material from 1681 to 1800; and the Parsed Corpus of Early English Correspondence. In this chapter, the authors concentrate on discussing issues which arose in the compilation of the original CEEC and the CEEC Sampler.

Although, like the Corpus of Late Eighteenth-Century Prose and parts of the NEET corpus, the CEEC corpora consist of letters, issues of transcription are not so important because CEEC consists of letters from edited collections rather than manuscript versions. The compilers are therefore dependent on the original editors, some of whom were historians rather than linguists, and so cannot always be sure that the 'diplomatic' text aimed at by Fitzmaurice and by van Bergen and Denison (this volume) has been achieved. However, a coding is provided to alert the user as to the extent of 'authenticity' of the text, from A ('autograph letter in good original-spelling edition') to D ('doubtful or uncertain authorship; problems with the edition, the writer's background, or both') (pp. 154–5).

The advantage of using edited collections is that, for the most part, the texts could be scanned in, allowing for a much larger corpus to be compiled in the time available. Given the team's intention of testing sociolinguistic methods on historical data, this is important, as a large number of informants would be needed if cells containing speakers sharing social attributes such as gender, age and social level were to be filled for successive historical periods. The chapter contains a discussion of the difficulty of providing a 'balanced' sample from letters, when literacy was much less common amongst women and the lower social orders.

One disadvantage of using edited rather than manuscript materials is that issues of copyright arise. As the Authors explain, this is not a problem when a corpus is intended only for private research, but gaining copyright clearance becomes a major task if the corpus is to be widely accessible. The creation of a smaller corpus of texts out of copyright (the CEEC Sampler) has provided an interim solution to this problem.

There is considerable discussion of the problems encountered in coding and the solutions arrived at. As was the case for the NEET and NECTE corpora, the compilers of the CEEC found that automatic parsing programs designed for use with (Standard) present-day English were not suitable for use with early texts. In this case, the Penn Treebank program (see Taylor, this volume) proved successful. The authors also describe their solution to the problems posed by the need to include a wide range of background information on the letter-writers, given that the corpus was designed for use in socio-historical investigations. The authors argue that neither the Cocoa format used in the Helsinki Corpus of English Texts, nor the TEI model used in the NECTE corpus (Allen *et al.*, this volume) would allow the user to conduct searches of the data within combinations of parameter values. They therefore decided to create a database of social information on the senders of letters which could be searched separately.

The authors conclude with an overview of research which has made use of the CEEC corpora. What is evident here is that, by conducting pilot studies from an early stage of the project, as reported in Nevalainen and Raumolin-Brunberg (1996), the team has been able to use the results from these studies to inform the principles of compilation. Like most of the corpora discussed in this volume, the CEEC is a work in progress rather than a 'once and for all' finished article.

Naomi Standen and Francis Jones describe a project 'which will create and store in a database English translations for a set of five interlinked histories written in China between 974 and 1444 CE' and, when completed, 'will form an invaluable resource for historians' (p. 172). The authors are aware that, in describing a corpus intended primarily for historical study, their work appears to sit uncomfortably in a volume devoted to the creation of corpora for linguistic and more specifically sociolinguistic research. They point out, however, that translation from one language to another 'like all linguistic communication, has sociolinguistic significance': 'we use translation as an analytical tool to highlight the evolving relationships between terms and concepts in the Chinese originals' (pp. 172–3). Their chapter develops this sociolinguistic dimension of the project in aiming to 'track the linguistic socio-ethnography of our own interpretative processes as translator-historians within a framework of cross-border and post-colonial power relations' (p. 173).

The discussion is in four main parts. The first part, 'The database project: issues and aims', describes the historical context, role and nature of the Chinese texts to be translated, paying special attention to the complex textual and conceptual interrelationships of their narratives, and to the challenge of designing the translation database in a way that 'retains an openness to the multiple readings of events generated by the various source texts and their translations' (p. 173). The title of the second part, 'Ideology, history, and translation', gives a good indication of its content. Starting from the assumption that 'communication involves interpretation', and extending it to the observations that 'historians do not describe "what happened", but give their own reading of data' and that, because no two languages have identical grammatical structures, 'translators, too, give their own reading of the textual and paratextual evidence of their source text' (p. 181), the authors discuss such issues as 'terminology and attitudes' (the concept of barbarianism and its ideological application), 'translation as closure' ('how translation can fix and conceal the ideological subtexts inherent in any historical reading', p. 183), 'translation as opening' (ways of avoiding translational closure in the preceding sense), and 'terminology control and multiple meanings' (terminological standardization and its relation to translational openness and closure). The third part of the discussion, 'Technical solutions', outlines the design and high-level implementation of the project as (i) a collection of interlinked passages, (ii) a relational database of the links to permit the standard relational search operations on the corpus, and (iii) a glossary 'which will chiefly document multiple English translations of a single Chinese word' (p. 191). Finally, the fourth part, 'Creating the database', describes procedural aspects of the creation of the corpus. The Conclusion points out the fruitfulness of their 'methodological synergy between the "core" discipline of historical textual analysis on the one hand, and translation-studies approaches to textual transformation on the other' (p. 193), and suggests that similar approaches in other cases of complex intertextuality or difficult-to-align texts might prove useful in other applications, citing in particular the York–Helsinki corpus described in this volume.

Ann Taylor describes the York–Toronto–Helsinki Parsed Corpus of Old English Prose (YCOE), a 1.5 million-word syntactically annotated corpus of Old English prose texts produced at the University of York in the UK from 2000 to 2003 by Ann Taylor, Anthony Warner, Susan

Pintzuk and Frank Beths. The YCOE is part of the English Parsed Corpora Series. It is the third historical corpus to be completed in this format and follows the same kind of annotation scheme as its sister corpora, the Penn–Helsinki Parsed Corpus of Middle English II and York–Helsinki Parsed Corpus of Old English Poetry. In addition, two other corpora of the series, the Penn–Helsinki Parsed Corpus of Early Modern English and the parsed version of the Corpus of Early English Correspondence, are currently under construction at the University of Pennsylvania in the USA and the University of York in cooperation with the University of Helsinki, respectively.

The description is in five parts. The first part, 'Background', outlines the motivation for the creation of YCOE. The discussion begins with the observation that the corpus series to which YCOE belongs 'was designed particularly with historical syntacticians in mind, and more particularly, those who use quantitative methods in their work' (p. 197), and goes on to develop the specific need for syntactically annotated electronic corpora. The argument, in brief, is that, relative to paper-based corpora, electronic corpora offer well-known advantages of accessibility and amenability to fast and reliable computational analysis, but that 'virtually all the questions that interest syntacticians require structural information about language that is not accessible from word strings' (p. 193), and that this necessitates the insertion of grammatical tags, thereby making the general advantages of electronic corpora available to syntactic analysis. The subsection 'Research applications' identifies the main research uses for YCOE: 'studies of the sentential syntax of the various stages of English, either synchronic or diachronic' and more generally 'any sort of syntactic study, as well as many morphological studies' (p. 200). The second part, 'Methodology and representation', describes the content of YCOE (a subset of the 3,037 texts in the Old English corpus created for the *Dictionary of Old English*, using complete texts rather than samples), how these texts were formatted for part-of-speech tagging by the Brill system, the error correction procedure, and, finally, automatic parsing into Penn Treebank format. The third part, 'Structure', gives a detailed account of the YCOE annotation scheme and the principles that underlie it. The fourth part, 'Distribution and end-user issues', deals with availability of the text of YCOE and of documentation for it, and describes the features of CorpusSearch, an analytical tool developed in part by the author that will search 'any corpus in the correct format, including all corpora in the English Parsed Corpora Series' (p. 219). The Conclusion briefly summarizes the significance of YCOE in 'the programme of creating syntactically parsed corpora for the whole attested history of the English language' (p. 225).

Linda van Bergen and David Denison's chapter describes the genesis of a relatively small (300,000-word) corpus of unedited letters, designed from the outset to be of interest to non-linguists, particularly historians, as well as linguists. Like the NEET corpus (Fitzmaurice, this volume), the Corpus of Late Eighteenth-Century Prose (CLEP) plugs the gap between the major corpora of earlier English and larger modern corpora such as the British National Corpus. The authors here describe their corpus as 'opportunistic in origin' (p. 228), presumably because the material was available in the archive of the John Rylands University Library in Manchester, but, as such, it provides an example of the kind of project which could be replicated with material from archives elsewhere in the UK. Van Bergen and Denison discuss in detail the decision-making processes involved in selecting material for their corpus, which consists of letters written to Richard Orford, a steward to the Legh family of Lyme Hall, Cheshire. Unlike the letters included in NEET, which were written by and to literary figures, and chosen to facilitate investigations into standardization and the effects of prescriptivism, those in CLEP represent the 'everyday' language of informal business transactions. Although the purpose of the letter-writers is primarily to conduct business, personal matters often intrude, so that, as the authors state, 'the dividing line between business and personal letters turned out to be very fuzzy' (p. 233). The decision to include rather than exclude material has led to what the authors admit is an 'unbalanced and heterogeneous' (p. 232) corpus, but, as with other corpora making use of historical and/or archive data (see, for instance, Allen *et al.*, this volume), the richness of the data included in the corpus leads us to question whether 'balance' is after all essential in diachronic corpora.

With regard to transcription, van Bergen and Denison report that, like Fitzmaurice (this volume), they aimed for a 'diplomatic' edition of the text, that is, one as close as possible to the original. The inclusion in this chapter of illustrations of the actual manuscript for comparison with the 'diplomatic' texts allows us to judge the closeness of the latter to the originals. However, as was the case for the NECTE corpus (Allen *et al.*, this volume), transcription was not straightforward, in this case because the handwriting was not always easy to decipher, so tentative or dubious readings are marked as such.

The discussion of coding in this chapter foregrounds an issue which was extensively debated in the workshop at the Fifteenth Sociolinguistics

Symposium with which these volumes are closely associated. The compilers of CLEP decided to use coding based on that of the Helsinki Corpus, because most users would be familiar with this. The corpus is available in two versions: a plain text file for concordancing and an HTML version designed for use with web browsers. There is an illustrated account of the advantages of HTML, followed by a discussion of the pros and cons of using TEI-conformant coding such as XML (as used in the NECTE corpus). In this case, the authors argue that potential users are not sufficiently familiar with XML to make this a practical option for the first release.

3 Acknowledgements

The editors would like to close by acknowledging the financial support provided to various phases of this project by: (i) the School of English Literature, Language and Linguistics, Newcastle University; (ii) Newcastle Institute for the Arts, Humanities and Social Sciences; (iii) Palgrave Macmillan; (iv) the Arts and Humanities Research Council (grant no. RE11776); and (v) the British Academy (grant no. BCG-37408).

We would also like to express our deeply felt gratitude to our authors who have gracefully endured our cajoling and actively engaged with us in pursuing a research agenda in corpus linguistics, the ultimate goal of which is to foster 'international standards for metadata', and articulate 'best practices for the collection, preservation, and annotation of corpus data for language archives' (Kretzschmar *et al.*, 2005 and 2006.

There are also a number of other people who deserve special thanks, including: Jill Lake, the commissioning editor responsible for these companion volumes, for her helpful feedback from inception to completion; to production staff at Palgrave Macmillan for their patience with our many technical queries; Tina Fry, Alison Furness, Kaycey Ihemere, Adam Mearns and Naglaa Thabet for their assistance with formatting and indexing; the organizing and scientific committees of SS15 and our anonymous reviewers who submitted the SS15 workshop papers and the chapters in these volumes to critical, stylistic and formal scrutiny. Finally, we are indebted to Shana Poplack for writing the foreword to this volume and for the many discussions we have had with her regarding the shape that these volumes should take since the idea for this project was first mooted back in 2002. Any remaining shortcomings are, as usual, our own.

Note

1. See, for instance, Francis and Kučera (1964); Johansson *et al.* (1978); Aarts and Meijs (1984); Garside (1987); Garside *et al.* (1987); Leech (1992); Hughes and Lee (1994); Burnard (1995); Haslerud and Stenstrom (1995); Sampson (1995); Knowles *et al.* (1996); Aston and Burnard (1998); Biber *et al.* (1998); Condron *et al.* (2000), inter alia.

References

Aarts, Jan and Willem Meijs (eds). 1984. *Corpus Linguistics*. Amsterdam: Rodopi.

Aston, Guy and Lou Burnard. 1998. *The BNC Handbook*. Edinburgh: Edinburgh University Press.

Biber, Douglas, Susan Conrad and Randi Reppen. 1998. *Corpus Linguistics: Investigating Language Structure and Use*. Cambridge: Cambridge University Press.

Burnard, Lou. 1995. *Users' Reference Guide to the British National Corpus*. Oxford: Oxford University Computing Services.

Condron, Frances, Michael Fraser and Stuart Sutherland. 2000. *Guide to Digital Resources in the Humanities*. Oxford: Humanities Computing Unit, Oxford University.

Filppula, Markku. 1999. *The Grammar of Irish English*. London: Routledge.

Francis, W. Nelson and Henry Kučera. 1964. *Manual of Information to Accompany a Standard Corpus of Present-Day Edited American English, for Use with Digital Computers*. Providence, RI: Dept. of Linguistics, Brown University.

Garside, Roger. 1987. 'The CLAWS word-tagging system'. *The Computational Analysis of English: A Corpus-Based Approach*, ed. by Roger Garside, Geoffrey Leech and Geoffrey Sampson, pp. 30–41. London: Longman.

Garside, Roger, Geoffrey Leech and Geoffrey Sampson (eds). 1987. *The Computational Analysis of English: A Corpus-Based Approach*. London: Longman.

Haslerud, Vibecke and Anna-Britta Stenstrom. 1995. 'The Bergen London Teenage Corpus (COLT)'. *Spoken English on Computer*, ed. by Geoffrey Leech, Greg Myers and Jenny Thomas, pp. 235–42. London: Longman.

Hickey, Raymond. 2003. *Corpus Presenter. Processing Software for Language Analysis with a Manual and A Corpus of Irish English as Sample Data*. Amsterdam: John Benjamins.

Hickey, Raymond (ed.). 2004. *Legacies of Colonial English: Studies in Transported Dialects*. Cambridge: Cambridge University Press.

Hughes, Lorna and Stuart Lee (eds). 1994. *CTI Centre for Textual Studies Resources Guide 1994*. Oxford: CTI Centre for Textual Studies.

Johansson, Stig, Geoffrey N. Leech and Helen Goodluck. 1978. *Manual of Information to Accompany the Lancaster–Oslo/Bergen Corpus of British English, for Use with Digital Computers*. Dept. of English, University of Oslo.

Knowles, Gerry, Briony Williams and Lolita Taylor. 1996. *A Corpus of Formal British English Speech*. London: Longman.

Kretzschmar, William A., Jean Anderson, Joan C. Beal, Karen P. Corrigan, Lisa-Lena Opas-Hänninen and Bartek Plichta. 2005. 'Collaboration on corpora for regional and social analysis'. Paper presented at AACL 6/ICAME 26, University of Michigan, Ann Arbor, 12–15 May 2005.

Kretzschmar, William A., Jean Anderson, Joan C. Beal, Karen P. Corrigan, Lisa-Lena Opas-Hänninen and Bartek Plichta. (2006). 'Collaboration on corpora for regional and social analysis'. Special Issue of *Journal of English Linguistics* 34:172–205.

Labov, William. 1994. *Principles of Linguistic Change: Volume 1, Internal Factors*. Oxford: Blackwell.

Leech, Geoffrey N. 1992. '100 million words of English: the British National Corpus'. *Language Research* 28(1):1–13.

Mair, Christian. (forthcoming). *Standard English in the Twentieth Century: History and Variation*. Cambridge: Cambridge University Press.

McEnery, Tony and Andrew Wilson. 2001. *Corpus Linguistics*, 2nd edn. Edinburgh: Edinburgh University Press.

Milroy, James. 2001. 'Language ideologies and the consequences of standardization'. *Journal of Sociolinguistics* 5(4):530–55.

Milroy, Lesley. 1987. *Language and Social Networks*. Oxford: Blackwell.

Milroy, Lesley and Matthew Gordon. 2003. *Sociolinguistics: Method and Interpretation*. Oxford: Blackwell.

Milroy, James, Lesley Milroy and Gerard Docherty. 1997. 'Phonological variation and change in contemporary spoken British English'. ESRC, unpublished Final Report, Dept. of Speech, Newcastle University.

Nevalainen, Terttu and Helena Raumolin-Brunberg. 1996. *Sociolinguistics and Language History: Studies Based on the Corpus of Early English Correspondence*. Amsterdam and Atlanta, Ga: Rodopi.

Nevalainen, Terttu and Helena Raumolin-Brunberg. 2003. *Historical Sociolinguistics: Language Change in Tudor and Stuart England*. Longman Linguistics Library. London: Longman.

Ochs, Elinor. 1999. 'Transcription as theory'. *The Discourse Reader*, ed. by Adam Jaworski and Nikolas Coupland, pp. 167–82. London: Routledge.

Sampson, Geoffrey. 1995. *English for the Computer: The SUSANNE Corpus and Analytic Scheme*. Oxford: Clarendon.

Strang, Barbara M. H. 1968. 'The Tyneside Linguistic Survey'. *Zeitschrift für Mundartforschung*, NF 4 (Verhandlungen des Zweiten Internationalen Dialecktologenkongresses), pp. 788–94.Wiesbaden: Franz Steiner Verlag.

Tagliamonte, Sali A. 2000–03. 'Back to the roots: the legacy of British dialects'. Unpublished report to the ESRC, grant no: R000239097.

Tieken-Boon van Ostade, Ingrid. 1996. 'Social network theory and eighteenth-century English: the case of Boswell'. *English Historical Linguistics 1994*, ed. by David Britton, pp. 327–37. Amsterdam and Philadelphia: Benjamins.

Tieken-Boon van Ostade, Ingrid. 2000a. 'Social network analysis and the history of English'. *European Journal of English Studies* 4(3):211–16.

Tieken-Boon van Ostade, Ingrid. 2000b. 'Social network analysis and the language of Sarah Fielding'. *European Journal of English Studies* 4(3):291–301.

Websites

Bank of English: http://titania.cobuild.collins.co.uk/boe_info.html
British National Corpus: http://info.ox.ac.uk/bnc

2

A Linguistic 'Time Capsule': The Newcastle Electronic Corpus of Tyneside English

Will Allen, Joan C. Beal, Karen P. Corrigan, Warren Maguire and Hermann L. Moisl[1]

1 Introduction

The general goal of this chapter is to outline the models and methods underpinning the Newcastle Electronic Corpus of Tyneside English (NECTE), created by the amalgamation of two separate corpora of recorded speech from the same geographical location. The earliest of these was collected in the late 1960s and early 1970s as part of the Tyneside Linguistic Survey (TLS) funded by the Social Science Research Council (SSRC) (see Strang, 1968; Pellowe *et al.*, 1972; Pellowe and Jones, 1978; and Jones-Sargent, 1983). The more recent of the two was created between 1991 and 1994 for a project entitled Phonological Variation and Change in Contemporary Spoken English (PVC), which was supported by the Economic and Social Research Council (ESRC) (see Milroy *et al.*, 1997). More specifically, the chapter addresses four topics: (i) the objectives of the NECTE enhancement programme and the original aims of the TLS and PVC projects that are its foundation; (ii) the initial state of the sources on which the NECTE corpus is built; (iii) procedures for the amalgamation of these sources; and (iv) projected further developments of the resultant corpus and preliminary linguistic analyses of it.

2 NECTE aims and objectives

In 2001, the NECTE project was funded by the AHRB with the aim of providing an enhanced electronic corpus resource. It was to be Text Encoding Initiative (TEI)-conformant and would eventually be made available to the public and to the research community in a variety of formats: digitized sound, phonetic transcription, orthographic transcription and grammatical markup, all aligned and downloadable from the Web.

2.1 TLS aims and objectives

The chief aim of the TLS was to determine the 'ecology' of urban varieties of English (that is, what kinds of variation exist), using a radical and rigorous statistical methodology that had evolved in opposition to the already predominant Labovian paradigm (see Labov, 1972, and Trudgill, 1974, for instance). Rather than pre-selecting 'salient', linguistic variables and correlating these with a narrow range of external indices, such as social class, the TLS grouped speakers and analysed their similarity to one another by comparing their data sets across a multitude of variables simultaneously. Each informant would thus be assigned a unique position in linguistic 'space', and differences between speakers would be evident in the manner in which these clustered relative to one another. 'Linguistic' clusters (grammatical, phonological and prosodic variants) could then be mapped onto 'social' clusters, likewise arrived at by multivariate analyses of the subjects' scores on a wide range of social and lifestyle factors from 'educational level' to 'commitment to taste in décor'.[2]

While the theoretical approach, methodology and initial outcomes from the TLS aroused a certain amount of interest, the project was perceived to be overly complex at the time, as Milroy (1984, p. 207) articulates in her statement:

> Although many would feel sympathetic to the aims of this ambitious project, the very punctiliousness of the Tyneside Linguistic Survey researchers has led to an imbalance in favour of methodology and theory and a relative weakness on results.

It is unsurprising, therefore, that despite some 'stimulating and innovatory' public outputs (Milroy, 1984, p. 207), the research programme was never fully completed and, indeed, remained largely forgotten until the archiving and transcription projects of Beal and Corrigan between 1994 and 2001 (see Beal (1994–5), Beal and Corrigan (1999), Beal and Corrigan (2000–2001), Beal, Corrigan, Duchat, Fryd and Gerard (1999–2000), Corrigan (1999–2000), and also section 3.1 below).[3] Thus, as well as preserving and disseminating what has become a valuable historical record of Tyneside English, the NECTE project brings closure on the one hand and a new beginning on the other to an important, but neglected, chapter in the history of sociolinguistics.

2.2 PVC aims and objectives

As noted in section 1 above, we have also incorporated and enhanced spoken data collected under the auspices of the PVC project. In contrast to the TLS, this latter research produced substantial outputs, which together have made a very significant contribution both to the methodology of sociophonetics and to our understanding of the nature of dialect levelling in late twentieth-century Britain (see, for instance, Milroy *et al.*, 1997; Docherty and Foulkes, 1999; Watt and Milroy, 1999; Watt, 2002). However, although the focus of research by the PVC team was on *phonological* variation and change, the data hold a great deal of valuable and exploitable analytical information for other fields of research. In our efforts to encourage more divergent linguistic investigations of this resource, the NECTE project has, therefore, made the PVC corpus available to a wider range of end-users than those envisaged when the interviews were originally conducted. We believe that doing so is crucial, given the richness of the data for morphosyntactic studies, for instance, as has already been demonstrated in Beal and Corrigan (2002, 2005a, 2005b) and Beal (2004b).

Above all, the amalgamation of these two data sets incorporating Tyneside speakers from different age, class and sex groupings between the middle and end of the twentieth century makes the NECTE corpus invaluable for both real- and apparent-time studies of internal and external variation on a number of linguistic levels, as argued in Beal and Corrigan (2000a, 2000b, 2000c).[4]

3 The sources on which the NECTE corpus is built

3.1 The Tyneside Linguistic Survey (TLS)

To judge from the unpublished papers and public output of the TLS, its main aim, as described in section 2.1, was to determine the nature and extent of linguistic variation among Tynesiders and how this might be correlated with a range of social and lifestyle factors. To realize this research aim, the TLS team created a corpus of materials relating to Tyneside English consisting of the following components:

- A collection of audio-taped interviews with speakers who were encouraged to talk about their life histories and their attitudes to the local dialect. In addition, at the end of each interview, informants were asked for acceptability judgements on constructions containing vernacular morphosyntax, and whether they knew or used a range of traditional dialect words. Interviews varied somewhat in length but lasted 30 minutes on average, and were recorded onto analogue reel-to-reel tape, the standard audio-recording technology of the time.

- Detailed social data for each speaker.
- Orthographic and phonetic transcriptions recorded onto index cards. Approximately 200 of these were completed for each interview, equating to the first ten minutes or so of the recording session. Index card transcriptions conveyed interviewee turns only and each brief section of audio was annotated for the following types of information: (i) Standard English orthography; (ii) a corresponding phonetic transcription of the audio segment; and (iii) some associated grammatical, phonological and prosodic details (see Figure 2.4 below).
- Digital electronic text files containing encoded versions of the phonetic transcriptions (1-Alpha codes) as well as separate ciphers conveying grammatical, phonological and prosodic (2-Alpha and 3-Alpha) information (see Figure 2.3 below).
- Digital electronic text files including additional codes that conveyed different kinds of social data for each speaker.[5]

Following the end of the SSRC award, the audio tapes and index card sets were stored in the Department of English Language (now part of the School of English Literature, Language and Linguistics) at the University of Newcastle upon Tyne. In addition, John Local, one of the TLS researchers, deposited six audio recordings with the British Library Sound Archive. The electronic files, which had been crucial to implementing the unique variationist methodology of the TLS project, were lodged with the Oxford Text Archive (OTA).

In 1994–95, Joan Beal at Newcastle University secured funding from the Catherine Cookson Foundation to: (i) salvage the rapidly deteriorating reel-to-reel audio tapes by re-recording them onto cassette tape, (ii) catalogue them alongside the social data, and (iii) archive the tapes, the index card sets and documentation associated with the TLS project in a new Catherine Cookson Archive of Tyneside and Northumbrian Dialect at the University of Newcastle. Had it not been for this funding, these 'hard-won sounds' of mid-twentieth-century Tyneside would, as Widdowson (2003, p. 84) puts it, have simply become dispersed 'particles of ferric oxide'.

Since 2001, the NECTE project has based the TLS component of its enhancement scheme on the material in the Catherine Cookson Archive and the British Library Sound Archive and on the electronic holdings of the digital files at the OTA. As restoration and digitization efforts progressed, it became evident that only a fragment of the projected TLS corpus had survived. Unfortunately, it still remains unclear exactly how much material has, in fact, been permanently lost. The crux of the matter is that the information in unpublished TLS project documentation (as well as that in the public domain) does not allow one to decide with any certainty how large the corpus originally was. We are not sure, for example, how many interviews were conducted, and the literature gives conflicting reports. Pellowe *et al.* (1972, p. 24), for example, claim that there were 150, whereas Jones-Sargent (1983, p. 2) mentions the higher figure of 200. It is also unknown how many of the original interviews were orthographically and phonetically transcribed. Jones-Sargent (1983) used 52 (digitally encoded) phonetic transcriptions in her computational analysis, but the TLS material includes seven electronic files that we recovered from the OTA, but that she did not use. As such, there were clearly more than 52 phonetic transcriptions, but was the ultimate figure 59, or were further files digitized but never passed to the OTA?

All one can reasonably do in this situation, therefore, is catalogue and enhance what currently exists and, to date, NECTE has been able to identify 114 interviews, but not all corpus components survive for each. Specifically, there remain:

- 85 audio recordings, of which three are badly damaged (110, 111 and 113 in Table A2.1 of the Appendix). For the remaining 29 interviews, the corresponding analogue tape is either blank or simply missing
- 57 index card sets, all of which are complete
- 61 digital phonetic transcription files
- 64 digital social data files.

The distribution of these materials across interviews is shown with an 'X' in Table 2.A1 of the Appendix. There is no natural order to the interviews as such, so they are arranged there in descending order depending on how many corpus components they still retain. Those interviews that have all four components are at the top of the table, followed by others with only three components, and so on. When the interviews are arranged in this way, it is easily seen that, out of 114 interviews, only 1–37 are complete in the sense that an intact audio recording, an index card set, and electronic phonetic transcription and social data file exist, all the others (38 onwards) being fragmentary to greater or lesser degrees.

3.2 The Phonological Variation and Change in Contemporary Spoken English (PVC) corpus

The primary PVC materials comprise 18 digital audio-taped interviews, each of up to 60 minutes' duration. Self-selected dyads of friends or relatives conversed freely about a wide range of topics with minimal interference from the fieldworker. As such, the interview format was that which, in the terms of Macaulay (2005, pp. 21–2), 'lies between the monologues of individual interviews and the polyphony of group sessions'. It has the advantage of generating 'unstructured conversations in optimal recording situations' which also delimit the observer's paradox and the concomitant possibility of accommodation.

In contrast to the detailed phonetic transcriptions provided by the TLS, the PVC team restricted their transcription to those specific lexical items in phonetic context that they were interested in analysing from auditory and/or acoustic perspectives. No systematic orthographic transcription of the material, such as that produced by the TLS, was ever attempted. As Table 2.1 (adapted from Watt and Milroy, 1999, p. 27) demonstrates, the PVC project did, however, record some social data, though it was not as detailed as that of the TLS team, since they restricted their categorization of subjects to age, gender and 'broadly defined socio-economic class' (Watt and Milroy, 1999, p. 27).

4 Procedures for the amalgamation of these sources

One of the most complex aspects of the NECTE encoding project is that the resultant digital corpus aimed to provide four different levels of data representation, namely, (i) audio, (ii) orthographic transcription, (iii) grammatical markup, and (iv) phonetic transcription. In what follows below, we provide a description of the methods used to create

Table 2.1 Design of PVC fieldwork sample

Working class (WC)				Middle class (MC)			
Younger (15–27)		Older (45–67)		Younger (15–27)		Older (45–67)	
Male	Female	Male	Female	Male	Female	Male	Female
4	4	4	4	4	4	4	4

these digital representations and a discussion of the most significant problems encountered when devising or recreating each level.

4.1 The audio data

Both the TLS and PVC corpora are preserved on audio tape and, unsurprisingly therefore, we view the primary NECTE data representation as being audio. The relative 'youth' and high sound quality of the PVC recordings has enabled a largely trouble-free, though still fairly time-consuming, preparation of the data for the purposes of the NECTE project. The TLS recordings, on the other hand, have been rather more problematic, since they required a considerable degree of restoration. The original analogue recordings, both reel-to-reel and the cassette versions, which came about as a result of their 'rescue' in 1994–95 (as outlined in section 3.1 above), were first digitized at a high sampling rate. All the TLS recordings included in NECTE were digitized from the cassette versions in WAV format at 12000 Hz 16-bit mono and were enhanced by amplitude adjustment, graphic equalization, clip and hiss elimination, as well as regularization of speed.[6] All PVC recordings were digitized in WAV format direct from the original DAT tapes and required no additional adjustment.

4.2 Orthographic transcription

The audio content of the TLS and PVC corpora has been transcribed orthographically and this is also included as a level of representation in the NECTE corpus. As noted in Preston (1985), Macaulay (1991), Kirk (1997) and, more recently, in Cameron (2001) and Beal (2005), representing vernacular Englishes orthographically, by using 'eye-dialect', for example, can be problematic on a number of different levels. Attempting to convey 'speech realism', in Kirk's (1997, p. 198) sense, can lead, for example, to an unwelcome association with negative racial or social connotations and there are theoretical objections too in that devising non-standard spellings to represent certain groups of vernacular speakers can make their speech appear more differentiated from mainstream colloquial varieties than is actually warranted. With these caveats in mind, we outline below the 'trade-offs' (see Tagliamonte, Volume 1) adopted for the NECTE project in this regard. Two issues, in particular, have exercised us in our attempt to transcribe the audio data orthographically in a maximally efficient and accurate manner that simultaneously encodes the nuances particular to spoken Tyneside English which a range of end-users might conceivably want annotated for them. The first of these relates to the application of the conventional spellings associated with standard written British English to a non-standard spoken dialect. Leaving aside, for present purposes, the question of writing as opposed to speaking conventions, Tyneside English speech differs significantly from standard spoken English across all linguistic levels, from phonetic to pragmatic. As such, it would have been uneconomic in the extreme to attempt to render all of these potential differences in the NECTE Orthographic Transcription Protocol (OTP). This seemed particularly justified with respect to the phonetic level, since it was always our intention to provide International Phonetic Alphabet (IPA) transcriptions for a carefully selected cohort of the PVC corpus sound files and because the TLS project had already bequeathed to us a highly detailed phonetic transcription of much of their material which we planned to authentically reformulate (see section 4.4 below). As such, no attempt was made to represent the non-standard phonology of Tyneside English with semi-phonetic spelling, for example. Hence, we have chosen to ignore popular representations such as the distinctive Tyneside pronunciation /na:/ as <knaa> for Standard English <know>. However, in cases where local vernacular renditions are either lexically or morphologically distinct from standard British norms, a representation was agreed by way of an OTP (see Poplack, 1989; and Lawrence *et al.*, 2003) and adhered to consistently. For instance, if a particular lexeme had an established tradition, having been recorded in a published dialect glossary such as Brockett (1825), Heslop (1892–94), Geeson (1969), Dobson (1974), Graham (1979), Griffiths (1999), Douglas (2001) or Moody (forthcoming), then this spelling was adopted. A lexicon of dialectal lexical items was compiled and added to the OTP as transcription proceeded, with cross-references, where appropriate, to the established glossaries, as in the examples from a range of semantic fields given in Table 2.2.

Table 2.2 Orthographic representation of dialectal lexical items

Gloss	**Moody** (forthcoming) **spelling**	**NECTE protocol spelling**
'food, packed lunch'	*Bait* (p. 38)	*bait*
modifier, e.g. 'canny few', meaning 'a lot'	*Canny* (p. 112)	*canny*
'sticky/slimy'	*Claggy* (p. 132)	*claggy*
'street chasing game'	*Kick-the-block* (p. 345)	*kick the block*
'sledge-hammer'	*Mell* (p. 395)	*mell*
'birds, especially sparrows'	*Spuggies* (p. 535)	*spuggies*

As Poplack (1989) rightly points out, any large-scale textual transcription exercise is subject to human error of various sorts. Our particular problems in this regard are exacerbated by the fact that the TLS tapes are now several decades old and, as noted already, have become degraded in various ways, so that it is often difficult or even impossible to hear what is being said. Acoustic filtering in the course of digitization, such as that described immediately above, improved audibility in some, but by no means all, cases. To offset these difficulties, we have availed ourselves of certain orthographic transcriptions made by the TLS project team back in the 1960s and 1970s when the original tapes were still in good condition, but, as Table A1 reveals, these cover only part of the corpus.[7] To ensure accuracy, therefore, we found it necessary to conduct four transcription passes through the audio files. The first of these established a base text, the second and third were correction passes to improve transcription accuracy, and the fourth established uniformity of transcription practice across the entire corpus.

4.3 Part-of-speech tagged orthographic transcription

Grammatical tagging was crucial to the NECTE programme as a level of data representation. The annotation scheme chosen was determined by what was possible within the timescale of the project, subject to the following constraints:

- Existing tagging software had to be used.
- The tools in question had to encode non-standard English reliably, that is, without the need for considerable human intervention in the tagging process and/or for extensive subsequent proofreading.

Having reviewed the full range of tagging software currently available and with these constraints in mind, the CLAWS tagger, developed for annotating the BNC by UCREL (University Centre for Computer Corpus Research on Language) at Lancaster University, UK, was selected. It fulfils NECTE's requirements in that it is a mature system developed over many years, which has consistently achieved an accuracy rate of 96–97 per cent in relation to the BNC corpus. The NECTE (that is, not the TLS) orthographic transcriptions of the TLS and the PVC audio were part-of-speech tagged by the CLAWS4 tagger using the UCREL C8 tagset and Figure 2.1 contains a sample of the resulting tagged output for the sentence: *and eh I lived in with my mother for not quite two year but varnigh.*[8]

```
<u who="informantTL Sg37">
<w type="CC" lemma="and">and</w>
<w type="UH" lemma="eh">eh</w>
<w type="PPIS1" lemma="i">i</w>
<w type="PPIS1" lemma="i">i</w>
<w type="VVD" lemma="live">lived</w>
<w type="RP" lemma="in">in</w>
<w type="IW" lemma="with">with</w>
<w type="APPGE" lemma="my">my</w>
<w type="NN1" lemma="mother">mother</w>
<w type="IF" lemma="for">for</w>
<w type="XX" lemma="not">not</w>
<w type="RG" lemma="quite">quite</w>
<w type="MC" lemma="two">two</w>
<w type="NNT1" lemma="year">year</w>
<w type="CCB" lemma="but">but</w>
<w type="VV0" lemma="varnigh">varnigh</w>
</u>
```

Figure 2.1 CLAWS output

4.4 Phonetic transcription

NECTE includes partial phonetic transcriptions of the TLS and PVC interviews. The TLS phonetic transcriptions require some detailed discussion, so they will be treated in section 4.4.2 below after a brief description of the phonetic transcription practices used for the PVC data.

4.4.1 *PVC phonetic transcription*

Sample phonetic transcriptions of the PVC materials are provided for comparison with the TLS transcriptions. These are far less extensive than TLS on account of the extremely time-consuming nature of the process (as articulated in section 4.4.2 below). Previous research, such as Kerswill and Wright (1990), as well as consultation with sociophoneticians (Gerard Docherty, Paul Foulkes, Paul Kerswill and Dom Watt) with expertise in north-eastern dialects and other potential end-users, confirmed that most researchers whose primary interest was in phonetics would prefer to do their own analyses, so a decision was taken to provide only broad transcriptions of a stratified subsample. The first five minutes of each of six PVC tapes was transcribed, giving samples of twelve speakers in all. This was done at a 'broad' phonetic level.

4.4.2 *TLS phonetic transcription*

To realize its main research aim stated in section 2 above, the TLS had to compare the audio interviews it had collected at the phonetic level of representation. This required the analogue speech signal to be discretized into phonetic segment sequences, in other words to be phonetically transcribed. The standard method is to select a transcription scheme, that is, a set of symbols each of which represents a single phonetic segment (for example, that of the IPA), and then to partition the linguistically relevant parts of the analogue audio stream such that each partition is assigned a phonetic symbol. The result is a set of symbol strings each of which represents the corresponding interview phonetically. These strings can then be compared and, if also given a digital electronic representation, the comparison can be done computationally.

The TLS team generated phonetic transcriptions of a substantial part of its audio materials, and they are included in the NECTE corpus. However, in order to make them usable in the NECTE context they have required extensive restoration. The sections below describe the TLS phonetic transcription scheme (4.4.2.1) and the rationale for and the restoration of the TLS electronic phonetic files (4.4.2.2).

4.4.2.1 *TLS phonetic transcription and digital encoding schemes*

The TLS made the simple, purely sequential transcription procedure described above the basis for a rather complex hierarchical scheme that would eventually represent the phonetics and phonology of its corpus. That scheme has to be understood if its phonetic data are to be competently interpreted, and it is consequently explained in detail below.

The TLS team developed its hierarchical phonetic transcription scheme in order to capture as much of the phonetic variability in the interviews as possible. To see exactly how this might be achieved, consider what happens when data generated by a sequential transcription procedure are analysed and, more specifically, the transcribed interviews are compared. An obvious way to do the comparison is to count, for each interview, the number of times each of the phonetic symbols in the transcription scheme being used occurs. This process yields a phonetic frequency profile for each of the interviews, and the resulting profiles can then be compared using a wide variety of methods. Unfortunately, such profiles fail to take into account a commonplace of variation between and among individual speakers and speaker groups, namely that different speakers and groups typically distribute the phonetics of their speech differently in distinctive lexical environments. Frequency profiles of the sort in question here only say how many times each of the various speakers uses phonetic segment *x* without regard to the possibility that they distribute *x* differently over their lexical repertoires. The hierarchical TLS transcription scheme was designed to capture such distributional variation.

The scheme is similar to the manner of specifying the lexical distribution of vowels in any given English accent used by Wells (1982), whereby comparisons are made using a number of standard 'lexical sets'. As the name implies, the latter is a set of words which can be related in some respect. Those described by Wells (1982) define sets of words which, taking RP and General American as reference points, have shared phonological histories, and give extensional definitions of the phonemes of those accents. Hence, the KIT set {*ship, rib, dim, milk, slither, myth, pretty, build, women, busy* ...}, for example, defines the phoneme /ɪ/ in Standard American and Received Pronunciation British English. In a similar way, the TLS used the phonemes of RP (only) as a basis for the definition of lexical sets.

The TLS hierarchical transcription scheme, which exploits a similar method, has three levels:

- The top level, designated 'Overall Unit' (OU) level, is a set of lexical sets where OU = $\{\{ls_1\}, \{ls_2]\ldots\{ls_m\}\}$, such that each $\{ls_i\}$ for $1 < i < m$ extensionally defines one phoneme in RP, and *m* is the number of phonemes in RP. The purpose of this level was to provide a standard relative to which the lexical distribution of Tyneside phonetic variation could be characterized.

- The bottom level, designated 'State', is a set of phonetic symbol sets where State = {{ps_1}, {ps_2}...{ps_m}}. There is a one-to-one correspondence of lexical sets at the OU level and phonetic symbol sets at the State level such that the symbols in {ps_i}, for $1 < i < m$, denote the phonetic segments that realize the OU {ls_i} in the fragment of Tyneside English that the TLS corpus contains.
- The intermediate Putative Diasystemic Variable (PDV) level proposes (thus 'putative') groupings of the phonetic symbols in a given State set {ps_i} based (as far as the existing TLS documentation allows one to judge) on the project's perceptions of the relatedness of the phonetic segments that the symbols denote. These PDV groups represent the phonetic realizations of their superordinate OUs in a less fine-grained way than the State phonetic symbol sets do. A detailed example of the scheme taken from Jones-Sargent (1983, p. 295) is given in Figure 2.2.

OU	PDV	(code)	states	lexical examples
1 [i:] (NL)	i:	0002	i i̥ i̱ i̞ ɨ i̟	week, treat, see
	I	0004	i̱ i̥ i̳ i̞ ɨ	week, relief
	ɛ	0006	e̱ ɛ̱ e̞ ɛ̝	beat
	eI	0008	ɛ̱i əɨ e̟ɪ ɛ̱i̥	see
	Iə	0010	iɛ̝ɪ iɛ̝ i̞ə	feed
	Ii	0012	ii(back) ii(low) i̱	we, see
2 [I] (NL)	I	0014	i̱ i̟ i̳ i̟̞ ɨ	fit, big, till
	ɐ	0016	ə ə̟ ə̳ ə̝ ɜ̱ʿ ɜ̝ʿ	shilling
	Iə	0018	i̞ə i̱ə i̞ə	did
	3:	0020	ɜ̱ ɜ̞ ɛ̳	shilling
	ɛə	0022	ɛ̱ɨ ɛ̱ɨ	miss, big

Figure 2.2 TLS coding scheme for realizations of the OUs [i:] and [I]

The OU [i:] defined by the lexical set (from which there are examples in the rightmost column of Figure 2.2) can be realized by the phonetic segment symbols in the States column, and these symbols are grouped by phonetic and lexical relatedness in the PDV column. This transcription scheme captures the required distributional phonetic information by allowing any given State segment to realize more than one OU. Note that several of the State symbols for OU [i:] occur also in the OU [ɪ]. What this means is that, in the TLS transcription scheme, a State phonetic segment symbol represents not a distribution-independent sound, but a sound in relation to the phonemes over which it is distributed.

The implications of this can be seen in the encoding scheme that the TLS developed for its transcription protocol so that its phonetic data could be computationally analysed. Each State symbol is encoded as a five-digit integer. The first four digits of any given State symbol designate the PDV to which the symbol belongs, and the fifth digit indexes the specific State within that PDV. Thus, for the OU [i:] there are six PDVs, each of which is assigned a unique four-digit code.[9] For a given PDV within the [i:] OU, say [ɪ], the first of the state symbols in left-to-right order is encoded as 00041, the second as 00042, and so on. Now, note that the State symbols 00023 and 00141 are identical, that is, they denote the same sound. Crucially, however, they have different codes because they realize different phonemes relative to OU, or, in other words, the different codes represent the phonemic distribution of the single sound that both the codes denote.[10]

4.4.2.2 Restoration of the TLS phonetic transcriptions

The phonetic transcriptions of the TLS interviews survive in two forms, that is, as a collection of index cards and as electronic files. Each electronic file is a sequence of the five-digit codes just described, a random excerpt from one of these files being given in Figure 2.3.

```
02441 02301 02621 02363 02741 02881 02301 01123 00906 02081-&&&& *
02322 02741 02201 02383 02801 02421 02501 01443 01284 00421 02021 00342
02642 02164 02721 02741 04321-&&&&
02621 02825 02301 02721 02341 02642 02541 00503 00161 00246 12601 01284
02781 02561 02363 02561 02881 07641 02941-&&&&
```

* The sequences designated by the *TLS* coders as '-&&&&' are end-of-line markers.

Figure 2.3 A sample of a TLS electronic file of five-digit codes

Initially, from NECTE's perspective, these electronic files appeared to be a labour- and time-saving alternative to keying in the numerical codes from the index cards. However, a peculiarity that stems from the original electronic data entry system used by the computing staff who had been entrusted with the task of creating the files from the TLS team's original index cards meant that they had to be extensively edited by NECTE personnel when the files were returned to us from the OTA. The problem arose from the way in which the five-digit codes were laid out by the TLS researchers on the index cards, as in Figure 2.4.

For reasons that are no longer clear, all the consonant codes (beginning (0220(1)) in line 4 of Figure 2.4) were written on one line, and all of the vowel codes appear on the line below ((0062(7)) of line 5 in Figure 2.4). When the TLS gave these index cards to the University of Newcastle data entry service, the typists entered the codes line by line, with the result that, in any given electronic line, all the consonant codes come first, followed by the vowel codes. This difficulty pervades the TLS electronic phonetic transcription files. While it had no impact on the output of the TLS team (given that they were examining codes in isolation and since phonetic environment was already captured by their hierarchical scheme), it was highly problematic for the NECTE enhancement of the original materials.

Simply to keep this ordering would have made the phonetic representation difficult to relate to the other types of representation planned for the NECTE enhancement scheme. The TLS files were therefore edited with reference to the index cards so as to restore the correct code sequencing, and the result was proofread for accuracy.[11]

Gateshead. Nelson Street.
HRB HRC
AA OF
0244(2)0230(1)0262(1)0236(4)0274(1)0282(5)0262(3)0274(1)0262(3)0226(1)
0112(3) 0024(2) 0202(1) 0002(3)
0286(1) 0230(1)
BS BS
ZF CY

Figure 2.4 A sample of a TLS index card

The only exception to this restoration procedure is the files for the Newcastle speakers. Because neither the audio recordings nor the index card sets for these speakers survive, restoration of the correct sequencing would have been a hugely time-consuming task, and one that could not be undertaken within the limited time available to the NECTE project. Even in their unordered state, however, these files are still usable for certain types of phonetic analysis such as those that involve segment frequency counts, and they are included in NECTE in their present state for that reason. Moreover, the formatting of numerical codes in these files differs from that in the other TLS-based files, where the codes are in a continuous sequence. For the Newcastle files, the original TLS formatting has been retained: the numerical codes are arranged in a sequence of code strings each of which is terminated by a line break, where a code string in the sequence corresponds to a single informant utterance. The motivation was to facilitate reordering of the codes if this is ever undertaken in future (if, for example, the audio files or the index card sets for the Newcastle group should ever come to light).

4.5 Content alignment

The NECTE project felt that the usefulness of its corpus would be considerably enhanced by the provision of an alignment mechanism relating the representational types described in sections 4.1–4.4 above to one another, so that corresponding segments in the various layers can be conveniently identified and simultaneously displayed. The decision to provide such an instrument immediately raises the question of granularity: how large should the alignment segments be? Should the representational types be aligned at the level of the phonetic segment or would it be more appropriate to set the alignment at a lower level of granularity such as sentence or even utterance? In addition to considering the divergent discourse dynamics of the TLS and PVC corpora, our evaluation of this crux also had to take into account research utility on the one hand, and feasibility in terms of project cost on the other, that is, would word-by-word alignment, say, be useful enough from the perspective of potential research on the corpus to justify the considerable effort required to manually insert the numerous markers necessary for so fine-grained a resolution?

For the TLS materials, the format of the interviews made alignment at the granularity of utterance the natural choice. This is because a typical interview consists of a succession of interviewer–question, interviewee–answer pairs in which the utterance boundaries are generally clear-cut (as is the norm for adjacency pairs more generally, according to Sacks *et al.*, 1974). There is some degree of overlap on account of interruption and third-party intervention, but this is infrequent enough to be handled fairly straightforwardly within an utterance-aligned framework.

The PVC materials, however, presented a rather different discourse situation since the interviews were considerably more loosely structured. In the first place, the interviewer's role is to monitor rather than participate, making their contribution almost negligible. Second, the setting is designed such that a majority of the conversation emanates from pairs of subjects who are either friends or relatives and therefore knew each other very well in advance of the interview. Unsurprisingly, therefore, overlaps in this case are the norm rather than the exception. Attempting to disentangle the speakers would, on the one hand, require very detailed markup (with consequent additional project costs), and, on the other, would necessitate ad hoc decisions about conversational structure, thereby imposing an undesirable pre-analysis on the data (see Stenstrom and Svartvik, 1994). Assuming the need for a uniform alignment mechanism across the entire corpus, it was clear that alignment at the utterance level was, therefore, impractical.

What were the alternatives? More detailed alignment at the granularity of the phonetic segment or of the word was ruled out on account of excessive manual effort. So too was alignment on the basis of syntactic unit, since this would have necessitated either manual syntactic markup (which would once again have been expensive) or access to a reliable automatic parser for the highly vernacular English that the corpus contains, which, to our knowledge, does not yet exist. The one choice remaining, which seemed both appropriate to the distinctive discourses of the TLS and PVC and was feasible in terms of cost, appeared to be alignment by 'real-time' interval, which was therefore the method that the NECTE team eventually adopted.

Our real-time interval alignment mechanism works as follows. It begins with the observation that real time (that is, time as it is conceived by humans in day-to-day life) is meaningful only for the audio level of representation in the corpus. By contrast, text, be it orthographic, tagged, or a sequence of phonetic symbols, has no temporal dimension. A time interval t is therefore selected and the audio level is partitioned into some number n of length-t audio segments s: $s(t \times 1)$, $s(t \times 2)$ ... $s(t \times n)$, where '×' denotes multiplication. Corresponding markers are then inserted into the other levels of representation such that they demarcate substrings corresponding to the audio segments.

Hence, for the audio segment $s(t \times i)$, for some i in the range $1...n$, there are markers in the other representational levels which identify the corresponding orthographic, phonetic and part-of-speech tagged segments. In this way, selection of any segment s in any level of representation allows the segments corresponding to s in all the other levels to be identified.

A time interval of 20 seconds was selected for this procedure on the grounds of project cost and end-user need. With regard to the former, it is obvious that the shorter the interval, the greater the effort of marker insertion. The increase is more than linear as the interval shrinks, that is, markup for a one-second interval takes more than 20 times longer than markup for a 20-second interval, due to the simple mechanics of starting and stopping the audio stream in exactly the right place and then deciding where to put the markers in the other levels. A 20-second interval was thus felt to be a cost-effective choice that also coincided with the potential demand for usability. With respect to the latter, 20-second chunks were found to yield about the right amount of aligned text from the various levels of representation on a typical computer screen when all the levels are simultaneously displayed, as in Figure 2.5 in the next section.[12]

4.6 Document structuring

NECTE is encoded using Text Encoding Initiative (TEI)-conformant Extensible Markup Language (XML) syntax. XML (http://www.w3.org/XML/) aims to encourage the creation of information resources that are independent both of the specific characteristics of the computer platforms on which they reside (Macintosh versus Windows, for example), and of the software applications used to interpret them. To this end, XML provides a standard for structuring documents and document collections. TEI defines an extensive range of XML constructs as a standard for the creation of textual corpora in particular. Together, these are emerging as world standards for the encoding of digital information, and it is for this reason that NECTE adopted them.

Specifically, the NECTE corpus is a TEI-conformant XML document in the TEI local processing format sense, as specified in the *Guidelines for Text Encoding and Interchange* (Sperberg-McQueen & Burnard, 2002, ch. 28).[13] To be TEI-conformant, an XML document has to be validated relative to the TEI Document Type Definition (DTD). NECTE's selection of a validator was based on information provided by Thijs van den Broek's technical report *Benchmarking XML-editors* (2004), a version of which is available on the Arts and Humanities Data Service (AHDS) website (http://ahds.ac.uk/creating/information-papers/xml-editors/). We chose the oXygen XML Editor (http://www.oxygenxml.com/) since it provides facilities not only for the creation of XML documents but also for their validation in relation to user-defined DTDs. The NECTE corpus document has, therefore, been validated relative to the TEI DTD by oXygen.[14]

To make all of this more concrete, consider the following severely truncated excerpt from the actual NECTE corpus in Figure 2.5.

```
<teiCorpus.2>
<teiHeadertype='corpus'>
<fileDesc>…</fileDesc>
<encodingDesc>…</encodingDesc>
<profileDesc>…</profileDesc>
<revisionDesc>…</revisionDesc>
</teiheader>
<TEI.2id="tlsg37"><teiHeader type="text">…</teiHeader>
<text>
<group>
<text id="tls37audio'>
<body>
<p>tls37 audio file</p>
<audio entity="tlsaudiog37"/>
</body>
</text>
<textid="tls37necteortho">
<body>
<u who="informantTlsg37"><anchor id="tlsg37necteortho0000"/>
tIs what's that </u>
<u who="interviewerTlsg37">g</u>
<u who="informantTlsg37">e<pause/>five two</u>
<u who"interviewerTlsg37">thanks<pause/>ta<pause/>eh could you tell
us first eh where you were born please<event desc="interruption"/>
<unclear/></u><u who="informantTlsg37">i was born at eleven
victoria street<pause/>gateshead
</u>
…
</body>
</text>
<text id="Tlsg37tlsortho">
<body>
<u who="informantTlsg37"><anchorid="tlsg37tlsortho0000"/>
I was born at eleven Victoria Street Gateshead thats just
against the</u>
…
```

Figure 2.5 Truncated excerpt from the XML version of NECTE

```
</body>
</text>
<textid="tlsg37phonetic">
<body>
<u who="informantTlsg37"><anchorid="Tlsg37phonetic000"/>
01304 02941 02641 02201 00626 02741 02301 02081 02781 00244
02561 02021 02741 02561 00144 02421 02263 00626 02861 17801
02621 02262 02861 00023 02301 02442 01123 02301 02623 02365
02603 00342 02301 02521 00823 02623 02442 11202 02741 02623
</u>
...
</body>
</text>
<textid='Tlsg37tagged'>
<body>
<u who="informantTlsg37">
<anchorid="tlsg37tagged0000"/>
<w type="ZZI"lemma="t">t</w>
<w type="ZZI"lemma="1">1</w>
<w type="ZZI"lemma="S">S</w>
<w type="DDQ"lemma="what">what</w>
<w type="VVBZ"lemma="be">'S</w>
<w type="DD1"lemma="that">that</w>
</u>
<u who="interviewerTlsg37"
<w type="ZZ1" lemma="e">e</w>
<pause/>
<w type="MC" lemma="five">five</w>
<w type="MC" lemma="two">two</w>
</u>
...
</body>
</text>
</group>
</text>
</TEI.2>
```

Figure 2.5 Continued

As can be seen, the textual content is surrounded by and interspersed with a multitude of tags enclosed by angle brackets. These serve to specify the many features of the NECTE corpus structure: <u who="informantTLSg37">, for instance, identifies a particular TLS informant and indicates that the speaker turn is about to begin; <w type="NN2"lemma="picture"> pictures </w> identifies 'pictures' as a word (<w>) of lexical type NN2 and lemma 'picture', and so on.

5 Projected further developments of NECTE and preliminary linguistic analyses

5.1 Further enhancement plans

Two developments of NECTE are currently projected in the short to medium term.

5.1.1 Provision of visualization and transformation facilities

Adoption of TEI-conformant XML requires no justification in principle as it is a world standard, but it can be an obstacle to users of the corpus in practice. The documentation page of the project website (http://www.ncl.ac.uk/necte/documentation.htm) observes, rather economically, that 'familiarity with XML and TEI is assumed throughout'. Users not familiar with these standards may find the pervasive markup tags in the NECTE files a distracting encumbrance and yearn for the good old days of plain text files. This is not an unreasonable position. XML was never intended to be reader-friendly. It is a markup language that provides a standard for the structuring of documents and document collections, and, though XML-encoded documents are plain text files that *can* be read by humans, in general they should not be. For an XML document to be readily legible, software that can represent the structural markup in a visually accessible way is required. For example, XSLT (Extensible Stylesheet Language Transformations) (http://www.w3.org/TR/xslt) can transform an XML-encoded document into an HTML-encoded one that can then be viewed using any standard web browser. Similarly, search and analysis of NECTE or any other XML-encoded corpus requires software to interpret the markup.

XML-aware software visualization and analysis tools are gradually becoming available. The Oxford University Computing Service's Xaira system (http://www.oucs.ox.ac.uk/rts/xaira/), for instance, is 'a general purpose XML search engine, which will operate on any corpus of well-formed XML documents. It is, however, best used with TEI-conformant documents'.[15] For user convenience, therefore, in further developing the NECTE corpus, our next priority is to provide XSLT style sheets that generate, on the one hand, HTML versions of the corpus content for accessible visualization using standard web browsers, and, on the other, plain text versions that can be used with existing applications that are not XML-aware.

5.1.2 Addition of materials

The catalogue of TLS materials described in section 3.1 above and outlined in Table 2A.1 of the Appendix shows that, in addition to the core of complete interviews that NECTE now contains, there is a penumbra of fragments, the inclusion of which could usefully augment the corpus in various ways (though, of course, they can never be subject to an identical alignment procedure since certain levels of representation are unavailable). Hence, interviews 38 and 39 can be included despite the missing phonetic transcriptions and while the audio files do not exist for interviews 40–57, there are other levels of representation that do. More crucially, since the audio files for 65–107 survive (though in a degraded state), some enhancement will be possible via digitization and, once this has been done, orthographic transcription can be attempted. We aim, therefore, to incorporate these materials into the corpus once the XSLT phase described immediately above has been completed.

5.2 Preliminary linguistic analyses

One aspect of the NECTE project, which is particularly gratifying, is that it has already begun to further the objectives of the original TLS and PVC research agendas (see section 2.1 and 2.2 above). Preliminary linguistic analyses of various kinds have been performed by the NECTE team on different aspects of the data. We describe below two areas that have proved fruitful in this regard and which we, therefore, intend to pursue further.

5.2.1 Corpus linguistics, dialectology, (historical) (English) linguistics and English language

Previous research prior to the establishment of this resource provided evidence suggesting that certain dialects preserve historical features of English that are no longer extant in standard and other regional varieties. In published research by Beal (2004a, 2004b) and Beal and Corrigan (2002, 2005a, 2005b), arising from the NECTE programme, we have demonstrated that the corpus is an extremely useful tool in this regard. It has permitted us, for example, to track the development of relative clause markers, adverbs and patterns of negation in real time (by comparing speakers across the 1969 and 1994 corpora).

Indeed, we have also begun cross-dialectal investigations (between NECTE and the Corpus of Sheffield Usage (CSU) (Beal, 2002)) that have allowed us to uncover morphosyntactic variation in the system of relativization in non-standard Englishes across regional space (see particularly Beal & Corrigan, 2005b). An important finding of these investigations has been that some language features are similar across the two dialects (such as the use of *nowt* as a negator, discussed in Beal and Corrigan, 2005a), whereas others distinguish dialects quite strikingly (as does the use of *what* as a relative marker found to be extremely rare in NECTE but fairly common in the CSU (Beal and Corrigan, 2002, 2005b)).

Although we have been fortunate with respect to the congruities between NECTE and the CSU, a real impediment to the advancement of knowledge as regards tracking the development of English more globally has been the lack of standardization with respect to the manner in which electronic vernacular corpora are encoded. As Bauer (2002, pp. 107–8) notes:

> On the whole, corpora have been built for national varieties of English rather than for regional dialects within one country. Thus we do not have public electronic corpora that would allow us to investigate differences in the syntax of Newfoundland and Vancouver Englishes, or of Cornish and Tyneside Dialects.

His motivation for this statement partly arises from the fact that 'diverse collections may be comprised of slightly different types of data'. As such, an important contribution to this subject area that NECTE has made is in the creation of protocols and guidelines regarding the collection, transcription, annotation and long-term preservation of vernacular corpora. When applied by other researchers to their own data sets, these will allow cross-variety comparisons of exactly the sort Bauer is lamenting the lack of. There is evidence of a perceived need internationally for such standards, as argued in Kretzschmar *et al.* (2005 and 2006).

5.2.2 Exploratory multivariate analysis

The highly detailed phonetic transcriptions of the Tyneside Linguistic Survey interviews that we have now restored offer a unique opportunity for applying exploratory multivariate analytical techniques, such as cluster and principal components analysis as well as various non-linear methods, to the interrogation of linguistic corpora.

Hence, some members of the NECTE team have begun to develop the empirical methodology based on exploratory multivariate analysis that the TLS used for selection of linguistic variables, described in section 2.1 above. Published work thus far evaluates the reliability of the results generated by hierarchical cluster analysis, the analytical method used by the TLS, and proposes the application of more recently developed methods such as the Self-Organizing Map to analyses of the TLS phonetic transcription data (Moisl and Beal 2001; Moisl and Jones,

2005). More recently, in papers presented at ICLAVE 3 (Moisl *et al.*, 2005) and UKLVC 5 (Maguire and Moisl, 2005) and currently being prepared for publication, the TLS results reported in Jones-Sargent (1983) have been replicated and extended. These outputs have demonstrated that the TLS speakers fall into clearly defined groups on the basis of their phonetic usage and that these groups correlated well with the socio-economic backgrounds of individual informants. These results are congruent not only with the interrogation of the corpus at the morphosyntactic level outlined in section 5.2.1 above, but are also interesting from the perspective of the social dynamics of Newcastle speech captured in research by the PVC team some thirty years after the collection of the TLS data.

6 Conclusion

The past two decades or so have resolved many of the corpus creation difficulties that beset the original TLS team in particular, and we have been at pains to enhance both the TLS and PVC corpora in these respects. For data entry, verification and correction we have made use of optical character recognition, graphical user interfaces, text processing systems, and a variety of text analysis and diagnostic software. For standards, we have adopted XML and TEI. Our plans for dissemination have moved considerably beyond what might have been imagined by either of the original research teams whose data we inherited, in that we have taken full advantage of the connectivity of the internet and the ever-developing facilities of the Web. It is now, in fact, possible to construct electronic corpora in the manner in which the TLS project intended, and to publish it as a resource for the research community in a way that its members did not, and could not, have conceived.

Appendix

Table 2.A1 Existing TLS source materials

Interview number	Tape exists	Index card set exists	Electronic phonetic transcription file exists	Social data file exists
1	X	X	X	X
2	X	X	X	X
3	X	X	X	X
4	X	X	X	X
5	X	X	X	X
6	X	X	X	X

Table 2.A1 Continued

Interview number	Tape exists	Index card set exists	Electronic phonetic transcription file exists	Social data file exists
7	X	X	X	X
8	X	X	X	X
9	X	X	X	X
10	X	X	X	X
11	X	X	X	X
12	X	X	X	X
13	X	X	X	X
14	X	X	X	X
15	X	X	X	X
16	X	X	X	X
17	X	X	X	X
18	X	X	X	X
19	X	X	X	X
20	X	X	X	X
21	X	X	X	X
22	X	X	X	X
23	X	X	X	X
24	X	X	X	X
25	X	X	X	X
26	X	X	X	X
27	X	X	X	X
28	X	X	X	X
29	X	X	X	X
30	X	X	X	X
31	X	X	X	X
32	X	X	X	X
33	X	X	X	X
34	X	X	X	X
35	X	X	X	X
36	X	X	X	X
37	X	X	X	X
38	X	X		X
39	X	X		X
40		X	X	X
41		X	X	X
42		X	X	X
43		X	X	X
44		X	X	X
45		X	X	X
46		X	X	X
47		X	X	X
48		X	X	X
49		X	X	X
50		X	X	X

Table 2.A1 Continued

Interview number	Tape exists	Index card set exists	Electronic phonetic transcription file exists	Social data file exists
51		X	X	X
52		X	X	X
53		X	X	X
54		X	X	X
55		X	X	X
56		X	X	X
57		X	X	X
58			X	X
59			X	X
60			X	X
61			X	X
62			X	X
63			X	X
64			X	X
65	X			
66	X			
67	X			
68	X			
69	X			
70	X			
71	X			
72	X			
73	X			
74	X			
75	X			
76	X			
77	X			
78	X			
79	X			
80	X			
81	X			
82	X			
83	X			
84	X			
85	X			
86	X			
87	X			
88	X			
89	X			
90	X			
91	X			
92	X			
93	X			
94	X			

Table 2.A1 Continued

Interview number	Tape exists	Index card set exists	Electronic phonetic transcription file exists	Social data file exists
95	X			
96	X			
97	X			
98	X			
99	X			
100	X			
101	X			
102	X			
103	X			
104	X			
105	X			
106	X			
107	X			
108	blank			
109	blank			
110	damaged			
111	damaged			
112	blank			
113	damaged			
114	blank			

Notes

1. The authors would like to acknowledge the financial support of the Arts and Humanities Research Board (AHRB) (grant no: RE11776) in funding this resource enhancement project entitled: A Linguistic 'Time-Capsule': The Newcastle Electronic Corpus of Tyneside English. We also appreciate the helpful comments generated by an oral version of this chapter delivered at the Models and Methods panel, which took place at Sociolinguistics Symposium 15, Newcastle University, April 2004. Thanks especially to Shana Poplack for her helpful comments on this paper.
2. The intentions and theoretical stance of the TLS team are discussed at length in Jones-Sargent (1983). As well as preserving the data from the TLS project, the NECTE team has revisited its methodology and sought to devise new methods capable of achieving the original aims of the TLS team (Allen *et al.*, 2003a, 2003b; and Jones and Moisl, 2003, for instance). As our preliminary analyses in section 5 demonstrate, the much greater computer power available today has allowed us to implement computationally more demanding cluster analysis algorithms, such as self-organizing maps, which could not have run within a reasonable time span in the 1960s, and they have already produced quite remarkable results. We note that Shana Poplack was to develop a methodology for multivariate analysis within the Labovian paradigm.

3. In this regard, there are some significant publications arising from the research, including: Local (1982), Jones (1985), and Local *et al.* (1986), as well as those mentioned in section 1 above.
4. Requests for access since the release of the corpus in July 2005 suggest that NECTE is also valuable to linguists in the fields of discourse analysis and language and gender, given the informal and unstructured nature of the dyadic interaction captured in the data and the mixture of same and differently gendered pairs of subjects. Scholars from other disciplines (folklore and history, for example) have also shown interest and it is expected that the impact of the corpus will increasingly be more wide-ranging as it becomes better-known outside English language and linguistics.
5. These materials are more fully described than we have space for in Jones-Sargent (1983).
6. We are grateful to Jonathan Marshall of the University of Gloucester for his assistance with the acoustic filtering procedures.
7. The NECTE amalgamation scheme also included these, partly for preservation purposes. Electronic copies of the orthographic transcription text on the index cards were made, and the copies were proofread relative to the cards. No changes of any kind, including corrections, were made as per normal practice in linguistic archaeology (see Meurman-Solin, this volume). The reader should also note that the TLS team only ever transcribed the interviewees' utterances, ignoring the interviewer entirely, though this has not been NECTE's practice.
8. Because it was specifically designed for handling Standard English text, there is no guarantee that tagging accuracy comparable to that for the BNC has been achieved for NECTE using the CLAWS software. We have, however, performed an amount of subsequent proofreading and found the error rate to be not unduly high. Specific accuracy levels, of course, remain to be determined by subsequent detailed study of this level of the corpus, which is beyond the scope of the NECTE project. For further details on the software itself than we have space for here, see http://www.comp.lancs.ac.uk/computing/research/ucrel/
9. The reader should be aware that the specifics of which numbers are used in the code are irrelevant in each case, and could have been anything else.
10. It is crucial to note that the Gateshead TLS transcriptions were done exclusively by a single member of the project, Vince McNeany, who was both a trained phonetician and a native speaker of the Tyneside dialect. This is important for subsequent analyses of the phonetic level because it minimizes the subjectivity and variation that inevitably compromises phonetic transcriptions. It still remains unclear who exactly undertook the Newcastle transcriptions and this may significantly impact upon their reliability, in comparison with the Gateshead sample.
11. We should point out that no attempt has been made by the NECTE team either to review the TLS phonetic transcriptions relative to the original audio recordings, or to extend/further refine the phonetic representation to accommodate what the TLS did not originally encode. The TLS transcriptions are, rather, offered as an historical artefact, and the reason they are included in NECTE is principally because of their intrinsic interest to researchers who want to study the phonetics of the TLS material. The phonetic analysis encoded is extremely detailed (much more so than that

of current practice within auditory sociophonetic research, for instance), providing from one to ten realizations of any given phonological segment, and this will no doubt be extremely useful to certain kinds of end-user.

12. It is, of course, a straightforward matter to decrease granularity by multiples of 20 if required. Finer granularity would, however, require insertion of markers at the appropriate places in all levels of representation and while this is possible, of course, it requires considerable additional human intervention.
13. An online version can be viewed at: http://www.tei-c.org
14. Further details of the TEI-conformant XML encoding are available from the NECTE website: http://www.ncl.ac.uk/NECTE/index.htm
15. Some additional directories of XML-aware software include: _http://xml.coverpages.org/publicSW.html; http://www.xmlsoftware.com/__http://www.garshol.priv.no/download/xmltools/__http://www.wdvl.com/Software/XML/

References

Allen, W., J. C. Beal, K. P. Corrigan, H. L. Moisl and C. Rowe. 2003a. 'A linguistic "time-capsule": *The Newcastle Electronic Corpus of Tyneside English*'. Poster presented at the 2nd International Conference on Language Variation and Change in Europe, University of Uppsala, June 2003.

Allen, W., J. C. Beal, K. P. Corrigan, H. Moisl and C. Rowe. 2003b. 'A linguistic "time-capsule": *The Newcastle Electronic Corpus of Tyneside English*'. Website display presented at NWAVE, University of Philadelphia, October 2003.

Bauer, L. 2002. 'Inferring variation and change from public corpora'. *The Handbook of Language Variation and Change*, ed. by J. K. Chambers, P. Trudgill and N. Schilling-Estes, pp. 97–114. Oxford: Blackwell.

Beal, J. C. 1994–95. *The Catherine Cookson Archive of Northumbrian Dialect*. Catherine Cookson Foundation.

Beal, J. C. 2002. *The Corpus of Sheffield Usage*. British Academy Small Research Grant.

Beal, J. C. 2004a. 'The phonology of English dialects in the North of England'. *A Handbook of Varieties of English*, Volume I, ed. by B. Kortmann, pp. 113–33. Berlin: Mouton.

Beal, J. C. 2004b. 'The morphology and syntax of English dialects in the North of England'. *A Handbook of Varieties of English*, Volume II, ed. by B. Kortmann, pp. 114–41. Berlin: Mouton.

Beal, J. C. 2004c. 'Geordie nation: language and identity in the North-East of England'. *Lore and Language* 17:33–48.

Beal, J. C. 2005. 'Dialect representation in texts'. *The Encyclopedia of Language and Linguistics*, 2nd edn, ed. by K. R. Brown, pp. 351–8. Oxford: Elsevier.

Beal, J. C. and K. P. Corrigan. 1999. *Investigating the Social Trajectories of Modal Verb Usage in Tyneside English*. Newcastle University Research Committee, Vacation Scholarship Panel.

Beal, J. C. and K. P. Corrigan. 2000a. 'A dynamic re-modelling of linguistic variation: the social trajectories of syntactic change amongst young Tynesiders, 1969–1994'. Paper presented at the Sociolinguistics Symposium, University of the West of England, Bristol, April 2000.

Beal, J. C. and K. P. Corrigan. 2000b. 'The Newcastle–Poitiers Electronic Corpus of Tyneside English'. Paper presented at the 11th International Conference on English Historical Linguistics, University of Santiago de Compostella, August 2000.

Beal, J. C. and K. P. Corrigan. 2000c. 'New ways of capturing the "Kodak moment": Real-time vs. apparent time analyses of syntactic variation in Tyneside English, 1969–1994'. Paper presented at the 2nd Variation is Everywhere Workshop, University of Essex, September 2000.

Beal, J. C. and K. P. Corrigan. 2000–01. *The Newcastle–Poitiers Corpus of Tyneside English*. British Academy Small Grant no.: SG-30122.

Beal, J. C. and K. P. Corrigan. 2002. 'Relativisation in Tyneside and Northumbrian English'. *Relativisation on the North Sea Litoral* (LINCOM Studies in Language Typology, 7), ed. by P. Poussa, pp. 125–34. München: Lincom Europa.

Beal, J. C. and K. P. Corrigan. 2005a. '"No, nay, never", negation in Tyneside English'. *Aspects of English Negation*, ed. by Y. Iyeiri, pp. 139–56. Tokyo: Yushodo University Press, and Amsterdam: John Benjamins.

Beal, J. C. and K. P. Corrigan. 2005b. 'A tale of two dialects: relativisation in Newcastle and Sheffield'. *Dialects Across Borders: Selected Papers from the 11th International Conference on Methods in Dialectology (Methods XI), Joensuu, August 2002, CILT, 273*, ed. by M. Filppula, J. Klemola, M. Palander and E. Penttilä, pp. 211–29. Amsterdam: John Benjamins.

Beal, J. C., K. P. Corrigan, J.-L. Duchat, M. Fryd and C. Gérard. 1999–2000. *The Newcastle–Poitiers Corpus of Tyneside English*. British Academy and British–French Joint Projects with the Centre National de la Recherche Scientifique (CNRS), RSU Code: RES/3300/7001.

Brockett, J. T. 1825. *A Glossary of North Country Words, in Use*. Newcastle upon Tyne: E. Charnley.

Cameron, D. 2001. *Working with Spoken Discourse*. London: Sage.

Corrigan, K. P. 1999-2000. *Syntactic Change in Progress? The Newcastle–Poitiers Electronic Corpus of Tyneside English*. Newcastle University Research Committee, Vacation Scholarship Panel.

Corrigan, K. P., H. Moisl and J. C. Beal. 2001–05. *A Linguistic 'Time-Capsule': The Newcastle Electronic Corpus of Tyneside English*. Arts and Humanities Research Board (AHRB), Grant no.: RE11776 (http://www.ncl.ac.uk/NECTE).

Dobson, S. 1974. *The New Geordie Dictionary*. Newcastle: Frank Graham.

Docherty, G. and P. Foulkes. 1999. 'Derby and Newcastle: instrumental phonetics and variationist studies'. *Urban Voices: Accent Studies in the British Isles*, ed. by P. Foulkes and G. Docherty, pp. 47–71. London: Arnold.

Douglas, P. 2001. *Geordie–English Glossary*. London: Abson Books.

Geeson, C. 1969. *A Northumberland and Durham Word Book: The Living Dialect, Including a Glossary, with Etymologies and Illustrative Quotations, of Living Dialect Words*. Newcastle upon Tyne: H. Hill.

Graham, F. (ed.). 1979. *The New Geordie Dictionary*. Newcastle: Frank Graham.

Griffiths, B. 1999. *North-East Dialect: Survey and Word-List*. Gateshead: Athenaeum Press.

Heslop, R. O. 1892–94. *Northumberland Words: A Glossary of Words Used in the County of Northumberland and on the Tyneside.* London: English Dialect Society.

Jones, V. 1985. 'Tyneside syntax: a presentation of some data from the Tyneside Linguistic Survey'. *Focus on England and Wales*, ed. by W. Viereck, pp. 163–77. Amsterdam: John Benjamins.

Jones, V. and H. Moisl. 2003. 'Cluster analysis of the *Newcastle Electronic Corpus of Tyneside English*: a comparison of methods'. Paper presented at Web X: A Decade of the World Wide Web, Joint International Conference for the Association for Literary and Linguistic Computing, University of Georgia, Athens, Georgia, May–June 2003.

Jones-Sargent, V. 1983. *Tyne Bytes: A Computerised Sociolinguistic Study of Tyneside.* Frankfurt am Main: Peter Lang.

Kerswill, P. and S. Wright. 1990. 'The validity of phonetic transcription: limitations of a sociolinguistic research tool'. *Language Variation and Change* 2:225–75.

Kirk, J. 1997. 'Irish-English and contemporary literary writing'. *Focus on Ireland*, ed. by J. Kallen, pp. 190–205. Amsterdam: John Benjamins.

Kretzschmar, W. A. Jr, J. Anderson, J. C. Beal, K. P. Corrigan, L. Opas-Hänninen and B. Plichta. 2005. 'Collaboration on corpora for regional and social analysis'. Paper presented at AACL 6/ICAME 26, University of Michigan, Ann Arbor, May 2005.

Kretzschmar, W. A. Jr, J. Anderson, J. C. Beal, K. P. Corrigan, L. Opas-Hänninen & B. Plichta. (2006). 'Collaboration on corpora for regional and social analysis'. *Journal of English Linguistics* 34:172–205.

Labov, W. 1972. *Sociolinguistic Patterns*. Philadelphia: Pennsylvania University Press.

Lawrence, H., S. A. Tagliamonte and J. Smith. 2003. 'Transcription technicalities'. Paper presented to the NECTE workshop 'Deriving Standards for the Creation of Electronic Vernacular Corpora: Tagging and Transcription Issues' at the Fourth UK Language Variation and Change conference, University of Sheffield, September 2003.

Local, J. K. 1982. 'How many vowels in a vowel?' *Journal of Child Language* 10:449–53.

Local, J. K., J. Kelly and W. H. G. Wells. 1986. 'Towards a phonology of conversation turn-taking in Tyneside'. *Journal of Linguistics* 22:411–37.

Macaulay, R. K. S. 1991. '"Coz it izny spelt when they say it": displaying dialect in writing'. *American Speech* 66:280–91.

Macaulay, R. K. S. 2005. *Talk That Counts: Age, Gender and Social Class Differences in Discourse*. Oxford: Oxford University Press.

Maguire, W. and H. Moisl. 2005. 'Identifying the main determinants of phonetic variation in the Newcastle Electronic Corpus of Tyneside English'. Paper presented to the Fifth UK Language Variation and Change conference, Aberdeen, September 2005.

Milroy, L. 1984. 'Urban dialects in the British Isles'. *Language in the British Isles*, ed. by P. Trudgill, pp. 199–218. Cambridge: Cambridge University Press.

Milroy, J., L. Milroy and G. Docherty. 1997. 'Phonological variation and change in contemporary spoken British English'. ESRC, Unpublished Final Report, Dept. of Speech, University of Newcastle upon Tyne.

Moisl, H. and J. C. Beal. 2001. 'Corpus analysis and results visualization using self-organizing maps'. *Proceedings of the Corpus Linguistics 2001 Conference, UCREL Technical Papers 13 – Special Issue*, ed. by P. Rayson, A. Wilson, T. McEnery, A. Hardie and S. Khoja, pp. 386–91. UCREL: Lancaster University.

Moisl, H. and V. Jones. 2005. 'Cluster analysis of the Newcastle Electronic Corpus of Tyneside English: a comparison of methods'. *Literary and Linguistic Computing* 20:125–46.

Moisl, H. and W, Maguire. 2007. 'Identifying the main determinants of phonetic variation in the Newcastle Electronic Corpus of Tyneside English', *Journal of Quantitative Linguistics*, 14.

Moisl, H., W. Maguire and W. Allen. 2005. 'Phonetic variation in Tyneside: exploratory multivariate analysis of the Newcastle Electronic Corpus of Tyneside English'. Paper presented to the Third International Conference on Language Variation in Europe, Amsterdam, June 2005.

Moisl, H. L., W. Maguire and W. Allen. 2006. 'Phonetic variation in Tyneside: exploratory multivariate analysis of the Newcastle Electronic Corpus of Tyneside English', in Hinskens, F. (ed.) *Language Variation: European Perspectives*, Amsterdam. John Benjamins, 127–141.

Moody, T. (forthcoming) *Glossary of Tyneside and Northumbrian English*, ed. by J. C. Beal and K. P. Corrigan. Newcastle: Northumbrian Language Society.

Pellowe, J. and V. Jones. 1978. 'On intonational variety in Tyneside speech'. *Sociolinguistic Patterns in British English*, ed. by P. Trudgill, pp. 101–21. London: Arnold.

Pellowe, J., B. M. H. Strang, G. Nixon and V. McNeany. 1972. 'A dynamic modelling of linguistic variation: the urban (Tyneside) linguistic survey'. *Lingua* 30:1–30.

Poplack, S. 1989. 'The care and handling of a megacorpus: the Ottowa–Hull French Project'. *Language Change and Variation*, ed. by R. Fasold & D. Schiffren, pp. 411–51. Amsterdam: Benjamins.

Preston, D. 1985. 'The Li'l Abner syndrome: written representations of speech'. *American Speech* 60(4):328–36.

Sacks, H., E. Schegloff and G. Jefferson. 1974. 'A simplest systematics for the organization of turn-taking for conversation'. *Language* 50(4):696–735.

Sperberg-McQueen, C. and L. Burnard (eds). 2002. *Guidelines for Text Encoding and Interchange*. Published for the TEI Consortium by the Humanities Computing Unit, University of Oxford (http://www.tei-c.org)

Stenstrom, A.-B. and J. Svartvik. 1994. 'Imparsable speech: repeats and nonfluencies in spoken English'. *Corpus-based Research into Language*, ed. by N. Oostdijk and P. de Haan, pp. 241–54. Amsterdam: Rodopi.

Strang, B. M. H. 1968. 'The Tyneside Linguistic Survey'. *Zeitschrift für Mundartforschung,* NF 4 (Verhandlungen des Zweiten Internationalen Dialecktologenkongresses), pp. 788–94. Wiesbaden: Franz Steiner Verlag.

Tagliamonte, Sali. A. 2006. 'Representing real language: consistency, trade-offs and thinking ahead!' *Creating and Digitizing Language Corpora: Synchronic Databases (Volume 1)*, ed. by Joan C. Beal, Karen P. Corrigan and Hermann L. Moisl, pp. 241–76. Basingstoke: Palgrave Macmillan.

Trudgill, P. 1974. *The Social Differentiation of English in Norwich*. Cambridge: Cambridge University Press.

van den Broek, T. 2004. *Benchmarking XML-editors.* Electronic Publication, Arts and Humanities Data Service. http://ahds.ac.uk/creating/information-papers/xml-editors/

Watt, D. 2002. '"I don't speak with a Geordie accent, I speak, like, the Northern accent": contact induced levelling in the Tyneside vowel system'. *Journal of Sociolinguistics* 6(1):44–63.

Watt, D. and L. Milroy. 1999. 'Patterns of variation in Newcastle vowels', *Urban Voices: Accent Studies in the British Isles,* ed. by P. Foulkes and G. Docherty, pp. 25–46. London: Arnold.

Wells, J. 1982. *Accents of English I. An Introduction.* Cambridge: Cambridge University Press.

Widdowson, J. D. A. 2003. 'Hidden depths: exploiting archival resources of spoken English'. *Lore and Language* 17(1/2):81–92.

Websites

CLAWS4, part-of-speech tagger for English (UCREL): http://www.comp.lancs.ac.uk/computing/research/ucrel/

NECTE: http://www.ncl.ac.uk/NECTE

oXygen XML editor: http://www.oxygenxml.com/

TEI Guidelines: http://www.tei-c.org (see Sperberg-McQueen & Burnard, 2002)

Xaira (Oxford University Computing Service): http://www.oucs.ox.ac.uk/rts/xaira/

XML (Extensible Markup Language): http://www.w3.org/XML/

XSLT (Extensible Stylesheet Language Transformations): http://www.w3.org/TR/xslt

3

Questions of Standardization and Representativeness in the Development of Social Networks-Based Corpora: The Story of the Network of Eighteenth-Century English Texts

Susan Fitzmaurice

1 Introduction

In this chapter, I describe the rationale and theoretical basis for the design of the Network of Eighteenth-Century English Texts (NEET) corpus housed in the School of English Literature, Language and Linguistics at the University of Sheffield (currently at three million words). The NEET corpus is an unconventional corpus in a number of respects: it samples but does not represent the written language produced in England within a period of about 100 years; it contains all or at least a sizeable sample of the written repertoire of a network of individuals who were selected for inclusion primarily by virtue of their social connections with a single person, the essayist Joseph Addison.

NEET was designed to be a database for the sociohistorical investigation of topics such as register variation in relation to author identity, the relation of linguistic variation to the suppression of variation, the influence of social ties, relative social rank and sex on individuals' language, and the influence of literacy and printing practices on the shape of the language. In this chapter, I will elaborate the ways in which sociohistorical questions regarding the relationships among author identity and register or genre motivated the development of the corpus, and pay particular attention to the foundational role of social networks analysis in providing the basis for a social description of the historical community whose language is the target data. In order to illustrate the versatility of the corpus as a research tool for the study of the history of the English language, I offer a few sample analyses that address particular research questions, including the question of how a writer's treatment of his or her audience identity might possibly shape the text, thus introducing internal stylistic variation in a writer's *oeuvre*. As I work through these examples, I will discuss the procedures developed for text-formatting and forms of storage appropriate for these mini studies. I will attend to the coding practices adopted for including sociohistorical information, about the author of each text, but also about the addressee or recipient of each text, in the case of epistolary texts in the letters subcorpus. I will also report the procedures adopted to facilitate the use of automatic taggers on the corpus at the same time as ensuring that unique or specific physical and linguistic characteristics of the texts as collected, such as variant spellings, contractions and abbreviations (for instance, those used in autograph manuscript sources), can be recovered.

2 Social networks and the design of the Network of Eighteenth-Century English Texts corpus

The primary question that motivated the beginning of the construction of NEET in 1994 was how individuals affected the shape and construction of standard modern English in the prescriptive grammars in the second half of the eighteenth century. This long-term research programme is a sociohistorical linguistic study of the processes of linguistic standardization as the manifestation of social and cultural influence exerted by figures active in Augustan England. At the centre is Joseph Addison (1672–1719), one of the two principal figures behind the influential periodical *The Spectator*,[1] who is identified by prescriptive grammarians like Robert Lowth and Joseph Priestley as 'one of our best authors' (Wright, 1994; Tieken-Boon van Ostade, 1999). A manageable way to approach the very large question of influence is to consider the extent to which Addison's reputation influenced his own social circle, especially with respect to their language. Accordingly, I constructed an electronic corpus of texts produced by Addison and figures in his circle, as well as those on the periphery of his social network. The group currently comprises ten men and four women, most of whom contracted social ties with Addison between 1694 and 1713. These include Dryden, as well as his collaborator, Steele, university friend, Edward Wortley, and fellow Whig writers like Prior, Congreve and Stepney. Later, Addison acquired Swift and Alexander Pope among his literary acquaintance, and Lady Mary Wortley Montagu's marriage to Wortley in 1713 brought her into this circle. The early feminist Mary Astell was on the fringes of the Addison network, as a correspondent of Lady Mary Wortley Montagu (Grundy, 1999). In order to gain a perspective of the broader social and linguistic context that situates Addison's own cohort, I also collected the letters of contemporary figures who were never connected with Addison, including the political journalist and novelist Daniel Defoe, Sarah Churchill, Duchess of Marlborough, and Susannah Wesley, writer and wife of an Anglican preacher.[2]

The ties contracted between the actors within this network vary in terms of duration, strength of tie (weak or strong), purpose of connection (for example, patronage, friendship, professional collaboration), and the reciprocity and symmetry of tie.[3] For example, over time, Addison's network changed in its density (the number of connections between network members as a proportion of the maximum that could exist) and degree of multiplexity (the content of these connections). In the days of the Kit-Cat Club, all the writers knew one another and they encountered one another in a variety of settings. They collaborated with each other and socialized with each other, to make a dense, multiplex network. Figure 3.1 illustrates this network.

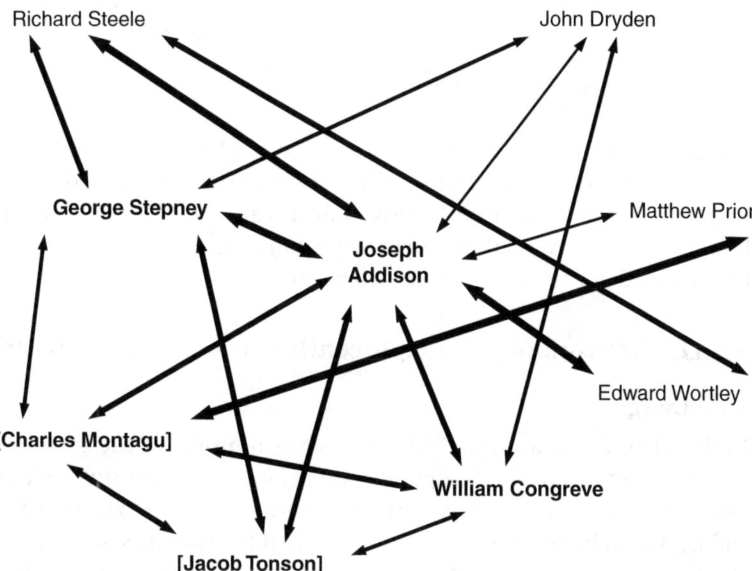

Figure 3.1 Joseph Addison and his circle, *c.*1700 (the Kit-Cat Club)

In contrast, in the heyday of *The Spectator*, younger authors separately sought connections with Addison as a likely literary sponsor and promoter of their work, and Addison himself cultivated the acquaintance of more powerful patrons than himself in order to advance his own standing in literary and political circles. Addison's network thus developed two tiers that rarely overlapped at more than one juncture, resulting in a less dense network of weaker ties. The relationships among these two groups of people described are summarized in the sociogram in Figure 3.2.

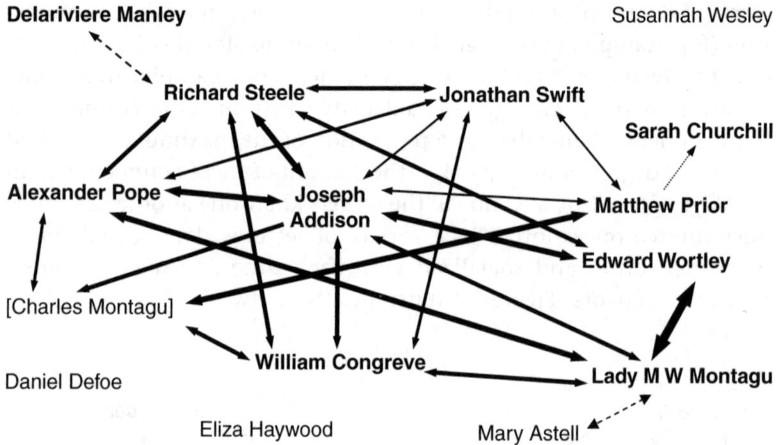

Figure 3.2 Joseph Addison and his circle, *c.*1711

The thicker the line, the stronger the relationship indicated. Accordingly, the weakest relationships are indicated by a dotted line. A line with arrowheads at both ends indicates a reciprocal relationship. In a non-reciprocal relationship, the person whose attentions are not reciprocated does not receive an arrowhead.

3 The Network of early Eighteenth-Century English Texts

3.1 Design

Table 3.1 provides a numerical and historical profile of the texts and writers in the corpus. The corpus consists of four prose registers: letters, essays, fiction and drama. Because the corpus design is grounded in and informed by social networks analysis and the specific social–historical ties that characterize the group, the texts collected in the corpus

Table 3.1 The NEET corpus

Writer	Dates of births and deaths	Letters: no. of words	Essays: no. of words	Fiction: no. of words	Drama: no. of words
John Dryden	1631–1700	23,068	57,299	N/A	28,266
Aphra Behn	1640–1688	N/A	N/A	59,797	24,597
Daniel Defoe	1660–1731	45,144	42,458	121,559	N/A
Sarah Churchill	1660–1744	50,728	16,213	N/A	N/A
George Stepney	1663–1707	19,690	N/A	N/A	N/A
Matthew Prior	1664–1721	20,848	14,520	N/A	N/A
Mary Astell	1666–1731	37,445	40,407	N/A	N/A
Jonathan Swift	1667–1745	48,143	43,043	N/A	N/A
Susannah Wesley	1669–1742	40,767	41,945	N/A	N/A
Delariviere Manley	1671–1724	N/A	N/A	41,562	N/A
William Congreve	1672–1729	26,382	20,479	21,235	28,604
Edward Wortley	1672–1761	25,396	N/A	N/A	N/A
Joseph Addison	1672–1719	50,791	42,248	N/A	N/A
Richard Steele	1672–1729	40,951	43,703	N/A	18,094
Alexander Pope	1688–1744	41,919	41,284	N/A	N/A
Mary Montagu	1689–1762	40,767	24,171	23,064	14,107
Eliza Haywood	1693–1756	N/A	N/A	13,698	19,426
Range	1631–1762	512,039	427,779	280,925	133,094

represent only the products of the writing practices of a group of peer figures (Fitzmaurice, 2002). The corpus was designed to facilitate the investigation of the role of author identity as well as register in linguistic variation in eighteenth-century English. To this end, it was important to include the kinds of writing produced by the figures in the group regardless of the fact that not all of the writers produce the same range or kinds of writing. Accordingly, 14 of the 17 figures are letter-writers, 12 are essay-writers, six are fiction-writers, and six (not the same six) are dramatists. William Congreve and Lady Mary Wortley Montagu alone among the 17 writers are exponents of all four registers. Congreve (1670–1729) was known principally as a dramatist, but he was also a member of the Kit-Cat Club, and a close friend and exact contemporary of fellow Whigs Joseph Addison and Richard Steele. He regarded John Dryden as a mentor and he knew Lady Mary Wortley Montagu (1689–1762) as a little girl when her father, Lord Kingston, introduced her to his fellow Kit-Cats as the Toast of the Club. As the second-youngest member of the set, and the last of the group to die,

Lady Mary Wortley Montagu represents the language of the mid eighteenth century. In contrast, Congreve's repertoire is emblematic of the language of the early part of the century (see Fitzmaurice, 2000b, for an assessment of Congreve's language status among his peers). Two of the oldest members of the set, John Dryden and Daniel Defoe, produce three registers each: Dryden produces letters, essays and plays, while Defoe produces letters, essays and fiction. These writers represent two very different social milieus. Although neither man seems to represent the mainstream (Dryden was a Catholic or Catholic sympathizer, and Defoe was a nonconformist Tory sympathizer), they occupy opposite ends of the social spectrum. Dryden had been the darling of James II, and the premier poet of the English court before the Glorious Revolution of 1688. In contrast, Defoe made a living as a journalist and spy for Robert Harley, but never attracted the attention or the patronage of the grandees who sponsored literary projects and the political careers of men like Addison or Steele.

A few comments about the contents of the registers, apart from the letters, are in order. In general, there are fewer texts in the fiction, drama and essay collections for each writer than in the letters collections. One obvious reason for this is that these people are less prolific in writing novels or plays than they are in writing letters, both professional and private. Thus the fiction collected for individual writers may consist of a single piece rather than a set of pieces or, indeed, a single piece selected on a principled basis. For example, Congreve's fiction is represented by his 1695 novella *Incognita*, the only piece of fiction he produced. Another obvious reason is that novels, unlike familiar letters, are sizeable documents, and therefore represent a substantial number of words in the register. Lady Mary Wortley Montagu's fiction is represented thus far in this corpus by *Princess Docile*, an autobiographical romance she wrote in retirement in Italy around 1756 (Grundy, 1999). In contrast, although Steele wrote a number of comedies, his drama is represented in NEET only by the 1705 comedy *The Tender Husband*. Lady Mary Wortley Montagu's drama is represented by her sole surviving attempt at playwriting, the 1734 comedy *Simplicity*.

It is striking how many of the writers are essayists: 12 out of the 17. Many of the eighteenth-century essays collected in NEET would most likely be regarded as journalism today. Defoe, Prior, Swift and Steele were political essayists, often producing propaganda and satire on behalf of the Whig or Tory parties. Defoe was editor of *The Review* (1704–13), a political journal published at the same time as Addison and Steele produced *The Spectator* (1710–12), followed by *The Guardian* (1713–14) and *The Freeholder* (1715–16). Lady Mary Wortley Montagu and Alexander Pope were occasional contributors to these journals. The essays written by Congreve and Dryden are different in focus and audience from those of the polemicists. Their essays are literary criticism, often written in response to reviews of their own work. The women writers in NEET are different again in terms of their essays' audience and concerns. Susannah Wesley, mother of John and Charles Wesley, founders of the Methodist movement, wrote instructional epistles for her children and conducted written theological debates with her sons. Mary Astell, a feminist and polemicist, wrote essays on women and education on the one hand, and conservative political essays on the other. These educated women writers, both reformers, differ markedly from Sarah Churchill, Duchess of Marlborough. Churchill's prose consists of political memoir: her own commentary on her experiences as a key political player in the court of Queen Anne by virtue of her role as the Queen's confidante.

3.2 Storage

The texts comprising the corpus are preserved as computer text files that can serve as digital facsimiles in the sense that all deletions and insertions, idiosyncratic spellings, abbreviations and historical conventions attending the eighteenth-century printed or autograph texts are preserved. I was anxious to ensure that the physical features of the texts were preserved as faithfully as possible, despite the impossibility of capturing the character of autograph manuscript documents. Transcribers preserved the spelling (however idiosyncratic it might be), abbreviations (whether conventional or not), deleted and inserted words and phrases, and syntax. Each text file has a fairly conventional header section consisting of information on the text, including the unique name of the text file, word count, the name of the author, the genre or register categorization of the text, the name of the text and the date of the text's production. The latter point warrants clarification: because the texts are drawn from manuscripts, printed texts, reprinted and edited texts, the date of production reflects the physical provenance rather than the actual composition of the text. This extremely rich format enables us to capture the physical characteristics of the source texts in sufficient detail for the historian, but these features do not make concordance work straightforward. Accordingly, as I attended to different analyses, I created 'clean' text files without deletions and insertions.

Additionally, for selected subcorpora, I made parallel modernized text files that can be subjected to grammatical tagging. It must be noted that a great deal of fix-tagging is required to make the results of tagging accurate. For example, in studies of modal expressions (Fitzmaurice, 2002), and the progressive construction (Fitzmaurice, 2004) in the language represented in the corpus, it was clear that modern taggers cannot accurately capture the historical nature of eighteenth-century British English lexis and lexico-grammar. I constructed special dictionaries for verbs and adverbs in order to ensure that the analysis was not skewed by misrepresentation. The latter point is particularly important for semantic–pragmatic analyses. For the letters subcorpus (as reported below in section 4.2), I added header data that enable the reader to place the letter as the product of a specific relationship between author and recipient. Some progress is being made to store parallel modernized versions of the texts to enable researchers to use standard corpus search software to answer particular questions.

4 Illustrative uses of the Network of Eighteenth-Century English Texts corpus

4.1 The progressive construction: variation and change

In Fitzmaurice (2004), I reported a comprehensive study of the nature and occurrence of the progressive construction in the NEET corpus. In this section, I illustrate the ways in which the corpus can serve as a database for the study of variation and change by offering a brief analysis of the construction's distribution and frequency in the idiolects of two writers, both exponents of all four registers represented in the corpus. These are William Congreve and Lady Mary Wortley Montagu. These writers belong to two distinct generations of writers in the corpus.

Table 3.2 summarizes the periods occupied by the three generations of writers whose work is collected in the corpus; it gives the lifespan of the generation first, and then gives the dates of the earliest and latest attested writings produced by each generation. The generational

Table 3.2 Writing periods

Generation	Dates of birth and death	Period of writing
Generation 1	1630–1700	1653–1700
Generation 2	1660–1745	1693–1731
Generation 3	1688–1762	1710–1762

periods are thus 1630–1700, John Dryden's dates of birth and death; 1660–1745, the birth dates of Daniel Defoe and Sarah Churchill and the date of Swift's death; and 1688–1762, Alexander Pope's date of birth and the date of Mary Wortley Montagu's death. The total period spanned by the writing in the corpus is over one hundred years: from 1653, represented by a letter from John Dryden to his wife, Honor, through to 1762, represented by a letter from Lady Mary Wortley Montagu to Lady Frances Steuart, written just before Lady Mary's death. The earliest drama text (out of a total of six) is John Dryden's *Marriage à la Mode,* produced in 1673, and the latest is Lady Mary Wortley Montagu's *Simplicity* (1734). The earliest piece of fiction in the corpus is Congreve's 1695 novella *Incognita,* and the latest is Lady Mary Wortley Montagu's *Princess Docile* (1756). The essays range from Dryden's *Essay on Dramatic Poesie* (1668) to Sarah Churchill's 1745 political memoir.

The expressions in (1) exemplify the way in which William Congreve and Mary Wortley Montagu use the progressive in their own language:

(1) a. They put me in mind (Tho at a different time of year) of the Roman Saturnalia, when all the Scum, and Rabble, and Slaves of Rome, by a kind of Annual and limited Manumission, were suffered to make Abominable Mirth, and Profane the Days of Jubilee, with Vile Buffoonry, by Authority. But I forget that *I am writing* a Post Letter, and run into length like a Poet in a Dedication, when he forgets his Patron to talk of himself.
(William Congreve to John Dennis [cclet053])

b. I beg your pardon, dear madam, for this long relation; but 'tis impossible to be short on so copious a subject; and you must own this action very well worthy of record, and I think not to be paralleled in any history, ancient or modern. I look so little in my own eyes (who *was at that time ingloriously sitting* over a tea-table), I hardly dare subscribe myself even,
(Lady Mary Wortley Montagu, to Lady Pomfret, 1739)

c. The Fairy *was always scolding* her, and never spoke of her without the epithet, that poor chatterbox; yet since it was she who sat up with her when she was ill or fancied herself so, and who gave her her potions, she had imperceptibly acquired the right to say whatever she wanted, and her perpetual babbling had more effect on the Fairy's mind than the greatest Eloquence could have had.
(Lady Mary Wortley Montagu, *Princess Docile*)

d. While the Marquess and Don Fabritio, *were wondering at, and lamenting* the Misfortune of her loss, Hippolito came towards Don Fabio and interceded for his Son, since the Lady perhaps had withdrawn her self, out of an aversion to the Match. (Congreve, *Incognita*, 1695 [ccfic001])

The quotations in (1a) and (1b), taken from personal letters, and (1c), from fiction, illustrate the most prevalent use of the construction in the period: as a backgrounding device marking duration or iteration of an activity in subordinate clauses. Examples (1b) and (1c) exhibit the ways in which the force of the verb in the progressive can be strengthened by lexical support, in these cases by manner and temporal adverbs respectively. Additionally, (1c) illustrates the use of the construction in a main clause context.[4] The quotations in (2) illustrate the construction's use in comic prose drama and in essays.

(2) a. Mrs. Fainall. Mirabell, there's a Necessity for your obedience, - You have neither time to talk nor stay. My Mother *is coming*; and in my Conscience if she should see you, wou'd fall into fits, and maybe not recover time enough to return to Sir Rowland, who as Foible tells me is in a fair way to succeed. Therefore spare your Extacies for another occasion, and slip down the back-stairs, where Foible waits to consult you. (Congreve, *The Way of the World* [ccdr011])

b. Bellinda: (sola) My heart *is breaking*. I hate every body, I hate my selfe, I could tear the whole world to pieces. (Wortley Montagu, *Simplicity, A Comedy* [mmdr001])

c. And such are they that only relish the obscene and foul things in Poets; which makes the Profession taxed But by whom? Men that watch for it, &c. Some thing farther in the same Discoveries, *He is speaking* again very much to our purpose for it is in justification of presenting vicious and foolish Characters: on the Stage in Comedy. (Congreve [ccess001])

d. Almeria, in the Play, oppressed and sinking beneath her Grief, adapts her words to her Posture, and says to Osmin One would think (says Mr. Collier) she *was learning* a Spaniel to set Learning a Spaniel to set! is an Aphorism of Julius Caesar, and Mr. Collier makes it plain. This poor Man does not so much as understand, even his own Dog language, when he says learn-

ing, I suppose he means teaching a Spaniel to set, a dainty Critick, indeed!
(Congreve [ccess002])

Figure 3.3 summarizes the relative distribution of the progressive across the four registers in the corpus by generation. This picture provides a little context for examining the occurrence of the construction in the work of Wortley Montagu and of Congreve, compared with the use of their generations and their sexes as represented in Figure 3.4.

Congreve and Montagu follow the general trends exhibited both by their own generations (generation 2 and 3 respectively) and by their own sexes across the registers. However, what is striking is that Congreve favours the progressive less in his essays and in his drama than all of the comparison groups, and (except for Montagu) he favours the progressive in his fiction more than any of the comparison groups. Montagu appears to use the progressive more frequently than her comparison groups in fiction and emphatically in drama. As far as register is concerned, both Congreve and Montagu exhibit a greater preference than their comparison groups for the construction. Now, it is important to remember that there are very few exponents of fiction represented in the corpus: Congreve and Montagu are two out of a total of six fiction writers. Accordingly, the size and shape of the sample might have the effect of highlighting the progressive's use by these writers. Only Montagu, the second youngest writer sampled for

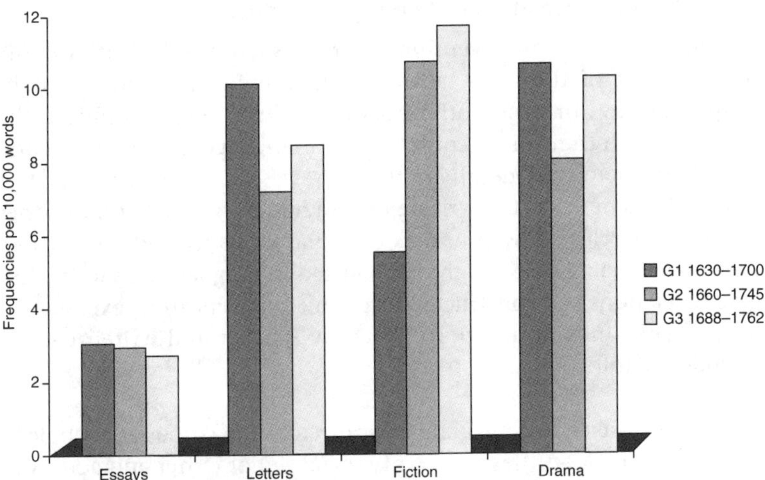

Figure 3.3 Mean frequencies across registers and generation

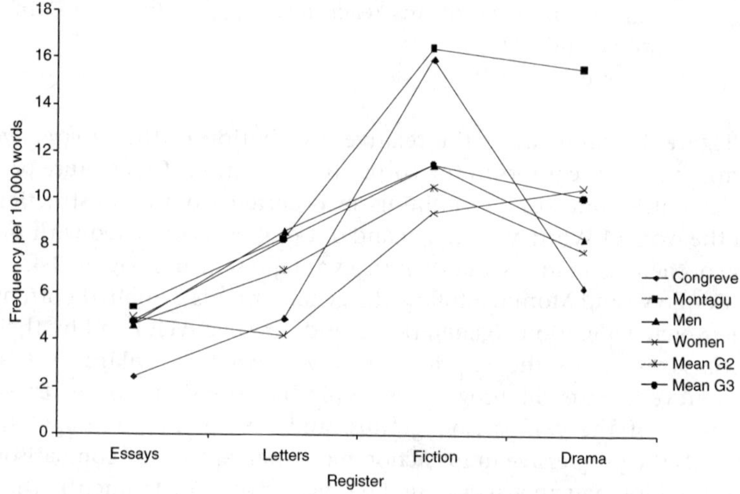

Figure 3.4 Congreve and Montagu (comparison with sex and generation)

NEET, exhibits a clear preference for the construction in her fiction and letters. It should be noted that because this corpus is *not* representative, it is impossible to extrapolate from the results reported generalizations regarding the performance or preferences of actual generations. However, it is possible to explore the idiolects of individuals, such as Montagu and Congreve.

4.2 The influence of identity on speaker attitude

The design of an unconventional corpus such as NEET affords the investigation of the ways in which an individual's identity might shape the ways in which others address him or her, and indeed the ways in which they might construct their language in order to accommodate the perceived identity of the addressee. In other words, the fact that NEET is built on the writing of individuals whose lives, histories and social circles are well understood enables us to study how those personal characteristics might be reflected in language and in the linguistic relationships constructed through communicative texts such as letters. The kinds of questions raised by speaker and writer identity include the following:

- How is speaker attitude grammaticalized in the corpus as a whole?
- How do the identities (sex, rank, social tie) of writer and addressee influence people's choice of attitude markers?

Table 3.3 Markers of speaker attitude

DESIRE Vto	desire verb + *to*-clause (e.g. *want, long, hope, desire to*)
ATT Vth	attitudinal verb + *that*-clause (e.g. *hope, seem that*)
PRED ADJ	predicative adjective (e.g. *be good, fine*)
EVALJ	evaluative adjective (e.g. *good, perfect, desirable*)
ATTADVL	attitude adverbial (e.g. *wisely, properly, decently, humbly, confusedly*)
DOWNTONER	downtoners (*barely, hardly, only*)
GEN HEDGE	hedges (*about, something like*)
AMPLIF	amplifiers (*very, absolutely, extremely, perfectly, mightily, entirely, heartily, infinitely, exactly*)
EMPH	emphatics (*indeed, sure, really*)

To approach these questions, I first of all conducted a search of the corpus to discover the ways in which speaker attitude is realized linguistically. Markers of speaker attitude turn out to be just that: constructions that encode speakers' desires, wishes, and evaluations of people, things and events. This investigation yielded the sample list of features shown in Table 3.3.

Importantly, the lexical study of the corpus indicated that a tagger designed for the grammatical analysis of present-day American English needed to be substantially adapted for the analysis of late seventeenth- and eighteenth-century British English. For example, the dictionary of general hedges for the NEET corpus does not include the periphrastic *sort of* or *kind of*; the adverb *nearly* in NEET is not a downtoner meaning 'almost', but a manner adverbial better construed as 'closely'. Similarly, the adverb *slightly* in NEET must be construed as an attitude adverbial meaning 'in a denigrating way' rather than an adverb construed as 'a bit'. Additionally, because the meanings of the modal auxiliary verbs in NEET vary pragmatically and situationally, the construction of a dedicated dictionary is not much help in counting categories of modal.[5] Accordingly, the modals were omitted from this study.

The next step in the study was to extract the letters subcorpus from the whole corpus to capture the correspondences of thirteen people. The details of the letters subcorpus are outlined in Table 3.4.

The dates for each letter-writer are given to indicate, principally, the end-date of an individual's correspondence, and the number of letters written by each writer is given to indicate that they vary quite considerably with respect to their *oeuvre*. In order to investigate the ways in which speaker identity might shape language, I created a header for

Table 3.4 Correspondences in NEET

Name	Dates	No. of texts
Dryden, John	1631–1700	64
Stepney, George	1663–1707	31
Defoe, Daniel	1660–1731	89
Churchill, Sarah	1660–1744	106
Prior, Matthew	1664–1721	45
Astell, Mary	1666–1731	48
Swift, Jonathan	1667–1745	65
Congreve, William	1670–1729	65
Wortley, Edward	1672–1761	48
Addison, Joseph	1672–1719	89
Steele, Richard	1672–1729	258
Pope, Alexander	1688–1744	63
Montagu, Lady Mary Wortley	1689–1762	57
Range	1631–1762	1,028

each letter that could be scanned for particular variables and the values extracted as context for the study of the language of the letter. The header of each letter thus consists of a set of variables designed to capture specific aspects of the author's identity, as well as those of the recipient of the letter. Some are straightforward to assess, others are harder to determine in the absence of knowledge of the ways in which status and rank work in eighteenth-century England on the one hand, and of the personal ties (nature as well as strength) between author and recipient on the other. I considered the variables shown in Table 3.5.

Table 3.5 Social variables represented in metadata headers

Author parameter	Values	Recipient parameter	Values
Author sex	1 (male) 2 (female)	Recipient sex	1 (male) 2 (female)
Author rank	1 (middling) 2 (upper middle) 3 (aristocratic/titled)	Recipient rank	1 (middling) 2 (upper middle) 3 (aristocratic/titled)
Author tie	1 (weak) 2 (medium) 3 (strong/intimate)	Recipient tie	0 (none) 1 (weak) 2 (medium) 3 (strong/intimate)

The sex variable is unproblematic: it consists of just two levels, 1 = male and 2 = female. Rank has three values or levels, determined in a relatively superficial and straightforward fashion. Level 3 is aristocratic or formal. This captures titles such as Earl, Duke, Bishop, Duchess and so on, and address forms such as 'My Lord', 'Your Lordship' and 'Your Ladyship'. Upper-middle-class rank was assigned a value of 2. This category includes people with civil service occupations and university educations. This is possibly the most difficult category to delineate accurately because the period sees the development of occupations that would become associated with what we now call upper-middle-class values, incomes and prestige. For example, it was only with Halifax's establishment of the London Stock Exchange in the last decade of the seventeenth century that the occupation of stockbroker (then 'stockjobber') emerged, but in its early manifestations the occupation was not a viable respectable occupation for the sons of gentlemen; the occupation was more likely to recruit the sons of merchants and tradesmen, members of what Defoe calls the 'middling sort'. In the early eighteenth century, professions such as banking and the law gathered prestige and recognition to be viable for the sons of the gentry. The category of tradesmen, secretaries like Joshua Dawson (Addison's secretary), and freelancing spies and journalists like Defoe belong to the rank of the middling sort, designated 1. They had non-university and nonconformist educations, and had no access to the civil service and thereby the patronage of the aristocracy. In addition, self-made, entrepreneurial women like Aphra Behn are members of this set. Rank can change over time. For example, Charles Montagu starts out as a member of the untitled gentry (among what we might describe as the upper middle classes: 2) but is elevated to 3 when he is made Earl of Halifax in 1704.

Social tie is infinitely more complicated. These are operationalized as directional. For example, Author tie is the value of the tie with the addressee of the letter, as perceived from the perspective of the author. Recipient tie is the opposite, namely, it is the value of the tie as perceived from the perspective of the recipient. This directional operationalization of the tie allows us to incorporate non-symmetrical ties into the mix, as well as tie strength. The value of 3 is strong, 2 is medium, 1 is weak, and zero (0) indicates no tie at all. The availability of a value of zero allows us to capture the function of a relationship that is not reciprocated. An example of such a tie is the gesture made by Matthew Prior to Sarah Churchill, the Duchess of Marlborough, which, though remarked upon by the recipient, was never returned.

Social ties may change over time just as acquaintanceships turn into friendships, so that Charles Montagu's recipient tie to Joseph Addison in 1699 [alet007] is 0, but by 1704 it has changed to 2.

A number of computer programs developed by Douglas Biber and his colleagues for the *Longman Grammar of Spoken and Written English* (Biber *et al.*, 1999) were used for the linguistic analysis of the tagged version of the NEET letters corpus. As mentioned, the problems we encountered concerned the mismatch of the tagger developed for the *Longman Grammar* and the eighteenth-century corpus, as far as lexicon is concerned. Simple form–class category tags were generally fine: the default category is N, and so any lexical item that was unfamiliar and seemed to be parsable as a Noun was identified as N. More problematic were abbreviations and spelling variations. The lack of standard abbreviations for expressions like *I'll* (for example, *Ile, I'le*) resulted in tag errors, and the spelling variations in Stepney's letters for modals (*cou'd, coud, could*) created tagging errors too. These were rectified by creating modernized spelling versions of the files specifically for the analysis. It is clear that in order to make the NEET corpus as versatile as possible, a parallel modernized version will have to be built.

Once the files were tagged, they were checked, and then they were scanned by a computer program to yield frequency counts for selected stance variables according to the different values of the social parameters: author sex, rank and tie, and recipient sex, rank and tie. I extracted selected attitudinal markers and surveyed the output to determine any patterns. I then examined various combinations of parameter values to try to figure out what parameters seem to condition or otherwise shape the expression of attitude in the letters. The analyses afforded can range from the straightforward to the very complicated: it is possible to examine attitude in terms of a single variable, such as author sex (Figure 3.5), two variables, such as author sex and recipient sex (Figure 3.6), and then by rank and tie (as exemplified in Figures 3.7 and 3.8).

Looking at the pattern of use in Figure 3.5, we can infer that women authors appear to use more predicative adjectives, amplifiers and general emphatics than do men authors. This pattern is illustrated in the following extract taken from a letter from Mary Wortley Montagu to her sister, Lady Mar (31 October 1723), in which I highlight the attitude markers in bold italics.

(3) I write to you at this time *piping hot* from the Birth night, my Brain, warm'd with all the ***Agreable*** Ideas that ***fine*** Cloths, ***fine***

> Gentlemen, brisk Tunes and lively dances can raise there. ***'Tis to be hoped*** that my Letter will entertain you; at least you will certainly have the ***freshest*** Account of all passages on that ***Glorious*** day. First, ***you must know*** that I led up the ball, which you'll stare at; but what's more, I think in my Conscience I made one of the ***best*** figures there. ***To say truth***, people grown *so* ***extravagantly ugly*** that we ***old Beautys*** are forced to come out on show days to keep the Court in Countenance. I saw Mrs Murray there, through whose hands this Epistle is to be conveyed. I don't know whither she'll make the same Complaint to you that I do. Mrs West was there, who is a ***great Prude***, having but 2 lovers at a Time; I think those are Lord Haddingtoun and Mr Lindsay, the one for use, the one show.

If we examine Figure 3.6, we see that authors tend to respond to women recipients by using slightly more predicative adjectives and general emphatics when they address them, compared with minutely fewer predicative and evaluative adjectives and emphatics when addressing men. In contrast, male addressees appear to elicit more amplifiers than do women.

In Figure 3.7, which illustrates the practices of authors in the upper middle ranks when addressing their betters, their peers and their inferiors, we see that inferior ranks elicit fewer infinitival complements with

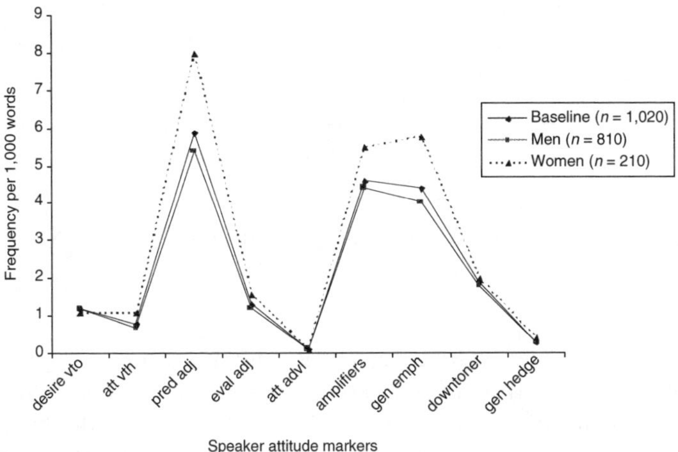

Figure 3.5 Speaker attitude by author sex

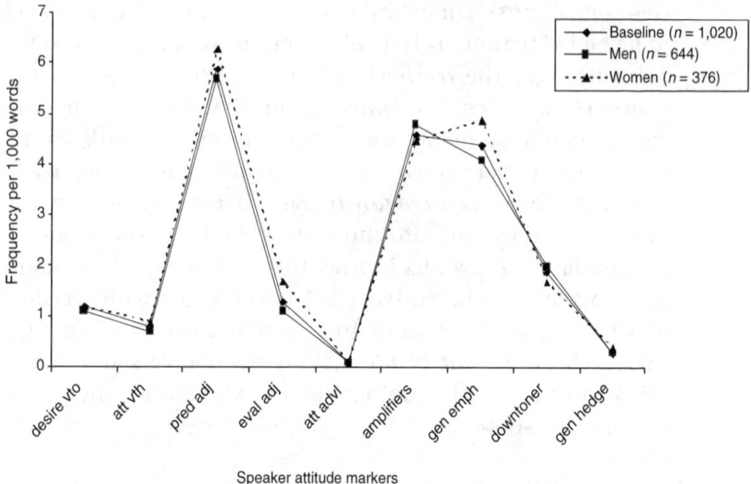

Figure 3.6 Speaker attitude by sex of recipient

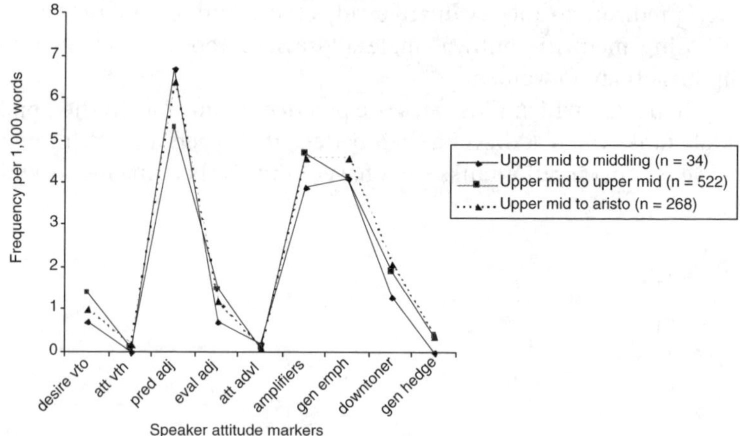

Figure 3.7 Speaker attitude by upper-middle rank of author

verbs of desire, evaluative adjectives, amplifiers, downtoners, and hedges, and slightly more predicative adjectives, than other addressees. In contrast, aristocratic recipients elicit more predicative adjectives and emphatics than upper-middle-ranking recipients, but comparable levels of amplifiers, downtoners and hedges.

This pattern is illustrated effectively in a letter from Joseph Addison to his superior, Charles Montagu, Earl of Manchester (4), in which he is hard at work thanking his recipient for favours rendered.

(4) I was *extremely* glad to hear your Lordship had entered on a post that would give you an occasion of advancing *so much* the Interest and Reputation of your Country: but I now find that I have *more particular* reasons to rejoice at your promotion Since I hear you have lately done me the honour to mention me *kindly* to my Lord Halifax. As this is not the first favour you have been pleased to show me I must confess I should be *very ambitious* of an opportunity to let you know how just a sense I have of the Gratitude and Duty that I owe to your Lordship.

What is striking about all of Figures 3.5–3.8 is that the patterning in the linguistic realization of speaker attitude does not vary much at all according to the variable(s) examined. However, there is minute and subtle variation: note that people with reciprocally strong ties differ depending upon the combination of author sex, the combination of author sex and recipient sex, or indeed rank of author.

This kind of analysis is interesting in that it paves the way for an in-depth analysis deploying a range of different linguistic features in order to investigate the extent to which author and recipient identity shape and affect the language chosen to represent the author. For example, it

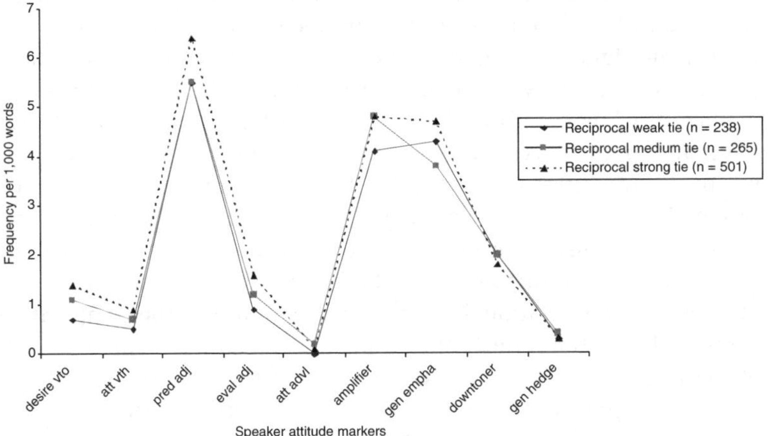

Figure 3.8 Speaker attitude by reciprocal tie

is possible to explore the difference between sex and gender by seeing whether men write more like women (as suggested by Figures 3.5 and 3.6) when they address women, than like men. Additionally, it is possible to refine this analysis considerably to examine whether authors change their language over time in response to a changing relationship with their addressee, or indeed in response to the changing status or rank of an addressee.

4.3 Standardization, literacy and print publication

My final illustration concerns the ways in which an unconventional corpus like NEET can afford the study of physical and cultural attributes of a range of registers and writers' practices in a convenient format. Sample questions that arise regarding matters of standardization and physical representation of language include:

- Do literacy practices normalize the language of individuals?
- Do printing practices suppress variation in the look of language?
- Does print publication of essays affect the representation of language?

Because these questions are not easily posed in the investigation of electronic corpora, I offer a brief survey of how we might answer such questions and, in so doing, illustrate the versatility of unconventional corpora. In order to examine literacy practices of individuals in the period covered by NEET, I extracted letters and essays for a subcorpus (see Table 3.6). We know a great deal about the letters produced by our authors: the identity and histories of their recipients, the relationships constructed by the authors with those recipients, the purpose of the letters, the duration of correspondences, where relevant, as well as whether the letters were collected into edited volumes to be printed mementos of their authors. Where letter-writers are also essayists, we have the opportunity to consider whether they treated the work of writing essays differently from that of corresponding with people. We can make inferences about their lives as amateur or professional authors, as publishers or printers of their own work, and about their practices and relationships with the book trade. For this study, the inclusion of two situationally distinct registers affords the comparative study of the possible effects of printing practices on the representation of the language in published essays, as well as the study of authors' own literacy practices adopted in autograph letters and essays.

For this illustrative survey, I select a couple of examples from a set of typical contractions that we encounter in texts of the period. The con-

Table 3.6 The subcorpus of letters and essays

Writer	Dates of births and deaths	Letters: no. of words	Essays: no. of words
John Dryden	1631–1700	20,721	57,299
Daniel Defoe	1660–1731	43,490	42,458
Sarah Churchill	1660–1744	51,520	16,213
George Stepney	1663–1707	19,392	N/A
Matthew Prior	1664–1721	19,676	14,520
Mary Astell	1666–1731	36,221	40,407
Jonathan Swift	1667–1745	47,377	43,043
Susannah Wesley	1669–1742	N/A	41,945
William Congreve	1672–1729	21,582	20,479
Edward Wortley	1672–1761	25,396	N/A
Joseph Addison	1672–1719	29,903	42,248
Richard Steele	1672–1729	20,689	43,703
Alexander Pope	1688–1744	40,799	41,284
Mary Montagu	1689–1762	37,175	24,171
Range	1631–1762	413,941	427,770

traction set includes both orthographic contractions that have a distinct phonological effect and orthographic contractions that are purely visual, and thus are relevant only for the impression left on the page. These are listed in Table 3.7. In the interests of brevity, I illustrate the relative distribution of the contracted and full representations of the object pronoun *them* in essays and letters, and that of the contracted and full representation of *though* in the same registers.

Figure 3.9 and Table 3.8 summarize the relative distribution of *'em* and *them* in the subcorpus.

If we assume that the handwriting characterizing the personal letter is likely to be marked by contractions that represent an economy of effort without risking disapproval of the implied informality, it would follow that late-seventeenth- and eighteenth-century letters are more likely to be marked by contractions than essays. And this is the case, although the letter-writers are by no means uniform in their preference for the contraction, ranging from zero use (Defoe, Swift and Congreve) to a high of 56 per cent in the letters of Edward Wortley. An observation

Table 3.7 Orthographic/graphological/linguistic features

Contractions (phonological)	*'em/em, 'tis/tis, 'twas/twas, don't/can't/won't/shan't*
Contractions (visual)	*Tho'/though, defy'd/defied*

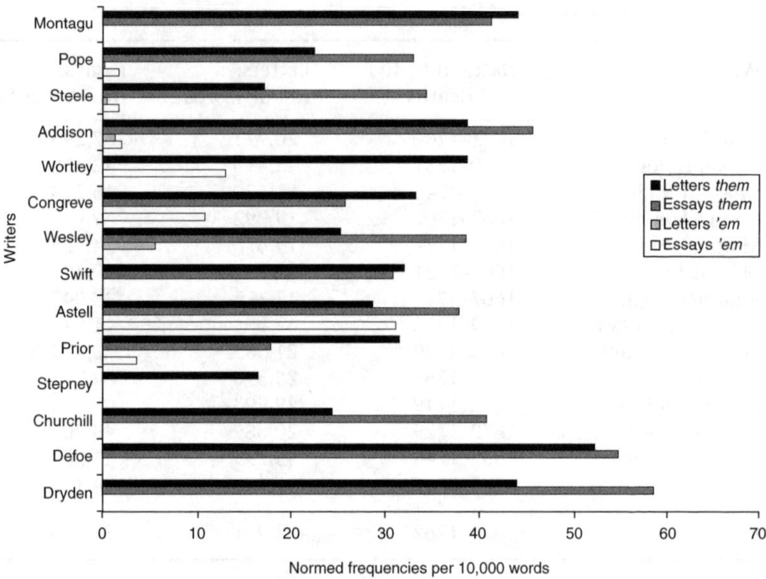

Figure 3.9 *'em* v. *them* in essays and letters

Table 3.8 Form of the third person plural object pronoun in letters and essays

	Essays ***'em***	**Essays** ***them***	**Letters** ***'em***	**Letters** ***them***
Dryden	0	58.64 (100%)	0.43 (1%)	45.24 (99%)
Defoe	0	54.88 (100%)	0	52.50 (100%)
Churchill	0	40.71 (100%)	0.18 (1%)	23.86 (99%)
Stepney			1.02 (6%)	15.32 (94%)
Prior	3.44 (16%)	17.91 (84%)	2.82 (9%)	28.68 (91%)
Astell	31.18 (45%)	37.86 (55%)	0.53 (2%)	28.04 (98%)
Swift	0	30.89 (100%)	0	27.42 (100%)
Wesley	0	38.62 (100%)	5.4 (18%)	25.28 (82%)
Congreve	10.74 (29%)	25.88 (71%)	0	32.21 (100%)
Wortley			12.99 (56%)	10.24 (44%)
Addison	1.89 (4%)	45.68 (96%)	12.18 (27%)	20.43 (63%)
Steele	1.83 (5%)	34.55 (95%)	2.20 (20%)	9.04 (80%)
Pope	1.69 (5%)	33.18 (95%)	4.77 (21%)	17.89 (79%)
Montagu	0	41.37 (100%)	3.86 (9%)	37.84 (91%)

that we might make about the patterns of preference exhibited for the reduced pronoun instead of the full form is that a number of the younger writers in the group appear to adopt the reduced form, albeit infrequently, in both registers. Of these, Addison, Steele and Pope select the reduced form more than 20 per cent of the time in their letters. This group is characterized by political and social affiliations as well as collaborating in periodical projects such as *The Spectator* and *The Freeholder*. It is interesting to speculate (and consider in further research) whether the level and intensity of the interaction among this group influences the frequency with which they adopt features such as this contraction. As I have shown elsewhere (Wright, 1997), Addison began to eschew use of the contraction around 1715, when he undertook to revise works such as his *Tour of Italy*, first published in 1703, which exhibited a marked use of the contraction.

Interestingly, the work of three other essayists (Prior, Mary Astell and William Congreve) exhibit more frequent use of the contraction but none at all in their letters. Indeed, despite the fact that Astell's essays exhibit a hearty use of the reduction (45 per cent), her letters show the reduced form just 2 per cent of the time.

The contrast in Astell's *oeuvre*, a contrast that would seem to be quite counter-intuitive, suggests that we might look at the practices followed by the printing house that produced her essays. If her autograph letters do not exhibit any clear preference for the reduced pronoun, it is reasonable to assume that the convention was introduced in the procedure that transformed the manuscript into print. Indeed, examination of the letters indicates that the only incidences of the contracted *'em* form appear in two (published) letters to John Norris of Bremerton:

(5) Reading the other day the Third Volume of your excellent Discourses, as I do every thing you Write with great Pleasure and no less Advantage yet taking the liberty that I use with other Books, (and yours or no bodies will bear it) to raise all the Objections that ever I can, and to make them undergo the severest Test my Thoughts can put *'em* to before they pass for currant, a difficulty arose which Without your assistance I know not how to solve.
(Mary Astell to John Norris of Bremerton, 21 September 1693 [malet001])

(6) Now I am loath to abandon all Thoughts of Friendship, both because it is one of the brightest Vertues, and because I have the noblest Designs in it. Fain would I rescue my Sex, or at least as many of them as come within my little Sphere, from that Meanness of Spirit into which the Generality of *'em* are sunk perswade them to pretend some higher Excellency than a well-chosen Pettycoat or a fashionable Commode and not

wholly lay out their Time and Care in the Adornation of their Bodies, but bestow a Part of it at least in the Embellishment of their Minds, since inward Beauty will last when outward is decayed.
(Mary Astell to John Norris of Bremerton, All Saints Eve, 1693 [malet043])

If we turn to look at the distribution of *though* and its visual contracted form *tho(')* in the subcorpus, we see that Mary Astell prefers the contraction in her essays, yet not in her letters. Again, this apparently counter-intuitive pattern seems to echo the preference she demonstrates for the contracted form *'em* in her essays, at the same time as she demonstrates a preference for the full form *them* in her letters. In the case of *tho'*, it appears that the only times that she uses the contraction in her letters is in unpublished letters (to Lady Anne Coventry and to John Walker). In contrast, all the occurrences of the full form *though* occur in five published letters to John Norris ([malet044], [malet045], [malet046], [malet047] and [malet048]), a fact that indicates that the choice of the form is less a matter of personal authorial preference and more one of editorial or publishing practice.

Table 3.9 presents a fuller picture of the extent to which the visual contraction *tho(')* and its full form *though* appear in the two registers in the subcorpus. All the essay-writers except Defoe adopt the contrac-

Table 3.9 Relative distribution of the visual contraction *tho/though* in essays and letters

	Essays ***tho(')***	**Essays** ***though***	**Letters** ***tho(')***	**Letters** ***though***
Dryden	0.17 (4%)	17.10 (96%)	2.15 (15%)	12.50 (85%)
Defoe	0	12.48 (100%)	11.74 (100%)	0
Churchill	0.62 (3%)	23.44 (97%)	15.07 (80%)	3.77 (20%)
Stepney			6.64 (100%)	0
Prior	11.70 (100%)	0	6.11 (100%)	0
Astell	8.91 (55%)	7.18 (45%)	10.68 (29%)	26.50 (71%)
Swift	2.32 (31%)	5.11 (69%)	4.16 (35%)	7.69 (65%)
Wesley	1.67 (8%)	18.59 (92%)	0	20.12 (100%)
Congreve	6.84 (64%)	3.91 (36%)	14.78 (65%)	7.96 (35%)
Wortley			14.18 (100%)	0
Addison	4.02 (49%)	4.26 (51%)	11.40 (92%)	0.98 (8%)
Steele	6.18 (67%)	2.97 (33%)	6.59 (79%)	1.71 (11%)
Pope	9.20 (84%)	1.69 (16%)	11.45 (91%)	1.19 (9%)
Montagu	12.83 (97%)	0.41 (3%)	15.67 (90%)	1.69 (10%)

tion, though the range is between a low of 3 per cent (in Sarah Churchill's memoir) and a high of 100 per cent (in Prior's essays). The essays in which the contraction appears most of the time include those of Mary Astell (55 per cent) as noted, William Congreve (64 per cent), Richard Steele (67 per cent), Alexander Pope (84 per cent) and Mary Montagu (97 per cent). It is at least possible that adopting *tho'* in place of *though* is an economy measure for the printer: not only does it use fewer graphs, and thus saves both paper and the number of letters needed to be typeset, it also saves space between lines because it does not consist of both ascenders and descenders.

When we examine the pattern of choice in letters, it appears that Defoe appears to use the contraction categorically in letters and the full form categorically in essays. In contrast, Matthew Prior uses the contraction all the time in both his essays and his letters. Additional categorical users of the contraction in their letters are George Stepney and Edward Wortley. Letter-writers who favour the contraction, using it more than 65 per cent of the time, include Sarah Churchill, William Congreve, Joseph Addison, Richard Steele, Alexander Pope and Mary Montagu. John Dryden demonstrates an overwhelming preference for the opposite, the uncontracted form, particularly in his essays, but also in his letters, where he opts for the uncontracted form 65 per cent of the time. Jonathan Swift is similarly consistent in preferring *tho(')*, though this preference is not as marked as Dryden's: he selects the uncontracted form about two-thirds of the time in his essays and in his letters.

The NEET corpus appears to provide a rich database for the study of standardization or normalization in the visual and stylistic representation of language, as well as in the lexico-grammatical system of the language. Such richness encourages the extensive study of other visual characteristics of the texts collected as part of the corpus. In section 4.2 above, I pointed out the need to develop a version of the corpus that has modernized spelling, to enable researchers to use taggers and parsers developed primarily for electronic corpora of modern English. In this section, the questions raised about the extent to which electronic corpora can support the investigation of literacy practices through the study of the physical and visual representation of language suggest that it is important to maintain a format that is faithful to the source materials. To illustrate the extent of the visual and physical richness of the texts collected in the corpus, I copy here two versions of the same text: a faithfully reproduced transcription of the autograph manuscript text found in the British Library, and a modernized version of the text.

(7) a. Transcript from Autograph letter:
(George Stepney to Henry Davenant, December 1706, British Library Add. MS. 4740: The Correspondence of Henry Davenant vol 1, f.166: autograph postscript to official news in his secretary's hand [gslet016])

Sir

I am to thank you for yr favrs of ye 12th & 23rd Inst

I spoke to my Ld Duke in ye Brat as I promisd you, & I learnd He had not reminded Ld Treasurer but woud upon his arrivall, & I hope he has done it. You must not be impatient, but take for granted you will be provided for when it can be done conveniently.

I have layd in for Lampoons, Plays, &c: & as soon as I receive any, you shall be servd.

Ime glad yr father has been informd by Mr Cardonnel that my honest endeavours have not been wanting; I faithfully performd all yr commands; & shall be ready to serve you when ever any occasion presents.

The Civill terms wherewith these people dismissed James might be according to ye Bruer Nil mali de mortui, for such they took ye Margrave, & every body here takes for granted that He is going the way of all flesh.

Wee are in our Holy Days, and have no news I wish you a Happy New Year

b. Modernized version with metadata of Stepney's letter to Davenant.

<Text type>Letters
<Author>George Stepney
<Author sex>1
<Author rank>2
<Author tie>2
<Recipient>Henry Davenant
<Recipient sex>1
<Recipient rank>2
<Recipient tie>2
<Date written>December 28, 1706, The Hague.
<# of words>216
<Comments>British Library Add. MS. 4740: The Correspondence of Henry Davenant

vol 1, f.166: autograph postscript to official news in his secretary's hand

Sir

I am to thank you for your favors of the 12th and 23rd Instant.
I spoke to my Lord Duke in the Brat as I promised you, and I learned He had not reminded Lord Treasurer but would upon his arrival, and I hope he has done it. You must not be impatient, but take for granted you will be provided for when it can be done conveniently.
I have laid in for Lampoons, Plays, &c: and as soon as I receive any, you shall be served.
I'm glad your father has been informed by Mr. Cardonnel that my honest endeavours have not been wanting; I faithfully performed all your commands; and shall be ready to serve you whenever any <[v]> occasion presents.
The Civil terms wherewith these people dismissed James might be according to the Bruer <Nil mali de mortui>, for such they took the Margrave, and every body here takes for granted that He is going the way of all flesh.

We are in our holidays <Holy Days>, and have no news I wish you a Happy New Year

5 Concluding remarks

I began this chapter with the promise to illustrate the uses of an unconventional corpus such as the Network of Eighteenth-century English Texts as a research tool and database for the linguistic investigation of variation and change. Although the corpus has proved plastic and versatile enough to accommodate the quite diverse kinds of analyses discussed and reported in this chapter, it is evident that the corpus is still under construction. There are several major tasks that remain for the NEET corpus to be a versatile and properly user-friendly research tool:

- One major task ahead is the completion of a parallel modernized version for each of the registers (in addition to the letters register).
- In order to ensure that the corpus is maximally useful, the tagger used thus far needs to be run through the entire corpus with extensive fix-tagging done, for two reasons. The first reason is to enable

the tagger to be adapted to capture as accurately as possible the range and nature of grammatical constructions in the corpus texts. The second is to enable me to extract all the lexical expressions that the tagger cannot recognize and complete a comprehensive dictionary of items.[6] The latter project would allow the corpus to be more accessible for large-scale semantic–pragmatic studies.[7]

- A properly comprehensive investigation of the effects of author and recipient identity on language would be greatly supported by the judicious expansion of the letters subcorpus to flesh out the correspondences already in the corpus. For example, the Pope and Swift subcorpora do not include a number of letters written to women friends. It would be ideal to expand the letters subcorpus in general to include more women writers.
- The registers should be better rounded out by adding prose dramas for all the writers who produce drama. Thus the corpus should include more prose comedies by Steele and Congreve.
- Finally, it would be ideal to provide as much historical, bibliographical and textual data as possible in the headers of each file in the corpus to make the corpus materials transparent and accessible for multiple research approaches.

Appendix: format of letters corpus for the analysis of speaker attitude

1. *Addison to Joshua Dawson* (man to man, upper middle to middle rank, reciprocally medium tie)

   <Text type>Letters
   <Author>Addison
   <Author sex>1
   <Author rank>2
   <Author tie>2
   <Recipient> Joshua Dawson
   <Recipient sex>1
   <Recipient rank>1
   <Recipient tie>2
   <Date written>December 14, 1709
   <Source>ed. Graham, 1941, pp. 196, letter 238
   <# of words>378

   Not having received the favour of a Letter from you since the 22nd past and not knowing but I may have lost one in the packet-boat

that is said to have been cast away this comes to enquire after Your Health and put you in mind that you have an Humble Servant at London who will be very glad to receive your Commands when he can be of any service to You in these parts. In your Last you told me Dr. that the Bishop of Killaloo had been <bin> at your Office for a Copy of Lord Wharton's Letter relating to Flemming. I wish you could intimate to me the Use that will be made of it, or any other particulars yet may be of service in case the Impeachment goes on which we are still threatened with. All that I can learn by whisper and Common fame is that His Lordship will be accused for Vacating Mr. Proby's Grant, Borguard's Commission, constituting a Governor of Wicklow and receiving exorbitant Sums from the Queen towards his Regiment of Dragoons with several other frivolous points. For my own part, though perhaps I was not the most obliged person that was near His Lordship, I shall think myself bound in Honour to do him what Right I can in case he should be attacked, and therefore should be glad if you would help me to any papers precedents or Answers that might be of Use in this particular, for doubtless you may hear more of the intended accusation than I can do. All that I have yet heard is I think impartially speaking very insignificant and Trifling. I am afraid if this matter comes on it will be necessary to have Copies of the Office Books during His Lordship's Administration and if such may be made I'll not only pay the price of your Copying but send one over on purpose to receive them.
Whenever you think your money you mention in your Last may be forthcoming if you please to let me know what you think the sum may be and when I may venture to draw upon you at Twenty days notice perhaps it may suit better with your and my convenience than to have it remitted hither.

2. *Addison to Edward Wortley* (man to man, upper middling to upper middling rank, reciprocally strong tie)

<Text type>Letters
<Author>Addison
<Author sex>1
<Author rank>2
<Author tie>3
<Recipient>Edward Wortley
<Recipient sex>1
<Recipient rank>2

<Recipient tie>3
<Date written>April 27, 1708
<source>ed. Graham, 1941, pp. 111–12, letter 123
<# of words>213

Dear Sir
I am very much obliged to you for the honour of Your Letter and am glad to hear that there is no occasion for acquainting you with the Issuing out of the Writs, which I hear will be on Thursday next. I sent you Enclosed a Print that is thought to be well-written. I fancy it is Manwarings. We hear that the D. of Florence furnished the Pope with the money that he contributed toward the intended Expedition. If so, His Minister will be sent hence very suddenly. You have doubtless heard of the affront offered your Cousin Manchester in searching his gondola for English cloth <Cloath> which was found in some Quantity on board of it by the Corruption of his Servants. It was done at the time when the Venetians had heard that the Invasion had succeeded. Their Ambassador is banished our Court and though he has desired Audience to explain the matter it is refused till Your Cousin Manchester has had the satisfaction he demands, which is that the Searchers stand in the Pillory and the cloth <Cloath> be put into the Gondola on the place where it was taken out. I long for some of your conversation in Country air and am Ever with the greatest Truth and Esteem Sir

3. *Addison to Charles Montagu, Earl of Manchester* (man to man, upper middle to aristocrat, reciprocal medium tie)

<Text type>Letters
<Author>Addison
<Author sex>1
<Author rank>2
<Author tie>2
<Recipient> Charles Montague, Earl of Manchester
<Addressee sex>1
<Addressee rank>3
<Addressee tie>2
<Date written>February 1702
<Source>ed. Graham, 1941, pp. 31–2. Letter 26.
<#words>194

I was extremely glad to hear your Lordship had entered on a post that would give you an occasion of advancing so much the Interest and Reputation of your Country: but I now find that I have more particular reasons to rejoice at your promotion Since I hear you have lately done me the honour to mention me kindly to my Lord Halifax. As this is not the first favour you have been pleased to show me I must confess I should be very ambitious of an opportunity to let you know how just a sense I have of the Gratitude and Duty that I owe to your Lordship. And if you think me fit to receive any of your commands abroad it shall not be for want of Diligence or Zeal for Your Lordships service if they are not executed to your satisfaction. I could not dispense with myself from returning my most humble thanks for the notice you have been pleased to take of me, as I dare not presume any longer to encroach upon your time that is filled up with affairs of so much greater Consequence, I am, My Lord,

Notes

1. The larger question guiding this research in the longer term is that of the extent to which Addison's reputation in his own time influenced those around him, especially with respect to their language. So I am interested in the extent to which those closely associated with him do (and do not) share particular linguistic traits, and the extent to which his network's linguistic behaviour differs from that of those people who remain unconnected with it. The connections (or ties, in the terminology of social networks analysis) that mark this group develop and change across time, in terms of their purpose, strength and longevity.
2. In contrast to the central network's key figures, Defoe's lower-class, nonconformist background and lack of university training hindered the access he desired to those more powerful people who shared common backgrounds with their clients. Unlike Richard Steele, whose connections won him a Membership of Parliament and a knighthood, Defoe's efforts did not gain him a position that gave him comparable status and political power. Instead, when preferment came to him, it was in the form of a job as an itinerant political worker for Robert Harley. At the opposite end of the social scale was Sarah Churchill, Duchess of Marlborough. She was Queen Anne's primary confidante until 1705, when her quarrel with Anne led to her replacement by Abigail Masham, a relative of Robert Harley. Matthew Prior had attempted to win her notice when he wrote a poem in praise of Marlborough in 1704, but the duchess returned his letter to him unopened. Prior endorsed the letter thus: 'Mem: dam She sent back the letter unopen'd and said she was sure yt Mr Prior write but what he would, He could not wish well to Her and her family' (Prior Papers (Marquess of Bath) vol 13: 55). Susannah Wesley, by virtue of her very different background as the outspoken wife of

an Anglican vicar in the provinces, was not connected at all with any of the circle. Daniel Defoe and Susannah Wesley remain outside the group at large, proving to be the only true outsiders in social terms.

3. For detailed discussion of the mechanisms of social network analysis as applied to sociohistorical linguistics, see the articles in the recent Special Issue (4.3) of *European Journal of English Studies* (ed. by Ingrid Tieken-Boon van Ostade and Terttu Nevalainen (2000)), and for detailed analysis of the social networks and coalitions constructed around Joseph Addison in particular, see Fitzmaurice (2000a, 2000b). The sociogram includes actors whose own written oeuvres are not included in the corpus, namely Charles Montagu and Jacob Tonson. Their names are bracketed to indicate this status. Note that their inletters are included in the letters subcorpus as part of the oeuvres of other actors, such as Addison and Steele.
4. In Fitzmaurice (2004), I also examine the ways in which the main clause progressive can be recruited to be an expressive device used in specific contexts to convey more, and often other than, the construction appears to do.
5. For a detailed discussion of this point, see Fitzmaurice (2002).
6. This process has been begun, notably for verbs across all the registers (see Fitzmaurice, 2004).
7. Hitherto, semantic pragmatic studies have been conducted by hand, as it were, on samples of texts included in broader samples for the purposes of counting features (Fitzmaurice, 2002).

References

Biber, Douglas, Stig Johansson, Geoffrey Leech, Susan Conrad and Edward Finegan. 1999. *The Longman Grammar of Spoken and Written English*. London: Longman.

Fitzmaurice, Susan. 2000a. 'Coalitions and the investigation of social influence in linguistic history'. *EJES* 4(3):265–76.

Fitzmaurice, Susan. 2000b. '*The Spectator*, the politics of social networks, and language standardisation in eighteenth-century England'. *The Development of Standard English, 1300–1800*, ed. by Laura Wright, pp. 195–218. Cambridge: Cambridge University Press.

Fitzmaurice, Susan. 2002. 'Politeness and modal meaning in the construction of humiliative discourse in an early eighteenth-century network of patron–client relationships'. *English Language and Linguistics* 6(2):1–27.

Fitzmaurice, Susan. 2004. 'The meanings and uses of the progressive construction in an early eighteenth-century English network'. *Studies in the History of the English Language II: Unfolding Conversations*, ed. by Anne Curzan and Kimberly Emmons, pp. 131–74. Berlin: Mouton de Gruyter.

Grundy, I. 1999. *Lady Mary Wortley Montagu, Comet of the Enlightenment*. Oxford: Oxford University Press.

Tieken-Boon van Ostade, I. 1999. 'Of formulas and friends: expressions of politeness in John Gay's letters'. *Thinking English Grammar: To Honour Xavier Dekeyser, Professor Emeritus*, ed. by G. A. J. Tops, B. Devriendt and S. Geukens, pp. 99–112. Leuven/Paris: Peeters.

Tieken-Boon van Ostade, I. and T. Nevalainen (eds). 2000. *Social Network Analysis and the History of English* Special Issue of *European Journal of English Studies* 4(3).

Wright, Susan. 1994. 'The mystery of the modal progressive'. *Studies in Early Modern English*, ed. by Dieter Kastovsky, pp. 467–85. Berlin: Mouton de Gruyter.

Wright, Susan. 1997. 'Speaker innovation, textual revision and the case of Joseph Addison'. *To Explain the Present: Studies in the Changing English Language in Honour of Matti Rissanen*, ed. by Terttu Nevalainen and Leena Kahlas-Tarkka, pp. 483–503. Helsinki: Mémoires de la Société Néophilologique de Helsinki.

4
The ONZE Corpus

Elizabeth Gordon, Margaret Maclagan and Jennifer Hay

1 Introduction

This chapter describes the Origins of New Zealand English corpus (ONZE) in the Linguistics Department of the University of Canterbury, Christchurch, New Zealand, which contains recordings of people born in New Zealand from the 1850s to the 1980s. The significance of these dates can be seen when it is noted that the European settlement of New Zealand is dated from 1840 when a representative of the British Crown signed the Treaty of Waitangi with a number of Maori chiefs. This means that the corpus contains recordings which represent the entire history of New Zealand English from the beginning of European settlement up to the present day.

The ONZE corpus consists of three separate collections. The earliest recordings are in the Mobile Unit archive of speakers (MU) born between 1851 and 1910; these were acquired by the University of Canterbury from the Radio NZ Sound Archives in 1989. The second collection is the Intermediate Archive of speakers (IA) born between 1890 and 1930; these were acquired in the mid 1990s. The third collection is the Canterbury Corpus (CC) of speakers born between 1930 and 1984; this collection began in 1994 and has been added to every year since. The ONZE project was set up initially to study the process of new dialect development in New Zealand using the MU archive; with the two additional archives it is now being used to produce both a diachronic and a synchronic study of New Zealand English.

2 Format and purpose of the archives

The three archives that make up the ONZE corpus are different in format and in original purpose. The Mobile Unit archive is an historical archive collected by members of the NZ National Broadcasting Service between 1946 and 1948. The intention was to broadcast pioneer reminiscences and stories from parts of New Zealand outside the main city centres. In the Intermediate Archive most of the recordings were collected as part of oral history research projects, and as with the MU archive we had no input into the choice of speakers or the content of the recordings. Two groups of IA recordings were collected for broadcast. One of these was obtained from the Radio NZ Sound Archives, and consists of recordings made on the West Coast of the South Island; the second group consists of interviews of old people which were recorded to be broadcast on a Christchurch community radio station. An additional small group of IA recordings were of the descendants of those recorded in the MU archive. The third archive, the Canterbury Corpus, is a deliberately structured sociolinguistic judgement sample collected by third-year students in the Linguistics Department of the University of Canterbury as part of their study of New Zealand English and the techniques of sociolinguistic field methods. Because the three archives were different in their original purpose, each raises different methodological issues. The issues associated with the MU archive centre round the reorganization of the spoken material, the identification of speakers and accurate transcription of names and places in the recordings. For the IA, the issues include working with the different types of recordings that cover the period. Because most of the speakers in the CC are still alive, issues of confidentiality are important. Such confidentiality issues are much less salient for the MU or the parts of the IA where the material was originally recorded for broadcast and most speakers were careful about the stories they told. Availability of the archives to people outside the University of Canterbury is also an issue in that we do not hold copyright for all of the material in the archives.

We turn now to a brief description of each of the individual archives in the ONZE corpus.

2.1 The Mobile Unit

The original task of the Mobile Disc Recording Unit of the NZ National Broadcasting Service was to record 'audio snapshots' of life in small rural towns and centres as a response to criticisms that early NZ broadcasting came mainly from Wellington. This meant that the plan was to collect recordings only in rural parts of New Zealand and not in any of the main cities. The MU archive comprises everything recorded on the three separate tours, and this also includes musical items and Maori ritual songs and prayers as well as interviews with old people. Only the latter have been the subject of ONZE research.

The first tour of the Mobile Unit in 1946 covered Wanganui, New Plymouth and rural districts of Taranaki (in the North Island). On this tour, the main intention was to collect music and only 19 interviews were conducted with elderly people. However, when these interviews of old New Zealanders were broadcast they were extremely popular with radio listeners, so in 1947, on the second tour, 55 interviews were recorded. This tour, also in the North Island, covered rural communities in the Waikato and the Thames valley. The third tour in 1948 was of rural towns in Otago in the South Island where 127 interviews were recorded. The Mobile Disc Recording Unit was disbanded at the end of 1948 because of changes in recording technology and the development of regional radio stations. Unfortunately for our purposes this means that many parts of New Zealand were not covered.

The Mobile Unit was a large van which carried two heavy disc recorders. These were operated in the van by a producer and a technical assistant but the microphones were connected to long cables so that the interviews could be carried out in people's homes, farms, schools and local town halls. The recordings were captured on 16-inch discs made of an acetate coating on an aluminium base, with most of the discs recording 10–11 minutes per side. Because acetate was a soft material, playing back was not encouraged, so most of those people recorded did not hear themselves unless their recording was later broadcast.

In general, the quality of the MU interviews is good, although in some there are extraneous noises such as ticking clocks, miaowing cats or rattling teacups. In some cases, people were interviewed alone, but in other cases group discussions were recorded, some with as many as eight speakers, making it difficult for researchers to identify all the participants. Some speakers spoke for extended periods of time and others only briefly. The interviews vary in their degree of formality, with some speakers reading from notes, others telling popular stories and still others engaged in casual conversations. Some of those interviewed sound quite nervous at first but then relax. Some seem completely oblivious of the fact they are being recorded, while others do not relax at all.

About 300 MU speakers were recorded singly and in groups. For ONZE research purposes, 108 New Zealand-born speakers and seven overseas-born speakers have been analysed. The reasons for the selection of the speakers changed over the years as the ONZE project progressed. At first those speakers born earliest were selected for auditory perceptual analysis. Later speakers were selected on the basis of the length and quality of their recordings. Because of the imbalance between the numbers of men and women in the archive, as many women as possible were selected for analysis. An attempt was made to have a reasonable coverage of age and type of settlement. For the purposes of quantitative analysis an attempt was made to make a stratified sample with male and female speakers born throughout the period of the archive and from different regions. However, with a historical archive such as this it is impossible to have a neatly balanced sample and we could only use the data available.

2.2 The Intermediate Archive

There are approximately 140 speakers in the Intermediate Archive born between 1890 and 1930. They come from four different sources and many come from geographical areas not covered by the Mobile Unit:

(a) Two researchers, Nicola Woods and Sandra Quick, recorded some of the descendants of the original speakers in the Mobile Unit archive. These recordings provide continuity with the MU archive and were collected in the 1990s. The interviewees were often able to add additional information about their ancestors recorded by the MU. These interviews were designed to parallel the interview style of the original MU recordings. Unlike some of those interviewed in the MU archive, none of these speakers reads from prepared notes.

(b) Rosemary Goodyear, a history student at the University of Otago, collected oral history accounts of early memories of old New Zealanders in Dunedin and Christchurch for her MA, and later for her PhD thesis. She was especially interested in accounts of childhood, both schooling and childhood games. These recordings were collected in the 1990s. Many of these interviews follow a schedule, with the speakers answering a set of questions from the interviewer. The interviews often lasted three to four hours. The ONZE corpus contains the entire interviews but only an hour from each has been selected for analysis.

(c) Lesley Evans, a volunteer radio programme-maker, collected interviews of 'interesting people' aged 60–100 living in Christchurch. Over 100 interviews were recorded in the speakers' own homes, and lasted from half an hour to over two hours. These were later edited down to 20-minute broadcasts called 'Life Stories' for Plains

FM, a community radio station. The interviewees were selected by the friend-of-a-friend method of contact (Milroy, 1987), although people listening to the broadcasts also rang the radio station to suggest more people to be recorded. Lesley Evans asked questions according to a schedule, though this was not strictly adhered to. The speakers were asked about 'life themes': places they had lived, early jobs, romance and married life, turning points in their lives and how things used to be. A number of the interviewees had come from rural backgrounds, though they had later retired to Christchurch, and they talked about farming matters. These interviews were recorded between 1990 and 1993 and acquired by the University of Canterbury in 2000.

(d) The NZ Broadcasting Service collected recordings of 13 speakers from the West Coast of the South Island (born 1880–1910) between 1960 and 1985. These recordings were broadcast on National Radio programmes and were obtained from the Radio New Zealand Sound Archives in 2004. They vary in length from ten minutes to an hour with the speakers telling stories of the small towns where they lived and interesting incidents in their lives.

2.3 The Canterbury Corpus

This archive has been collected since 1994 by students in the New Zealand English course at the University of Canterbury. The archive is structured according to a speaker quota and constitutes a judgement sample. Approximately equal numbers of men and women are included, equal numbers of younger (age 20–30) and older (age 45–60) speakers, and equal numbers of speakers from higher social classes (categorized as 'professional') and from lower social classes (categorized as 'non-professional'). This structure sets up eight cells in the database. In order to create an archive of New Zealand English speech, all the speakers were born in New Zealand, and none spent significant periods of time outside the country. No control was kept over the birthplace of the speakers. Most of them come from the Canterbury region, but some come from other parts of the country. Because these recordings were collected by students, the interviewing skills and quality of the recordings vary. The Canterbury Corpus recordings were deliberately collected to be part of an archive of New Zealand English. Each speaker reads the New Zealand English word list (see Maclagan and Gordon, 1999) designed to give examples of all the phonemes of New Zealand English and to provide information about sound changes in progress, such as the NEAR/SQUARE merger (Gordon and Maclagan, 2001). Extracts from the word list and examples of the ways in which it has been used are given in section 5.1. Student interviewers then engage their subjects in conversation for half an hour. The aim was to obtain material that is as close to casual speech as possible.

3 Preparation of the data

3.1 Preparation of the recordings

3.1.1 Mobile Unit

In 1989, copies of the original MU recordings were made on audio cassettes for the University of Canterbury. The Mobile Unit used two disc recorders. As a speaker was interviewed, the recording was made on side 1 of disc A. When this was full, the interview continued on side 1 of disc B. Disc A was then turned over and the interview was continued on side 2 of disc A and then side 2 of disc B. When the discs were transferred on to cassette tapes, however, side 1 of disc A was followed immediately by side 2 of disc A, then sides 1 and 2 of disc B. This meant that the order of the original recordings was completely scrambled. In addition, small items, or the ends of other interviews, were often recorded on the last few minutes of a disc. One speaker, or group of speakers, could sometimes be recorded in several different sessions, often on different days. The first step in preparing the recordings was, therefore, the very time-consuming task of identifying the sections of each interview and re-recording the interviews in their original order. Preservation copies of the cassette tapes were made first onto digital audio tapes (DAT) and later onto audio CDs. To facilitate analysis, DAT recordings were made for some individual speakers. In order to avoid loss of quality, the tapes were transferred to CD in real time, from a Sony TC-WE8055 Cassette Deck to a Fostex Professional CR300 CDR CD recorder. Copies of most of the CDs have also been made in WAV format. These are used for acoustic analysis. A complete copy of the ONZE corpus is now held on CD in the Macmillan Brown Library of the University of Canterbury in a temperature-controlled room.

3.1.2 Intermediate Archive and the Canterbury Corpus

The recordings for the Intermediate Archive and the Canterbury Corpus were all made on audio cassettes. The students collecting the data for the CC used tape recorders owned by the University of Canterbury to ensure that the quality was satisfactory. Preservation copies of both archives were made by transferring them to audio CDs in real time on a Fostex Professional CR300 CDR CD recorder. WAV format CDs have also been made, and are used for acoustic analysis.

3.2 Transcription of the recordings

All of the material in the ONZE corpus consists of oral recordings which needed to be transcribed. For reasons of readability and time, it was decided to transcribe them orthographically into conventional spelling rather than to use a phonetic or phonological script. The orthographic transcription required a certain amount of detective work, especially for the Mobile Unit recordings, where names of people and places were not immediately familiar to the transcribers. Historical archives around New Zealand were mined in order to check the spellings of ships and old hotels.

A decision was also made to use conventional spelling in the transcripts rather than to try to indicate dialectal pronunciations. Conventional spelling was adequate to indicate when <come> and <done> were used instead of <came> and <did>, but no attempt was made to indicate *-in* for *-ing*, and if someone said *me horse* it was transcribed <my horse>. H-dropping or the hyper-correct addition of an /h/ as in <hoven> for <oven> was similarly not indicated in spelling. These decisions were made in order to facilitate reading the transcripts and searching for instances of particular words across different speakers.

The guiding principle in the transcription was that the written version should follow the spoken as faithfully as possible. To this end, conventional punctuation was not used, except for a question mark to indicate a question, especially if question syntax was not used (see Figure 4.1). Features of spoken language such as pauses, overlapping speech, hesitation phenomena, fillers and paralinguistic features such as laughter were carefully included.

At first, individual speakers were not specifically identified in transcripts unless there were several people in the interview. The interviewer was identified by the use of bold, and ordinary type was used for the interviewee. Overlapping speech was indicated by italics. More recently, the transcripts have been reworked so that they are suitable for automatic searching. This has required a change in the formatting. All speakers are now identified by initials, though the convention of using bold for the interviewer has been maintained for the sake of readability. Symbols are included so that overlapping speech, unintelligible speech and paralinguistic features such as laughter can be unambiguously retrieved automatically as well as by eye. Figure 4.1 presents the transcription conventions currently used for all archives.

Transcription guidelines

Call the interviewer "A" and the interviewee "B". Type all of the interviewer's utterances in **bold**; the interviewee's in plain type.

> **A: how long have you lived here**
>
> B: about five years

- Start each major utterance on a new line. This isn't necessary for very small feedback responses like "mmm" or "yeah". Insert these where appropriate between angle brackets, remembering to use bold if the interviewer is providing the feedback, or plain type if the interviewee is.

  > B: Christchurch is really fun <**yeah**> and I like living here a lot.

- Break the transcript up into easily readable chunks by inserting blank lines after each pair of utterances, or when the interviewee changes topic in a lengthy turn.
- Use no capital letters except for proper nouns and "I", and use a minimum of conventional punctuation: Use question marks, especially if the grammatical structure does not indicate a question, but the intonation does, as in the second utterance here:

  > **A: do you have a cat?**
  >
  > B: yes . you have a cat too?

  Don't use commas or full stops to indicate clauses and sentences.

  Instead, use the following conventions to indicate pauses:

full stop	.	= very short hesitation
dash	-	= hesitation
two dashes	--	= long hesitation

- Use conventional spelling most of the time, but where necessary use colloquialisms such as "yeah" "gonna" "cos" "gotta" "dunno" etc. if this is what was said.

  Use these fillers where appropriate:

  mmm um er [for schwa] ahh

- Where you can't decipher, type *[unclear]* or ***[unclear]***, depending on who is speaking. Use this method of brackets and italics when you wish to record a comment, such as *[another person enters the room]* or *[laugh]*.
- When speech is overlapping, indicate this with italics, and place a single slash at each end of the overlapping parts of speech, for both speakers.

  > **A: so the best thing about Christchurch is */the nightlife /***
  >
  > B: */the nightclubs/* yeah [laugh]

- Don't tidy up the speech. Leave in the repetitions, fillers and errors.

Figure 4.1 Transcription conventions used in the ONZE project

A sample transcript is given in Figure 4.2. As will be discussed in section 4.2, this format has received further modification, in order to incorporate time-stamping information, which aligns the transcript with the audio file.

A: **is it alright for Joe to lick his . scar?**

B: it is as long as he doesn't do it */too roughly/*

A: ***/too much/***

B: a little bit . you're sitting on a wee nerve there darling hey -- a little bit's fine because it's um keeps it clean and and their tongue's quite sterile <**mmm**> dog's tongues . but if he did it a lot um . he has to have one of those bucket things on his head because .

A: **mm keep his eyes .**

B: because if they lick too often yhe tongue's rasping and it gets it quite raw <**mm**> and . you note that cut that's the main cut . and he's sort of got it like that and there's another one round here

A: **is that his cut over from . his past operations?**

B: same side . it's not on the same scar you can still see is that stopped or is it still going?

A: **still going I think**

B: thank you thank you--*[unclear]* down here there's another one he took it out and with . there <**yeah**> two incisions but got it out in one piece I don't know how he could . he must have cut the bone . perhaps loosened it away and then*/cut out the bigger one/*

A: ***/right . makes sense/***

B: but this the um the second . operation he had which was is a major one too . he had to wear a . a bucket after . several days because he was licking it a lot and it was getting quite raw - um . and so hopefully he won't do that cos those bucket things are annoying they . for them . they put one on on last time . that looked a bit like an upside down lampshade . have you ever seen one?

A: **yeah those */big circular column things/***

B: /oh oh right/ and it was quite big and when we brought him home if he didn't . if he wasn't careful . and aimed himself directly through a doorway . it was so big it would hit on the <**yeah**> on the door frame

Figure 4.2 Sample transcript

3.3 Content of the recordings

Because the MU recordings were all recorded for broadcast, they are in the public domain. Occasionally speakers will say 'You won't use that for broadcast, will you?', usually about a fairly innocuous anecdote they have just told, but most of the time the content covered is relatively matter of fact (lists of items sold in a local store, details about the building of a particular house, descriptions of towns in earlier times) or else good stories about the old days, often about people who were no longer alive. There is nothing in the archive with restricted access because of content. We use the full names of the MU interviewees in publications, partly because the recordings are already in the public domain, and partly to honour these early pioneers whose stories often reveal hardship endured courageously. Much of the IA is also relatively public. Lesley Evans's material and the West Coast tapes were originally collected for broadcast, and are similarly in the public domain. Rosemary Goodyear's material was collected for theses that are freely available from university libraries, and while it is not public in quite the same sense as the broadcast material, the interviewees were very aware that they were being interviewed for research. Because the IA recordings were made more recently, we usually do not use interviewees' real names in publications. The West Coast speakers, like the MU speakers, were recorded for broadcast, and so their names can be used in publication. The descendants of the MU speakers were recorded precisely because their forebears are part of the MU archive. They all understood this purpose and consented to have their relationship with the MU speaker identified in publications. The CC raises different issues. The interviewers for the other archives were all 'officials', broadcasters or postgraduate students, usually interviewing relative strangers. The interviewers for the CC, by contrast, were all undergraduate students, who often interviewed people they knew well. Although the interviewees all knew that they were being recorded, and had signed consent forms agreeing that the recordings would be held in the CC archive and made available for research, and even for public broadcast, it is clear that, as the recordings progressed, many of the interviewees completely forgot the purpose of the exchange. The material that is disclosed in the CC recordings is often much more personal than in the other archives. We have accounts of relationship break-ups and of prostitution, and descriptions of incidents which the speakers might later find very embarrassing. In addition, as far as we know, the interviewees are still alive, and New Zealand is a very small country, where someone will always be able to recognize a voice, no matter how careful we are to preserve anonymity. For this reason, we place embargoes on the public use of any recording where we feel that the interviewee may later be embarrassed and we do not use interviewees' real names in publications.

3.4 Information about the speakers

Information about the speakers is held in several databases. An ongoing task is keeping the databases up to date. We are still working on ways to fully integrate the databases that contain the background information about the speakers with those that contain the results of analyses. In order to be able to categorize the speakers, information was needed about age, birthplace and social class. This information was more difficult to find for speakers in the MU archive and required a great deal of extra research. The original interviewers for the Mobile Disc Recording Unit recorded some information about the speakers they interviewed. As time went on, they kept more detailed records, so that there is usually adequate information to enable easy identification of the speakers for the later interviews, but the information for some of the early recordings is rather sparse. In order to be able to use the interviews for research purposes, we sought genealogical information about the speakers and their parents. More detailed information about the family histories of the speakers was obtained from the NZ Registry of Births, Deaths and Marriages. Information about the towns where the recordings were collected and where the MU speakers were living was obtained from local museums and libraries as well as the relevant historical sources.

One of the unusual features of the MU archive is that the interviewers recorded women as well as men (though there are still more men than women recorded in the archive) and they recorded people from lower social classes. The criterion for selection was a person's ability to tell good stories. The interviewees were mainly manual workers on farms, or they worked in shops, and the women worked in the home. Many told stories of pioneer hardship and endurance. Although we do not have full social class information for the speakers, a great deal can be gleaned from what is said on the tapes and from other historical records.

Information about the speakers in the Intermediate Archive was generally acquired at the time the material was recorded, although, for the West Coast speakers obtained from Radio NZ Sound Archives, it has been necessary to adopt the strategy that was used for the Mobile Unit archive. Rosemary Goodyear kept full records of those she interviewed (including pen-and-ink portraits which she made of each speaker).

The students collecting the recordings in the Canterbury Corpus were required to get some personal information from their interviewees, including their education, occupation, and the occupations of their parents. As with recordings in the other archives, extra information is often obtained from the recordings themselves. Identifying the social class of speakers in the Intermediate Archive and the Canterbury Corpus is made easier because many of the speakers recorded for the IA, and all of the speakers in the CC, filled in detailed consent forms which enabled us to assign them to appropriate social groups.

However, assigning a social class to speakers in New Zealand immediately raises methodological issues in that New Zealand society does not divide easily into the social classes used in many other English-speaking countries. A social class classification was derived for the Canterbury Corpus that combined information about occupation with information about education level. The score for occupation was arrived at for each speaker using a six-point scale derived from the Elley–Irving codes for census occupations (Elley & Irving, 1985; NZ Ministry of Education, 1990). The lower the number, the higher the social class rating of the occupation. A six-point scale was devised along similar lines to code the speakers' educational attainments (see Gregersen and Pedersen, 1991, for a similar way of assessing social class). These two scores were added together to give a range from 2 (high) to 12 (low). For the Canterbury Corpus, the professional speaker groups have average scores between 4 and 4.5 whereas the non-professional speaker groups have average scores of 8.5 to 9.5, thus indicating that the archive does, indeed, contain speakers representing two very different social groups. 'While this method for assigning social class is widely used by social scientists in New Zealand, it has a number of shortcomings. The ranking of occupation is made according to level of income, but it is well-known that some very rich people (such as some farmers) are able to claim very low incomes for taxation purposes. The scale is also outdated and does not list some occupations popular today (such as counsellors).

4 Making the data available to researchers

4.1 Copyright issues

The Canterbury Corpus is the only archive for which the University of Canterbury holds full copyright. The University of Canterbury also holds copyright for the recordings collected by Sandra Quick and Nicola Woods in the Intermediate Archive. Rosemary Goodyear and

Lesley Evans have agreed to allow their recordings to be used for research purposes. The Sound Archives of Radio New Zealand holds the copyright for the MU archive and the West Coast recordings in the IA; the University of Canterbury has permission to use these recordings for research purposes, but not to pass them on to people outside the university. Similarly, we do not pass on to people outside the university material in the IA from Rosemary Goodyear or Lesley Evans. This limits the accessibility of the MU archive and parts of the IA for researchers outside the University of Canterbury. Permission to use the MU material and the Radio New Zealand material in the IA can be obtained from Radio New Zealand Sound Archives (PO Box 1531, Christchurch, New Zealand) but it is likely that a fee will be charged. Copies of the MU recordings are also available in the Alexander Turnbull Library in Wellington, where they can be accessed under the same copyright conditions as at the University of Canterbury; however the Turnbull Library does not hold transcriptions, and the recordings have not been reorganized so that complete recordings of the same speaker can be found in a single recording (see section 3.1.1 above). All of the recordings are available to researchers working at the University of Canterbury.

4.2 Towards a digital interactive format for the corpus

4.2.1 Time-alignment of transcripts

Since 2003, we have been working on techniques for interacting more directly with the sound files, via the orthographic transcript. That is, we wanted to introduce time-stamping information into the transcript, so that a researcher could directly access any particular utterance of interest. After an initial exploration of appropriate tools, we settled on Transcriber software (http://www.ldc.upenn.edu/mirror/Transcriber; see also Barras *et al.*, 2001). NXpeds Footpedals (www.nxpeds.com) have been programmed for use with the software, so that transcribing into Transcriber proceeds very similarly to the traditional use of a transcription machine. A screenshot of a MU transcript in this format is shown in Figure 4.3. We are in the process of migrating all of our existing transcripts to this format. This is being done by hand, and takes approximately double real time. That is, it takes a researcher approximately two hours to time-align a one-hour interview. We currently have approximately 200 hours' worth of transcripts in this format.

4.2.2 Conversion to Praat

Because the format of the Transcriber files is XML, it can be relatively easily transformed into other formats. We therefore developed a simple

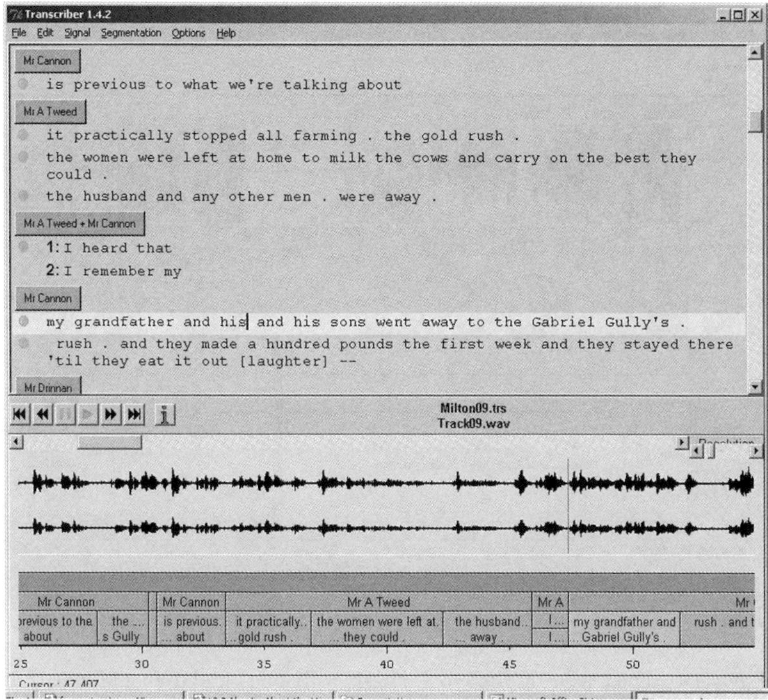

Figure 4.3 Time-aligned transcript, using Transcriber

JavaScript which would transform the Transcriber files into TextGrids for use with Praat acoustic analysis software (Boersma & Weenink, http://www.fon.hum.uva.nl/praat/). An example of a Mobile Unit interview displayed in this format is given in Figure 4.4. This format enables the researcher to search the transcript for relevant utterances, and immediately engage in acoustic analysis.

4.2.3 Development of a web-browser based transcript server

In 2004 we began to develop software which allows these time-aligned transcripts to be stored on a central database, from where they can be easily viewed, filtered and searched (Fromont and Hay, 2004). This software is now in place, and is proving highly successful, both for research and for using the corpus in teaching. Part or all of the corresponding recordings can now be played back or loaded into acoustic analysis software directly from the transcript.

Figure 4.5 shows the web page on which speakers can be filtered and selected. Once the initial speaker selection is made, a regular

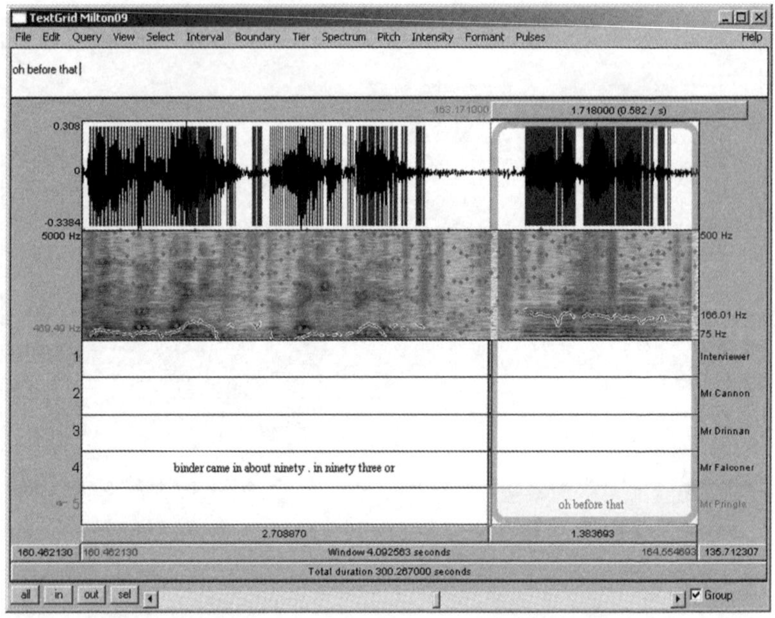

Figure 4.4 Praat acoustic analysis software, with a text grid from a Mobile Unit transcript which has been automatically generated from the Transcriber file

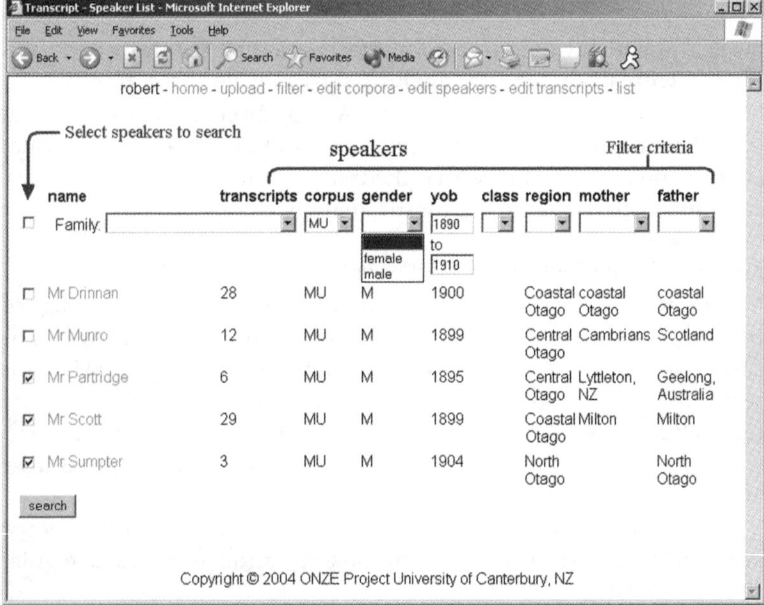

Figure 4.5 ONZE transcript server: initial speaker selection page

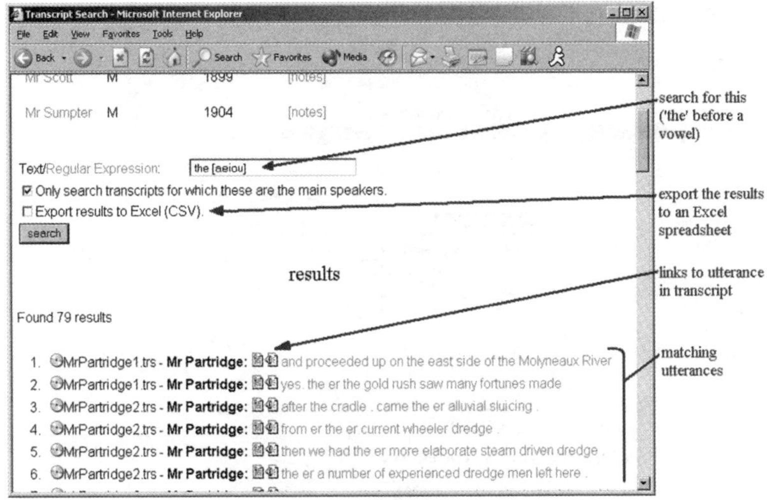

Figure 4.6 ONZE transcript server: sample search results

expression search can be entered (Figure 4.6). This returns a list of all of the utterances from the selected transcripts which match the query. If desired, this list can be exported (together with relevant speaker information) directly to Excel, ready for further analysis (Figure 4.7).

Clicking on an utterance returned by the search produces the full transcript for the speaker involved, positioned with the relevant utterance at the top of the screen. Any part of the transcript can be clicked on and listened to, although this currently requires access to the

Microsoft Excel - results__the_[aeiou].csv

	A	B	C	D	E	F	G	H	I
1	Num	Transcript	Speaker	Gender	YearOfBirth	Cla	Sync	URL	Text
2	1	MrPartridge1.trs	Mr Partridge	M	1895		64.315	http://trar	and proceeded up on th
3	2	MrPartridge1.trs	Mr Partridge	M	1895		185.395	http://trar	yes. the er the gold rush
4	3	MrPartridge2.trs	Mr Partridge	M	1895		88.726	http://trar	after the cradle . came th
5	4	MrPartridge2.trs	Mr Partridge	M	1895		141.66	http://trar	from er the er current wh
6	5	MrPartridge2.trs	Mr Partridge	M	1895		145.003	http://trar	then we had the er more
7	6	MrPartridge2.trs	Mr Partridge	M	1895		203.044	http://trar	the er a number of expe
8	7	MrPartridge2.trs	Mr Partridge	M	1895		275.667	http://trar	the box to catch the at th
9	8	MrPartridge3.trs	Mr Partridge	M	1895		30.905	http://trar	settled on the er point of
10	9	MrPartridge3.trs	Mr Partridge	M	1895		114.844	http://trar	to force . the spoil up thr
11	10	MrPartridge3.trs	Mr Partridge	M	1895		206.129	http://trar	no they weren't here as e
12	11	MrPartridge3.trs	Mr Partridge	M	1895		232.52	http://trar	and ahh it has been sai

Figure 4.7 Sample Excel file, generated by ONZE transcript server

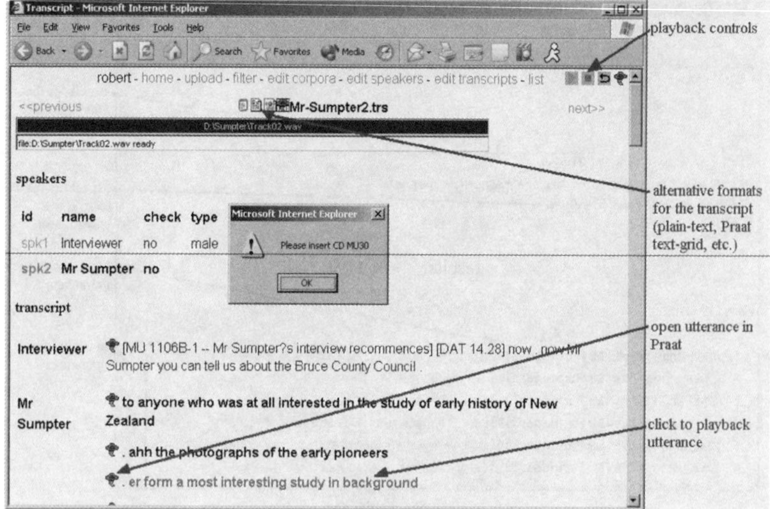

Figure 4.8 ONZE transcript server: interactive transcript

correct CD (Figure 4.8). Clicking on the 'Praat' icon to the left of any given utterance opens that utterance in Praat acoustic analysis software, so that its acoustic properties can be inspected (Figure 4.9).

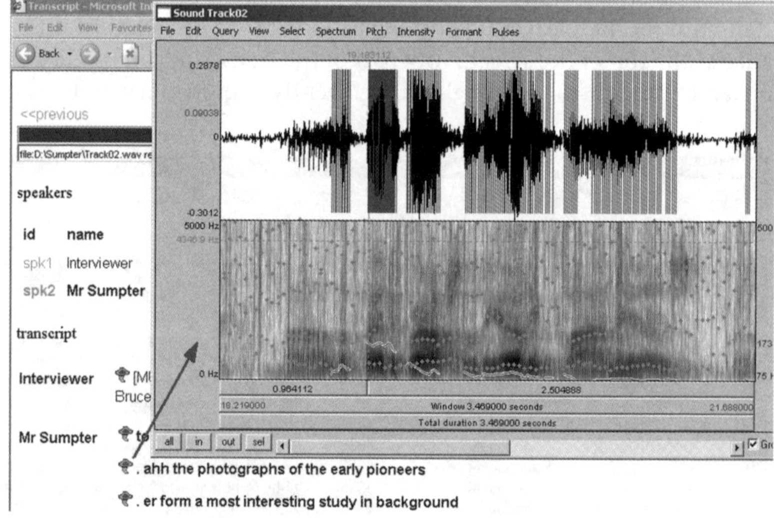

Figure 4.9 ONZE transcript server: clicking on the Praat icon opens an utterance in Praat acoustic analysis software

This system has already radically increased the efficiency with which we can interact with the corpus. It raises exciting new possibilities for research projects that would have previously been extremely time-consuming.

4.2.4 Future plans

The requirement for access to the correct CD places limitations on the usefulness of the transcript server. However, we have recently received funding for a high capacity server, on which all of the audio files can be stored. This will remove the requirement for access to the correct CD (researchers can simply click on the relevant part of the transcript) and will allow access by multiple researchers at once. We began the task of uploading the more than 1,000 hours of audio material onto this server in January 2005. This brings its own challenges. For example, many of the CDs are broken into tracks with generic names (Track 1, Track 2, Track 3 and so on). Such a naming convention is possible when each speaker is on their own CD, but is clearly not desirable when all are stored on a central server.

We are also currently applying for funding to develop the search mechanisms beyond orthographic searching. As a first step, we plan to use the CELEX lexical database (Baayen *et al.*, 1995) to do some automated crude phonological tagging. This would vastly increase the linguistic sophistication of potential searches.[2]

5 Use of the corpus

5.1 Phonetic/phonological analysis

The ONZE project was originally conceived as a project that traced the development of the New Zealand accent. The material consists of oral recordings and all the initial analyses were phonetic/phonological. Three different types of phonetic/phonological analyses have been carried out: auditory perceptual analyses, auditory quantitative analyses and acoustic analyses. Auditory perceptual analysis has been used to obtain an overall impression of a large number of speakers in the MU archive. In an auditory perceptual analysis, detailed phonetic notes are made of the different realizations of various phonemes and approximate indications are given as to their relative frequency, but token counts are not made. For the MU data, a template was prepared so that information was gathered systematically about the NZE vowels and all the items that were known to be important in the development of NZE (such as precursors to the NEAR/SQUARE merger, or the vocalization of

/l/). Although a template which is filled in manually is 'low tech' compared with the digital search facilities that are now available, it still has a place in providing an overview of the material to be analysed.

In an auditory quantitative analysis, precise counts are made of the occurrence of specific realizations of phonemes of interest. Auditory quantitative analysis is more time-consuming than auditory perceptual analysis, so fewer phonemes are usually covered. Auditory quantitative analysis was used with the stratified sample that was created within the MU archive (see section 2.1 above). It enabled statistical comparison of the usage of men and women of different ages and birthplaces. The word lists recorded as part of the Canterbury Corpus, extracts from which are shown in Figure 4.10, have also been subjected to auditory quantitative analysis. This analysis has enabled us to trace the development of the <growen> form of the <-own> past participles (Maclagan and Gordon, 1998), to investigate the relationship between conservative pronunciations for the closing diphthongs (MOUTH and PRICE) and innovative pronunciations for the front vowels (KIT, DRESS and TRAP)

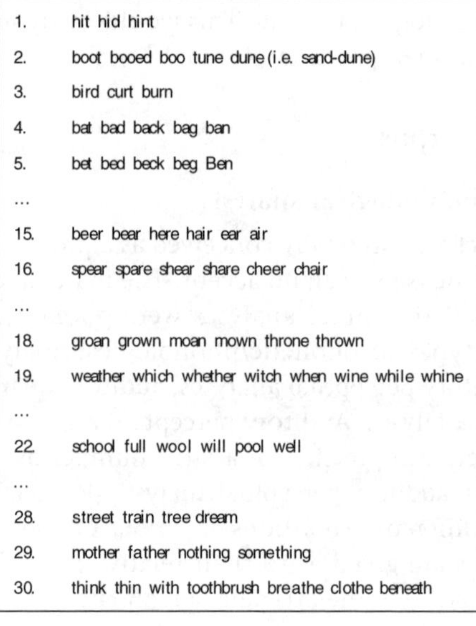

1. hit hid hint
2. boot booed boo tune dune (i.e. sand-dune)
3. bird curt burn
4. bat bad back bag ban
5. bet bed beck beg Ben

...

15. beer bear here hair ear air
16. spear spare shear share cheer chair

...

18. groan grown moan mown throne thrown
19. weather which whether witch when wine while whine

...

22. school full wool will pool well

...

28. street train tree dream
29. mother father nothing something
30. think thin with toothbrush breathe clothe beneath

Figure 4.10 Extracts from the New Zealand English word list

Source: Maclagan and Gordon (1999).

(Maclagan *et al.*, 1999) and to track the development of features such as affrication in /tr/, /dr/ and /str/ clusters and TH-fronting (Gordon and Maclagan, 2000; Maclagan, 2000) as well as to monitor the NEAR/SQUARE merger (Maclagan and Gordon, 1996). Auditory quantitative analysis has also been used to track the loss of /hw/ with speakers from the Intermediate Archive (Schreier *et al.*, 2003).

Acoustic analysis uses acoustic analysis programs to analyse phonemes of interest. The acoustic programs we have used are Soundscope 16, a commercially available program for Macintosh computers (GW Instruments), and two freely available programs, Emu (Cassidy, http://emu.sourceforge.net) and Praat (Boersma and Weenink, http://www.fon.hum.uva.nl/praat/). To date, acoustic analysis has been carried out on the vowel systems of five men and five women selected to be typical of the speakers in the MU archive, and analysis is under way on the word-list data from selected speakers in the CC. (For details of the analyses carried out to date on the MU archive, see Gordon *et al.*, 2004; and Maclagan and Gordon, 2004.)

Now that the digital format allows the transcriptions to be displayed as the sounds are played, different phonetic/phonological analyses are possible. It is now relatively straightforward to listen to all examples of a particular word throughout the entire ONZE corpus, from the first speakers of NZE to the most modern and innovative. This will facilitate a much broader perspective on sound change than has so far been possible.

5.2 Grammatical analysis

As we listened to the MU recordings, we noticed interesting grammatical features (such as the use of the Scottish *for to* infinitive or the use of *come* as a past tense) and plans were made to do grammatical analyses as well as phonological. We soon found that, when all analysis was carried out by listening to the tapes, it took an extremely long time to find sufficient examples of grammatical features to make an analysis feasible, and grammatical analysis was reluctantly put aside. Now that all the transcripts in the corpus have been recoded in a format that can be searched electronically, some types of grammatical searches can be carried out by computer, and grammatical analysis is proving to be a rich new area (for example, Hay and Schreier, 2004; Quinn, 2004). However, note that while the transcription conventions used for the MU recordings (see section 3.2) make it easy to search for individual words, they will obscure the use of some non-standard grammatical features. Such features can be identified by listening to the recordings and checking wherever the feature is possible. Now that the web-based server is operational, such auditory checking will no longer be impossibly time-consuming.

5.3 Other analyses

The corpus contains much material that is of interest to historians. The MU archive, for example, contains many stories of the relationships between early European settlers and the Chinese who settled on the outskirts of gold-mining towns. It also includes eyewitness accounts (from a child's perspective) of incidents in the New Zealand Wars of the 1860s, as well as a wealth of social information about the lives of people in the early NZ settlements. The CC archive contains interviews with people who would often be unlikely to be chosen for oral history research, but whose accounts of life in NZ today also provide interesting social material. Some of those interviewed were very pleased to think that their views and reflections on life might be preserved in a research archive. All the archives contain excellent examples of narrative, and it has been suggested that this could be used for comparative purposes with other narrative studies. There is also material for possible future research on the European settlers' pronunciation of Maori words and place names. This could provide interesting insights into attitudes and race relations between the settlers and the indigenous people.

6 Conclusion

This chapter has chronicled the development of the ONZE project from almost accidental beginnings (Elizabeth Gordon was told about the MU recordings at a conference on oral history in 1986) to its current status as a carefully planned corpus. Over time, the purpose of the archive has changed from a collection of recordings that would allow us to trace the development of the input dialects into a new variety of English to an archive that contains oral recordings of the entire history of New Zealand English. The use of the corpus has changed from solely phonological analysis of the oldest speakers (in the MU archive) to phonological and grammatical analyses across the whole time development of NZE. Although copyright issues restrict the extent to which much of the material can be accessed outside the University of Canterbury, the entire corpus is available to anyone who is able to come to Canterbury and use it here.

7 Acknowledgements

We gratefully acknowledge funding from the following sources, without which the ONZE project could not have happened. The acquisition of the MU tapes was made possible by a University of Canterbury Research Grant together with NZ$2,000 from the Macmillan Brown Trust. The first two years of the ONZE project were funded by the Foundation for Research, Science and Technology (the New Zealand Public Good Science Fund). Its continued operation has been supported by several University of Canterbury Research Grants, a University of Canterbury Teaching Grant, and two grants from the Marsden Fund of the Royal Society of New Zealand. The New Zealand Lotteries Board Fund and the Canterbury History Foundation provided money for data preservation. The development of the transcript web-server has been done by Robert Fromont, who is also to be thanked for producing the screenshots in this chapter.

Notes

1. More recently, we have used the New Zealand Socio-Economic Index for associating social class information with speakers.
2. As this goes to press, all the audio has been successfully uploaded onto the server, and approximately 400 hours are time-aligned and available in ONZEminer for searching. Transcripts are now automatically tagged with CELEX information as they are uploaded, and multi-level searching has been implemented. We are working on syntactic parsing, automatic word-alignment, and on methods for representing the results of analyses in the database itself.

References

Baayen, R. H., R. Piepenbrock and L. Gulikers. 1995. *The CELEX Lexical Database* (CD-ROM). Philadelphia: Linguistic Data Consortium, University of Pennsylvania.

Barras, C., E. Geoffrois, Z. Wu and M. Liberman. 2001. 'Transcriber: development and use of a tool for assisting speech corpora production'. *Speech Communication* 33(1–2):5–22.

Elley, Warwick B. and J. C. Irving. 1985. 'The Elley–Irving Socio-Economic Index: 1981 census revision'. *New Zealand Journal of Educational Studies* 20:115–28.

Fromont, R. and J. Hay. 2004. 'Development of a digital interactive corpus of New Zealand English'. Paper presented at the New Zealand Language and Society Conference, Palmerston North, September 2004.

Gordon, E. and M. A. Maclagan. 2000. '"Hear our voices": changes in spoken New Zealand English'. *TESOLANZ Journal* 8:1–13.

Gordon, E. and M. A. Maclagan. 2001. '"Capturing a sound change": a real time study over 15 years of the NEAR/SQUARE diphthong merger in New Zealand English'. *Australian Journal of Linguistics* 21(2):215–38.

Gordon, E., L. Campbell, J. Hay, M. Maclagan, A. Sudbury and P. Trudgill. 2004. *New Zealand English: Its Origins and Evolution.* Cambridge: Cambridge University Press.

Gregersen, Frans and Ilse Pedersen. 1991. *The Copenhagen Study in Urban Sociolinguistics*. Copenhagen: C.A. Reitzels Forlag.

Hay, J. and D. Schreier. 2004. 'Reversing the trajectory of language change: subject–verb agreement with BE in New Zealand English'. *Language Variation and Change* 16(3):209–35.

Maclagan, M. A. 2000. 'Where are we going in our language? New Zealand English today'. *NZ Journal of Speech-Language Therapy* 53–54:14–20.

Maclagan, M. A. and E. Gordon. 1996. 'Out of the AIR and into the EAR: Another view of the New Zealand diphthong merger'. *Language Variation and Change* 8:125–47.

Maclagan, M. A. and E. Gordon. 1998. 'How *grown* grew from one syllable to two'. *Australian Journal of Linguistics* 18:5–28.

Maclagan, M. A. and E. Gordon. 1999. 'Data for New Zealand social dialectology: the Canterbury Corpus'. *New Zealand English Journal* 13:50–8.

Maclagan, M. A. and E. Gordon. 2004. 'The story of New Zealand English: what the ONZE project tells us'. *Australian Journal of Linguistics* 24(1):41–56.

Maclagan, M. A., E. Gordon, E. and G. Lewis. 1999. 'Women and sound change: conservative and innovative behaviour by the same speakers'. *Language Variation and Change* 11(1):19–41.

Milroy, M. 1987. *Observing and Analysing Natural Language*. Oxford: Blackwell.

New Zealand Ministry of Education. 1990. 'Derivation of Elley-Irving codes from census occupations'. Unpublished MS, Wellington.

Quinn, H. 2004. 'Possessive have and (have) got in New Zealand English'. Paper presented at NWAV33, September 2004.

Schreier, Daniel, Elizabeth Gordon, Jennifer Hay and Margaret Maclagan. 2003. 'The regional and linguistic dimension of /hw/ maintenance and loss in early 20th century New Zealand English'. *English World-Wide* 24(2):245–70.

Websites

The onze project: http://www.ling.canterbury.ac.nz/onze

Emu (S. Cassidy): http://emu.sourceforge.net

NXpeds Footpedals: www.nxpeds.com

onzeminer software: http://www.ling.canterbury.ac.nz/jen/onzeminer

Praat (P. Boersma and D. Weenink): http://www.fon.hum.uva.nl/praat/; http://www.ling.canterbury.ac.nz/jen/onzeminer

Transcriber (C. Barras and E. Geoffrois): http://www.ldc.upenn.edu/mirror/Transcriber

5

Tracking Dialect History: A Corpus of Irish English

Raymond Hickey

1 Introduction

The present chapter attempts to describe the text corpus called *A Corpus of Irish English* (Hickey, 2003a) which contains some 90 texts that attest the history of Irish English from its beginnings (in written form) in the early fourteenth century to the early twentieth century. The considerations in this chapter are diachronic in nature and hence complement the synchronic examination of Irish English to be found in the chapter by Jeffrey Kallen and John Kirk in Volume 1 of the current work. Because of its historic nature, the corpus consists solely of texts, but again this kind of corpus could provide background information for corpora of present-day varieties of English such as that described by Anderson *et al.* (Volume 1). The corpus also links up with atlas-type projects such as that reported on for Dutch by Barbiers *et al.* (Volume 1) or that already published as Hickey (2004a).

The purpose of *A Corpus of Irish English* is to put at the disposal of interested students and scholars a set of texts, the linguistic examination of which can help to answer questions concerning the genesis of Irish English and to throw light on issues of dialect development, especially with reference to overseas forms of English in what has come to be known as 'new dialect formation' (Hickey, 2003b; Gordon and Trudgill, 2004).

The electronic files of *A Corpus of Irish English* consist of various types, depending on the source of the data and the literary genre they represent. The geographical source of some of the text types can be given: for instance, the glossaries for the dialect of Forth and Bargy all stem from the south-east corner of Ireland. Literary works by identified authors can also be located, at least going on their place of birth. In most cases this also provides an indication of the dialect of Irish English which is being represented as in the case of Sean O'Casey (1884–1964). However, in other cases, such as that of the playwright John Millington Synge (1871–1909) (see section 3.3 below), the question of dialect portrayed in plays is difficult to answer clearly as Synge maintained that he was representing the speech of uneducated peasants in the west of Ireland. The question of what dialect is represented is naturally of concern where works are anonymous, as with the many text fragments from the beginning of the early modern period, that is the late sixteenth and early seventeenth centuries. Another feature of many texts throughout the history of Irish English is that they are satirical in nature, that is, they use what is regarded as Irish English to parody the speech of the Irish. This matter is especially critical as many of the authors of such satirical works were in fact not Irish. It is fair to assume in such cases, for instance with Ben Jonson's *Irish Masque at Court* (1605) (see edition in Jonson, 1969), that the speech used is a caricature based on a small selection of features which the non-Irish noted in the speech of the Irish. While such texts are obviously not necessarily reliable descriptions of varieties of Irish English in the early modern period, they nonetheless reveal what features were salient to non-Irish observers.

2 Background to *A Corpus of Irish English*

The present corpus was compiled over a period of several years during which texts were collected, digitalized (largely through scanning) and prepared for easy manipulation by corpus analysis software (Hickey, 2003a). At the initial stage various decisions had to be made which determined the later form and content of the corpus. Among these early considerations was one about whether to include historical or just present-day material. The decision came down in favour of historical material, largely because this material had not been available in electronic form up to then. Another decision, independent of the first, concerned the representativeness of the texts chosen. Assuming that a historical element was to be included, it was decided to offer a cross-section of literature written in English by authors who were Irish by birth or affiliation. A further consideration was whether literary merit was to be a guideline for the quantity of material by a certain author to be entered. If this were the case then it would have been necessary, for instance, to give considerable weight to the works of W. B. Yeats and G. B. Shaw. But this matter was seen in a different light. Going on the assumption that users of a corpus of Irish English would be interested in determining what linguistic features are characteristic of just that variety, those texts which are linguistically representative of Irish English were given preference. There were cases where literary merit and the interest of the variety for linguists met, as in the writings of Sean O'Casey and perhaps John Millington Synge, but this was more the exception than the rule. Authors like Shaw and Yeats are not particularly interesting linguistically as both use very standard forms of English.

The purpose of *A Corpus of Irish English* is to illustrate the language traits of Irish English at their most salient, especially from a historical perspective. This has meant that some authors are included who are not normally regarded as particularly valuable from a literary point of view, for example Lady Augusta Gregory and Dion Boucicault. Others are represented by works which are not necessarily regarded as their masterpieces but which clearly show their portrayal of Irish English. This is evident in the case of Shaw whose *John Bull's Other Island* is the only work included by this author for just that reason. The same applies to Yeats who is represented by the plays *Cathleen ni Hoolihan* and *The Countess Cathleen*. As the corpus includes historical material, it seemed sensible to start from the earliest attestations of Irish English and divide the texts according to period and genre. In the older period of Irish English only poetry is to be found and it was included; although some of it is perhaps dubious in its dialectal authenticity, it must for want of other material, be accepted.

The texts of the current corpus are largely literary in nature. This has to do with availability and relative certainty of source. There are, however, some other possible avenues which could be explored in the construction of historical corpora. One of these is presented by court verbatim transcripts, from the Old Bailey for instance, which exist for Irish defendants over the centuries and which could be assumed to be a relatively accurate rendering of at least the syntax of Irish English during previous periods.

2.1 Structure of the corpus

The literary remains of Irish English can be traced back to the early fourteenth century. Despite the relatively long period for which there are documents their actual number is small, certainly when compared to that for England in the same period. The remnants of medieval Irish English can be counted on the fingers of one hand. The situation improves in the early modern period which can be seen as beginning around 1600. In the early seventeenth century the English put a policy of determined settlement (plantation) into effect (Palmer, 2000), first of all in the north of the country with Scots settlers (and some English) who were encouraged by James I of England to move to Ulster and fill the vacuum left behind after the defeat of the Gaelic forces in this region.

These plantations reached their culmination in the mid seventeenth century with the re-allocation of land in the east to English mercenaries and servants loyal to Oliver Cromwell. There was a parallel expulsion of the native Irish from these lands to the poorer west of the country which increased in population as a result and which was the area where Irish survived longest.

For the early modern period a number of text types are available. The most frequent are satirical pieces in which an Irish character makes an appearance and is usually ridiculed. Prose sketches in this vein are also common and one has direct portrayals, if somewhat brief, of Irish English by Irish writers as well. Swift's *Irish Eloquence* and *A Dialogue in Hybernian Stile* fit into the latter category.

Various prose fragments are contained in the present corpus as these document the transition period from a mainly Irish-speaking country to one in which the former native language is recessive and no longer of importance for the development of English. The formative early modern period is one in which much transfer from Irish into English can be observed, no doubt due to the considerable bilingualism which was typical for broad sections of the population during the changeover from Irish to English.

For the nineteenth century drama is the most important genre. It accounts for the large number of plays in the corpus for this period. With the literary revival at the end of the nineteenth century the emphasis is no longer on comic portrayals of more or less ridiculous Irish figures (see Duggan, 1969 [1937]; Leerssen, 1996; Romani, 1997) but with a more authentic representation of Irish characters as illustrated by the works of Synge. Dramatic realism is to be found in the plays of O'Casey which contain dialogue representing the language of the Dublin working classes.

Alongside the many plays of linguistic interest in the nineteenth century there are also novelists and short-story writers who used Irish English in their work for deliberate effect and in conscious contrast with more standard forms of English. This is true of another writer represented in *A Corpus of Irish English*, the northern Irish writer William Carleton (1794–1869) in whose *Traits and Stories of the Irish Peasantry*

(1830–33) Irish English is found in the speech of the socially low-standing peasants. This situation is different from that in Synge where there is no discrimination on the basis of language (Todd, 1989, p. 73), especially as there is no standard usage in the plays with which the more idiosyncratic forms of the language could contrast.

2.2 Questions of genre

A Corpus of Irish English consists largely of drama. Because the primary aim of the corpus is to offer written representations of Irish English it appeared sensible to concentrate on the genre in which the spoken word is central. The decision to concentrate on drama for the modern period meant that prose writers were largely excluded. Nonetheless some prose was integrated into the corpus. For instance, the nineteenth-century northern Irish writer William Carleton (see previous paragraph) is represented by a selection of tales. This is also true of the Banim brothers, John (1798–1842) and Michael (1796–1874), from whose *Tales of the O'Hara Family* (6 vols, 1825–26) a set of extracts was taken.

3 Periods represented in the corpus

3.1 Medieval period

The first period of Irish English began with the arrival of mercenaries from Wales in 1169 and lasted until the final defeat of the Irish by the English in 1601 (during the Tudor conquest of Ireland: Moody and Martin, 1994 [1967], pp. 174ff.). In this period the available linguistic material is scanty. Most of it is contained in a set of poems to be found in the Harley 913 manuscript of the British Museum (now in the British Library) and which are available in an annotated edition by Wilhelm Heuser from 1904 who took certain liberties in punctuation and expanding abbreviations (Kosok, 1990, p. 22). There is also a more recent edition by Angela Lucas (see Lucas, 1995). Going on some onomastic evidence, these poems are regarded as Irish in provenance and are referred to as the *Kildare Poems* after the mention of a monk, Michael of Kildare, as the author of one of the poems. They probably stem from the beginning of the fourteenth century. To these should be added the poems 'The virtue of herbs' and 'On blood letting' (Zettersten, 1967). From the fourteenth century there are the *Acts and Statutes of the City of Waterford*; from the sixteenth century there is the motley *Book of Howth* (Kosok, 1990, p. 28), comments on which are to be found in Henry (1958).

For the present corpus only the poetry just mentioned has been incorporated. An analysis of the linguistic features of these texts is to be found in Hickey (1997). For more general remarks on the initial stages of Irish English, see Hickey (1993).

The linguistic continuation of the medieval period is not to be found in the literature of the seventeenth and eighteenth centuries but in the attestations of an archaic dialect from the south-east of the country (Co. Wexford), called after the two baronies where it was spoken, Forth and Bargy (read/bargi/). This variety of English is more like a form of Middle English (Hickey, 1988) which has been influenced by Irish, at least lexically. It survives only in the form of glossaries (Vallancey, 1788; and Poole, published by Barnes in 1867) which were compiled at the end of the eighteenth and the beginning of the nineteenth centuries respectively, that is before the dialect died out. Both these glossaries are to be found in *A Corpus of Irish English*, along with one or two texts in the dialect (poems and songs). In the corpus the glossaries are available in database form which facilitates lexical examination. They may be processed as databases and/or converted into texts quite easily using the supplied database management software (see descriptions in Hickey, 2003a).

3.2 Early modern period

When considering the early modern period in Ireland (from 1600 onwards) a strict distinction in types of English must be made. This distinction has continued to be important up to the present day.

1. More or less genuine representations of Irish English by native Irish writers.
2. Stretches of texts by non-Irish writers where a non-native perception of Irish English is found.

There is a remarkable amount of material available, mostly in the form of drama, stretching in time from the very end of the sixteenth up to the mid eighteenth century (Bliss, 1979). This literature contains material of both of the above types and forms the bulk of this section of the corpus. Notable among the dramatists whose works are to be found here are William Congreve (1670–1729), Richard Brinsley Sheridan (1751–1816) and George Farquhar (1678–1707). There are a few prose samples from this period, such as *The Irish Hudibras*, probably by James Farewell, and Swift's *A Dialogue in Hybernian Stile*.

The value of the second type of literature should not be underestimated. It is interesting in that it reveals what features of Irish English were salient and thus registered by non-native speakers. These features have gone into forming the linguistic notion of the 'Stage Irishman', a stock figure in much drama from this period onwards (Duggan, 1969 [1937]; Kiberd 1983; Kosok, 1990, pp. 61ff.; Leerssen, 1996; Romani, 1997; Sand, 2000).

3.3 The nineteenth and twentieth centuries

The nineteenth and twentieth centuries are represented in the corpus mostly by drama because, as outlined above, this genre is likely to contain most examples of specifically Irish English features given that it is written speech.

The two main authors here are John Millington Synge and Sean O'Casey. These literary figures are in a way complementary. Synge is to rural Ireland what O'Casey is to urban Ireland, above all Dublin. O'Casey was himself a native of Dublin, while Synge, although not a native of the west of Ireland, studied the life and language of its inhabitants (see his *The Aran Islands*, 1899) and attempted to represent this faithfully, at least in his early plays. It is true of both authors that their later plays are stylistically more idiosyncratic and less typical of a general form of the rural or urban varieties of Irish English.

Other dramatists, some of whose typical works are included in this section, are Dion Boucicault (1820–90) and Lady Augusta Gregory (1852–1932), along with Shaw and Yeats (see remarks above).

4 Structure of the corpus

The sections of *A Corpus of Irish English* have been arranged in such a way that when the corpus has been installed using the software (known as Corpus Presenter) supplied in Hickey (2003a), the following hierarchical structure will be shown. The necessary control files for the tree to be shown within the software are supplied with the CD-ROM which accompanies Hickey (2003a).

Introduction
- Overview of Corpus

Middle Ages
- Kildare Poems (1)
- Kildare Poems (2)
- A Treatise on Gardening
- The Virtue of Herbs
- The Pride of Life

Forth and Bargy
- Vallancey's glossary (1788)
- Poole's glossary (early 19c)

Fingal
- The Fingallian Dance (1650–60)
- The Irish Hudibras (1689)
- Purgatorium Hibernicum (1670–5)

Drama
- 16th century
  - Anon.: Sir John Oldcastle (1599/1600)
  - Shakespeare: Henry V (1599/1623)
  - Anon.: Captain Thomas Stukeley (1596/1605)
- 17th century
  - Cuffe: The Siege of Ballyally Castle (1642)
  - Dekker: The Honest Whore Part II (1605/1630)
  - Dekker: Old Fortunatus (1599/1600)
  - Head: Hic et Ubique (1663)
  - Jonson: The Irish Masque (1613/1616)
  - Randolph: Hey for Honesty (c. 1630/1651)
  - Shadwell: The Lancashire Witches (1681/1682)
  - Anon.: The Welsh Embassador (1623)
- 18th century
  - Breval: The Play is the Plot (1718)
  - Centlivre: A Wife Well Managed (1715)
  - Congreve: The Way of the World (1700)
  - Farquhar: The Beaux' Stratagem (1707)
  - Farquhar: The Twin Rivals (1702/1703)
  - Goldsmith: She stoops to conquer (1773)
  - Michelbourne: Ireland Preserved (1705)
  - R. B. Sheridan: The School for Scandal (1777)
  - R. B. Sheridan: St. Patrick's Day or The Scheming Lieutenant
  - Th. Sheridan: The Brave Irishman (1740/1754)
- 19th century
  - Boucicault: The Colleen Bawn (1860)
  - Boucicault: Arragh na Pogue (1864)
  - Boucicault: The Shaughraun (1875)
  - Gregory: Hanrahan's Oath
  - Gregory: On the racecourse
  - Gregory: Spreading the news
  - Gregory: The workhouse ward
  - Wilde: The Importance of Being Earnest (1895)

Yeats: The Countess Cathleen (1899)
Yeats: Cathleen Ni Houlihan (1902)
20th century
Shaw: John Bull's Other Island (1904)
Synge: In the Shadow of the Glen (1903)
Synge: Riders to the Sea (1904)
Synge: The Well of the Saints (1905)
Synge: The Playboy of the Western World (1907)
Synge: The Tinker's Wedding (1909)
Synge: Deirdre of the Sorrows (1910)
O'Casey: The Shadow of a Gunman (1923)
O'Casey: Juno and the Paycock (1924)
O'Casey: The Plough and the Stars (1926)
O'Casey: The Silver Tassie (1928)
Behan: The Quare Fellow (1954)
Behan: The Hostage (1959)
Novels
19th century
Edgeworth: Castle Rackrent (1801)
Prose
19th century
Banim: O'Hara Tales (1825–26)
Carleton: Traits and Stories (1830–33)
Varia
17th century
Anon.: Bog-Witticisms (c.1687)
Anon.: Páirlement Chloinne Thomáis (1645–50)
Anon.: The Irishmen's Prayers (1689)
Anon.: John Dunton, Report of a Sermon (1698)
18th century
Anon.: Peadar Ó Doirnín, Muiris Ó Gormáin (1730–40)
Anon.: The Pretender's Exercise (?1727)
Anon.: A Dialogue between Teigue and Dermot (1713)
Swift: A Dialogue in Hybernian Stile (c.1735)

It is obvious from the above list that there are different text types contained in *A Corpus of Irish English*. These texts can be examined using the options contained in the Corpus Presenter software suite. For instance, there are modules for examining databases (which contain the glossaries for Forth and Bargy) and for interrogating the text files which contain prose and drama. Furthermore, when examining texts, one can specify if the entire collection (the whole tree as displayed on the computer screen) is consulted or just the texts in a single branch. One can also select individual files so that only these are subject to examination.

5 Interrogating the corpus

When specifying the parameters for a search with the supplied software various options are available to the user. One can search for simple strings, or one can carry out searches using spelling variants or grammatical variants of words or sets of words which are determined by the user. There are many additional means of organizing searches: for instance, it is possible to specify a syntactic frame and use this when examining files of the corpus. This option is especially useful in the context of Irish English. This variety and its sub-varieties are characterized more by non-standard syntactic features than by irregular morphology, a fact which is characteristic of varieties which owe their origin to language contact rather than to a long period of historical continuity, as is the case with Scots, for instance. In the latter one finds more non-standard grammatical forms than in Irish English: compare the morphological variants as described in McClure (1994) with the few non-standard morphological forms as discussed in Hickey (2003c). This fact is in keeping with observations on shift-induced varieties of languages as shown in the case studies contained in Thomason and Kaufman (1988).

Searches using syntactic frames are useful when trying to determine if syntactic structures occur in the texts of a corpus. For example, it is possible to search for attestations of the aspectual types known to occur in Irish English to see what the distribution is like diachronically. Consider the immediate perfective which is expressed in Irish English by using the temporal adverb *after* followed by a continuous form of the verb as in *He's after breaking the glass* 'He has just broken the glass' (Kallen and Kirk, Volume 1, also treat this structure). This structure is a calque on a source construction in Irish which uses the adverb *tar éis* 'after' with a non-finite verb form for the same purpose (for further details concerning the not entirely undisputed origin and present-day distribution of this structure in dialects of Gaelic, see Ó Sé, 2004).

To locate instances of the immediate perfective in *A Corpus of Irish English* with the Corpus Presenter software all one needs to do is enter a syntactic frame as indicated in the following. When specifying the information for a search one can furthermore say whether a string rep-

Table 5.1 Immediate perfective in Irish English

Syntactic frame	Entry	Scope
String 1	*after*	whole word
String 2	*ing*	end of word
Intervening items: 1		
Input list: no		
Type of return		
I'm [after] walk[ing] hundreds and long scores of miles... Father Reilly's [after] read[ing] it in gallous Latin... I'm [after] feel[ing] the last gasps quitting his heart. Aren't we [after] mak[ing] a good bargain... (Synge, *The Playboy of the Western World*)		

resents an entire word or just a part of one. If the latter is the case, one may specify if this occurs at the beginning or end of a word (see rightmost column in the Table 5.1). There are a number of other parameters which can be set for a search and which increase flexibility and the likelihood of accurate returns: for instance, one can determine the number of possible intervening items between String 1 and String 2 in a search and use an input list for each of the strings, if necessary (see below). This option allows one to search for strings using spelling variants, an important consideration when looking at historical texts (see Barbiers *et al.*, Volume 1, for similar discussions of the use of search engines used to interrogate databases).

The returns given in Table 5.1 show typical instances of the immediate perfective construction of Irish English (Hickey, 1995). As can be seen from the returns it would be possible to specify that no intervening items occur between Strings 1 and 2 as in this structure the continuous form follows immediately on the temporal adverb *after*. If more intervening items were allowed then spurious returns like the following might occur: '... and there were men coming [after] them, and they hold[ing] a thing in the half of a red sail ...' (Synge, *Riders to the Sea*), illustrating a different type of non-standard structure (Filppula, 1991), but not the immediate perfective of Irish English.

As mentioned above, it is often sensible to use not a single string but an input list, any member of which can occupy the position of the string it is associated with. If one were examining the plays of Sean O'Casey, for instance, one would need to use an input list as there are two forms in his dramas, *after* and *afther* (the latter indicating the dentalization of /t/ before /-r/ to [t̪] which is found historically in many forms of English; see the treatment of this issue in Hickey, 1987).

Input lists are also useful if one wishes to check on inflected forms in a corpus. To take an example from O'Casey again: the word *mot* 'girlfriend' is typical of local Dublin English (the meaning evolved from 'something very small' via 'something precious' to its present meaning: Dolan, 1998, p. 180). One might suspect that *mot* would occur in one of the plays. Indeed it does, but only in an inflected form: see 'Never held a mot's hand' from *The Plough and the Stars*. Now if one searched for *mot* as an entire word then there would be no return. However, one could construct a small input list with *mot, mot's* so that both forms would be searched for and the second would be returned from the play just mentioned. Yet another use of an input list would be to collect words which thematically belong together. For instance, one might be interested in words which indicate poor health and then devise an input list with items like 'weak, poorly, feeble, dawny', and so on. The last item is a regionalism from English which is first attested in the seventeenth century in Ireland, retaining its meaning of 'weak, of poor health' (Dolan, 1998, p. 93), and is attested in the plays of Sean O'Casey: 'I'm terrible dawny, Mrs. Burgess' (*The Plough and the Stars*).

A semantic issue in connection with the immediate perfective which has been the subject of discussion among scholars (see McCafferty, 2003) concerns the time reference it is embedded in. In present-day Irish English it has an exclusively past time reference but originally it seems to have referred to the future, perhaps because it was influenced, at the beginning, by the use of English *after* as in *He's after his dinner* 'He is looking for his dinner'. Again an examination of *A Corpus of Irish English* helps in this respect. The returns with Corpus Presenter (see Figure 5.1) show that the instances with future time reference declined rapidly in the mid 1700s while the past time reference increased dramatically and continues as the only interpretation of this aspect in present-day Irish English (Hickey, 2003a, pp. 18f.).

A further example of a syntactic search in *A Corpus of Irish English* is offered below. It concerns the possible occurrence of the habitual aspect which is frequently marked by *do* and *be* in the present in Irish English. For the search which is illustrated in Table 5.2, the forms *do, does, don't* and *doesn't* were used in an input list. As *be* is the only form found in habitual constructions, an input list was not necessary for the second string.

The returns show that this structure is attested quite frequently in the dramas of Synge (just one of which is quoted here for reasons of

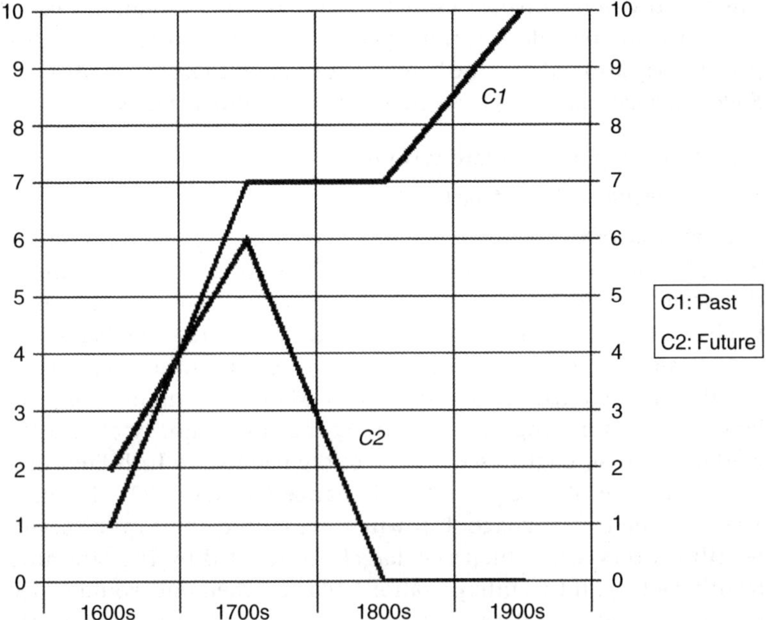

Figure 5.1 Shift in time reference for the *after* perfective as attested in *A Corpus of Irish English*

Table 5.2 Habitual aspect in Irish English

Syntactic frame	**Entry**	**Scope**
String 1	*do, does, don't, doesn't*	whole word
String 2	*be*	whole word
Intervening items: 1		
Input list: yes (for 1)		
Type of return		
Is it often the polis [do] [be] coming into this place, master of the house?		
the clumsy young fellows [do] [be] ploughing all times		
the like of them [do] [be] walking abroad with the peelers		
...the way the needy fallen spirits [do] [be] looking on the Lord?		
(Synge, *The Playboy of the Western World*)		

space). The matter of the habitual in Irish English does not rest here as there are a number of alternative expressions of this aspectual type. In the north of Ireland it is common to find the form *bees* for the habitual, for example *John bees working at the week-ends*, so any consideration of this category would involve a search for this as well. In addition a verbal *-s* on persons outside the third person singular, especially the first person, may also indicate the habitual, for example *I meets my sister on a Friday afternoon*. Searches for such forms would also be necessary.

5.1 Checking on standard wisdoms

5.1.1 The attestations of the habitual

The example of the habitual just discussed might appear fairly simple but it has far-reaching consequences. These result chiefly from the timescale of the attestations of the habitual in diachronic Irish English. The texts of *A Corpus of Irish English* show that the habitual is not attested before the middle of the nineteenth century (see Hickey, 2004b, for a detailed discussion of this). There are a number of problems with this finding. It is fair to say that the majority of scholars working on Irish English see the rise of the habitual in Irish English as a consequence of contact-induced change (Hickey, 1995; Filppula, 1999) during the language shift which set in in earnest in the seventeenth century and which was largely concluded by the late nineteenth century. If this interpretation is correct then one would expect to find attestations of the habitual in Irish English texts from the seventeenth century onwards. However, these are noticeably absent, something which is not true of the immediate perfective with *after* (although this initially had future reference). There are two possible conclusions from this fact. The first is that the habitual did indeed just arise at the beginning of the nineteenth century and hence is rightly only to be found from the early 19th century onwards. The second conclusion is that the textual attestations of Irish English are inaccurate, that is, that the habitual arose in the seventeenth century but did not find its way into texts until well into the nineteenth century. The value of text corpora like *A Corpus of Irish English* is in highlighting attestations and hence sharpening the awareness among researchers for the historical interpretation of well-attested features like the habitual aspect.

5.1.2 Second person plural distinctions

Non-standard varieties of English normally have some means to distinguish between singular and plural second person pronouns. One need only think of *y'all, y'uns, youse, ye, yez,* the Caribbean *unu* or Tok Pisin *yupela*. The form of interest in the current context is *youse* which is reputedly of Irish English origin. There is no doubt that *youse* is common today in Irish English and found colloquially in American,

Australian, New Zealand and South African English where it is assumed to be due to Irish speakers, though the relative quantities of Irish input at these different anglophone locations varied greatly.

With the demise of *thou* in Ireland, *you* came to be understood as the pronoun with singular reference and the gap to be filled therefore was that in the plural. The Irish second person plural pronoun is *sibh* [ʃiv], phonologically unlike anything available in English then or since. The Irish solution was to find a form which was different from *you* and which could function as a plural pronoun. Basically, there were two pathways open at that time. The first was to use the inherited *ye* as a marker of second person plural. The second, and apparently later, option was to create a synthetic plural by appending the regular plural suffix *-s* to the already present *you*, yielding *youse* [ju(:)z]. Later a combined form arose, *yez* [jiz] or with reduction to [jɛz] or [jəz]. There would seem to be a chronological sequence involved here as shown in Table 5.3 (see Hickey, 2003c, for more details).

Youse is a regular plural formation by simple attachment of suffixal *-s* to the existing pronoun *you*. If one is making a case for *youse* being a specifically Irish development then one must exclude any English source. With the help of available text corpora this issue can be resolved with reasonable certainty. For instance, the sampler of the Corpus of Early English Correspondence (Nevalainen, 1997; Raumolin-Brunberg, 1997; Nevalainen & Raumolin-Brunberg, 2003) does not reveal a single instance of *youse*, although *ye* and *thou* abound (*thou* is by far the most common second person pronoun, 372 instances, with *ye* occurring 19 times). This holds for the 23 texts in the public domain version of this corpus, covering letters from the end of the sixteenth to the end of the seventeenth century.

Equally in the 138 texts of the Early Modern English section of the Helsinki Corpus of English Texts there is not a single instance of *yous(e)* or *ye(e)z*. (a further Irish form from *ye* + {S}). The situation for Ireland can be seen by examining *A Corpus of Irish English*. Here the form *yous(e)* occurs abundantly in the plays of John Millington Synge (1871–1909) and with later writers like Sean O'Casey (1884–1964) and Brendan Behan (1923–64).

Table 5.3 Plural second person pronouns in Irish English

ye	From 12th century onwards
youse	Not before early to mid 19th century
yez	Not before mid 19th century

A further fact can be cited here to underline the Irish origin of *youse*. The form is found in England in only a few areas, Liverpool (Trudgill, 1986, pp. 139–41), Newcastle (Beal, 1993) and in Scotland in Glasgow and spreading out from there in central Scotland (Macafee, 1983, p. 51). It is hardly a coincidence that these are the areas of Britain with greatest Irish influence.

If the above considerations justify the assumption that *youse* is not English but Irish, the next question would be: when did it arise? When one looks at earlier writers a different picture emerges from that later on: Maria Edgeworth (1767–1849), in her novel *Castle Rackrent* (1800), which attempts to display the speech of the native Irish realistically, has many instances of *ye* (11) but not a single one of *yous(e)*. The *Oxford English Dictionary* gives the earliest attestations from Samuel Lover's novel *Handy Andy: A Tale of Irish Life* (1842). This in general concords with *A Corpus of Irish English* where no attestations are to be found before the mid nineteenth century, a similar picture to that for the habitual aspect (see above). The conclusion to be drawn from these observations is that while *youse* can be safely regarded as Irish in origin, it does not date from the beginning of the major language shift (seventeenth century), probably because the original *ye* was used initially by Irish speakers and only later did the analogical form *youse* arise (much as did negative epistemic *must* as in *She mustn't be Scottish*: Corrigan, 2000). Support for this contention comes from the greater occurrence and acceptance of the *ye* form along the western seaboard in areas where Irish maintained itself longest (see the discussion of *A Survey of Irish English Usage* in Hickey, 2004a).

6 Further results yielded by corpora

6.1 False assumptions

One obvious use of text corpora is to confirm or refute opinions which have perhaps been held without any serious degree of questioning by scholars in the field. The rise of such opinions may be justified in some original observation, but the continuation may not be supported by attestations in a dialect. A good example of this situation can be seen when looking at continuous forms of the type *a*-V-*ing*, for example *They were out a-playing on the strand*. When investigating such structures some authors have pointed out the structural parallel with Irish and Scottish Gaelic (Majewicz, 1984). Consider the Irish rendering of the English sentence just given: *Bhí siad amuigh ag imirt ar an trá* (was they out at playing on the strand). However, this obvious parallel would appear to be coincidental. The structure *a*-V-*ing* is well attested in British English during the colonial period, deriving historically from *on* V-*ing* with phonetic reduction of the preposition *on* much as in *asleep* from an earlier *on sleep*. This may well be the source for those varieties of American English which show this structure, as Montgomery (2000), who is sceptical of the Celtic origin, rightly points out. To consolidate this view one can examine the texts in *A Corpus of Irish English* which has only a very few attestations in the many historical texts where one might expect the type *a*-V-*ing* to occur. In an examination of all the plays from the nineteenth century in *A Corpus of Irish English*, only two of the 128 returns for the syntactic frame *a*-V-*ing* were instances of the structure being discussed here (the instances were *a-milking* and *a-waiting* in plays by Dion Boucicault where the author used a hyphen after the *a* to indicate the structure in question). Significantly, none of the plays of Lady Gregory, which are replete with putative Irish English structures, show instances of *a*-V-*ing*.

6.2 Slight attestations

The example just given is one where a small number of attestations suggest that Irish English is not the source of a feature found in varieties of English today, for instance in forms of American English (Montgomery, 2000). Such slight attestations may also be simply the remnants of a feature which died out completely. This is the case with archaic features of English morphology which may have been present with early settlers but which were later abandoned. For instance, there is a proclitic form for the first person singular, *ch* 'I' (first noted by Alexander Gil in his *Logonomia Anglica* from 1621: Ihalainen, 1994, p. 200), which is attested in the archaic dialect of Forth and Bargy (Hickey, 1988) but is confined to this one case in Ireland.

6.3 The neglect of distinctions

A small number of attestations may, however, have a further source in a dialect corpus. This is the relative neglect of distinctions found in other varieties, specifically in more widespread varieties of British English. A clear example of what is intended here is provided by the use of the so-called 'extended present' of Irish English (Filppula, 1997). By this is meant the use of a present form of a verb to encompass an action which stretches back into the past. In such cases, for instance in sentences with the temporal adverbial *since* (for example *He has been here since we moved to Dublin*), English requires the present perfect. However, Irish English only uses the present and so neglects the tense distinction found in standard English, for example *We're living here for ten years now.* A significant source for this usage in Ireland (it is also found in Scotland) may well be Irish where an equivalent to the present perfect of English does not exist.

Quantifying the neglect of distinctions is notoriously difficult and it must be admitted that corpora cannot always be of assistance here. Essentially, what is required is a list of contexts in which the distinction which is being examined might have occurred. Then one could count those in which it did actually occur. There are, however, ways of doing this with corpus-processing software. For example, one could search for all contexts with the temporal adverb *since* and then manually assess whether they would contain the present perfect in more standard forms of English and whether they do so in the corpus texts of Irish English.

6.4 Deciding oneself

The returns of a retrieval run frequently require interpretation by the user of the corpus. More often than not, it is necessary to manually assess whether the returns are genuine examples of the structure one is looking for. This fact should not, however, be regarded as a reason for not using a corpus in one's investigations. Sophisticated software with a user-friendly interface will allow users to decide quickly and easily what returns are spurious and what are not, and will provide the option of saving the genuine cases.

Table 5.4 shows an instance of information retrieval with manual assessment. The concern here was with the non-standard past tense forms *seen* and *done*. In the history of English the forms for the preterite and the past participle have varied considerably (Lass, 1994; Cheshire, 1994) and non-standard varieties have shown a tendency to use fewer different forms in the past, often just one for both finite and non-finite forms of a verb. This situation also applies to Irish English. Of the forms under consideration here, *seen* is by far the more common of the two.

The figures in Table 5.4 were gleaned by manually separating out the instances of the preterite from those of the past participle. The manual

Table 5.4 Occurrences of preterite *seen* and *done* in Irish English plays

Authors	*seen*	*done*
O'Casey (4 plays)	44	12
Synge (6 plays)	46	0

assessment of the returns did, however, reveal an interesting fact about the use of preterite *seen*. This is its almost exclusive occurrence in the first person. It would appear that it is favoured as a form for narration, that is, when a character in a play is recounting an incident or offering information. This type of finding is typical of manual evaluation of retrieval returns from a corpus: it was not what was being looked for and only came to light incidentally. As it turned out, 17 of the 44 instances in O'Casey's plays were from *Juno and the Paycock* which has a large amount of first person narration. The same is true for *The Playboy of the Western World* by Synge which accounts for 18 of the returns. The play *Juno and the Paycock* also had the highest incidence of preterite *done*, but here (as in the other plays) it occurred in the third rather than in the first person (the ratio was 5:1 in *Juno and the Paycock*). Furthermore, one can note that Synge has not a single incidence of preterite *done*. Neither Lady Gregory nor Dion Boucicault do either, going on the plays in *A Corpus of Irish English*. Boucicault does, however, have an incidence of first person preterite *seen*.

6.5 Shared features

Finally, it should be stressed that the attestation of a usage or structure in a dialect corpus like *A Corpus of Irish English* must be relativized and cross-checked in similar corpora for other varieties if such collections are available. For instance, the adverb *never* is used in Irish English to mark a punctual event in the past as in *She never called us yesterday*. Attestations of this usage are to be found in the Irish English corpus (and in present-day corpora of Irish English: see discussion by Kallen and Kirk in Volume 1), but the usage is common in northern England and in Scotland as well so that no exclusive claim can be made for it.

7 Conclusion

The present chapter presents an overview of a dialect corpus, in this case *A Corpus of Irish English*, which has been put at the disposal of interested scholars (Hickey, 2003a). The collection contains the majority of texts which are available for the history of this dialect, or, more accurately, this set of dialects. The different types of texts are discussed and the nature of the language which they represent is referred to. Some of the pitfalls and advantages associated with exploiting these texts for linguistic research are pointed out. In all, the latter seem to predominate and a number of sample analyses show the uses to which a careful and objective analysis of corpus data can be put and the benefits to be accrued from this.

References

Anderson, Jean, Dave Beavan and Christian Kay. 2006. 'SCOTS: Scottish Corpus of Texts and Speech'. *Creating and Digitizing Language Corpora: Synchronic Databases (Volume 1)*, ed. by Joan C. Beal, Karen P. Corrigan and Hermann L. Moisl, pp. 17–34. Basingstoke: Palgrave Macmillan.

Barbiers, Sjef, Leonie Cornips and Jan Pieter Kunst. 2006. 'The Syntactic Atlas of the Dutch Dialects (SAND): a corpus of elicited speech and text as an online dynamic atlas'. *Creating and Digitizing Language Corpora: Synchronic Databases (Volume 1)*, ed. by Joan C. Beal, Karen P. Corrigan and Hermann L. Moisl, pp. 54–90. Basingstoke: Palgrave Macmillan.

Barnes, William (ed.). 1867. *A Glossary, with Some Pieces of Verse, of the Old Dialect of the English Colony in the Baronies of Forth and Bargy, County of Wexford, Ireland Formerly Collected by Jacob Poole*. London: J. R. Smith.

Beal, Joan C. 1993. 'The grammar of Tyneside and Northumbrian English'. *Real English. The Grammar of the English Dialects in the British Isles*, ed. by James Milroy and Lesley Milroy, pp. 187–213. Real Language Series. London: Longman.

Bliss, Alan J. 1979. *Spoken English in Ireland 1600–1740: Twenty-Seven Representative Texts Assembled and Analysed*. Dublin: Cadenus Press.

Cheshire, Jenny L. 1994. 'Standardization and the English irregular verbs'. *Towards a Strandard English 1600–1800*, ed. by D. Stein and I. Tieken-Boon van Ostade pp. 115–34. Berlin: Mouton de Gruyter.

Corrigan, Karen. 2000. 'What bees to be maun be: aspects of deontic and epistemic modality in a northern dialect of Irish English'. *English World-Wide* 21(1):25–62.

Dolan, Terence P. 1998. *A Dictionary of Hiberno-English: The Irish Use of English*. Dublin: Gill & Macmillan.

Duggan, G. C. 1969 [1937]. *The Stage Irishman: A History of the Irish Play and Stage Characters from the Earliest Times*. New York: Benjamin Blom.

Filppula, Markku. 1991. 'Urban and rural varieties of Hiberno-English'. *English Around the World: Sociolinguistic Perspectives*, ed. by Jenny L. Cheshire, pp. 51–60. Cambridge: University Press.

Filppula, Markku. 1997. 'The influence of Irish on perfect marking in Hiberno-English: the case of the "extended-now" perfect'. *Focus on Ireland*, ed. by J. Kallen, pp. 51–71. Amsterdam: John Benjamins.

Filppula, Markku. 1999. *The Grammar of Irish English: Language in Hibernian Style*. London: Routledge.

Gordon, Elizabeth and Peter Trudgill. 2004. 'English input to New Zealand'. Legacies of Colonial English: Studies in Transported Dialects, ed. by R. Hickey, pp. 440–55. Cambridge: Cambridge University Press.

Henry, Patrick Leo. 1958. 'A linguistic survey of Ireland: preliminary report'. *Norsk Tidsskrift for Sprogvidenskap* [*Lochlann, A Review of Celtic Studies*] Supplement 5, 49–208.

Hickey, Raymond. 1987. 'The realization of dental obstruents adjacent to /r/ in the history of English'. *Neuphilologische Mitteilungen* 88:167–72.

Hickey, Raymond. 1988. 'A lost Middle English dialect. The case of Forth and Bargy'. *Historical Dialectology*, ed. by J. Fisiak, pp. 235–72. Berlin: Mouton de Gruyter.

Hickey, Raymond. 1993. 'The beginnings of Irish English'. *Folia Linguistica Historica* 14:213–38.

Hickey, Raymond. 1995. 'An assessment of language contact in the development of Irish English'. *Language Contact under Contact Conditions*, ed. by J. Fisiak, pp. 109–30. Berlin: Mouton de Gruyter.

Hickey, Raymond. 1997. 'The computer analysis of medieval Irish English'. *Tracing the Trail of Time: Proceedings of the Conference on Diachronic Corpora, Toronto, May 1995*,ed. by Raymond Hickey, Merja Kytö, Ian Lancashire and Matti Rissanen, pp. 167–83. Amsterdam: Rodopi.

Hickey, Raymond. 2003a. *Corpus Presenter: Processing Software for Language Analysis with a Manual and A Corpus of Irish English as Sample Data*. Amsterdam: John Benjamins.

Hickey, Raymond. 2003b. 'How do dialects get the features they have? On the process of new dialect formation'. *Motives for Language Change*, ed. by R. Hickey, pp. 213–39. Cambridge: Cambridge University Press.

Hickey, Raymond. 2003c. 'Rectifying a standard deficiency: pronominal distinctions in varieties of English'. *Diachronic Perspectives on Address Term Systems. (Pragmatics and Beyond, New Series, Vol. 107.)*, ed. by Irma Taavitsainen and Andreas H. Jucker, pp. 345–74.Amsterdam: Benjamins.

Hickey, Raymond. 2004a. *A Sound Atlas of Irish English*. Berlin/New York: Mouton de Gruyter.

Hickey, Raymond. 2004b. 'Standard wisdoms and historical dialectology: the discrete use of historical regional corpora'. *Methods and Data in English Historical Dialectology*, ed. by Marina Dossena and Roger Lass, pp. 199–216. Frankfurt am Main: Peter Lang.

Ihalainen, Ossi. 1994. 'The dialects of England since 1776'. *English in Britain and Overseas: Origins and Development* (The Cambridge History of the English Language, Vol. 5), ed. by R. Burchfield, pp. 197–274. Cambridge: Cambridge University Press.

Jonson, Ben. 1969. *The Complete Masques*, ed. by Stephen Orgel. New Haven, Conn./London: Yale University Press.

Kallen, Jeffrey L. and John M. Kirk. 2006. 'ICE-Ireland: local variations on global standards'. *Creating and Digitizing Language Corpora: Synchronic Databases (Volume 1)*, ed. by Joan C. Beal, Karen P. Corrigan and Hermann L. Moisl, pp. 121–62. Basingstoke: Palgrave Macmillan.

Kiberd, Declan. 1983. 'The fall of the stage Irishman'. *The Genres of the Irish Literary Revival*, ed. by R. Schleifer, pp. 39–60. Norman, Oklahoma: Pilgrim Books.

Kosok, Heinz. 1990. *Geschichte der anglo-irischen Literatur* [*The history of Anglo-Irish literature*]. Berlin: Erich Schmidt.

Lass, Roger. 1994. 'Proliferation and option-cutting: the strong verb in the fifteenth to eighteenth centuries'. *Towards a Strandard English 1600–1800*, ed. by D. Stein and I. Tieken-Boon van Ostade, pp. 81–114. Berlin: Mouton de Gruyter.

Leerssen, Joep. 1996. *Mere Irish and Fíor-Ghael: Studies in the Idea of Irish Nationality, Its Development and Literary Expression Prior to the Nineteenth Century*. Cork: University Press

Lucas, Angela (ed.). 1995. *Anglo-Irish Poems of the Middle Ages*. Dublin: Columba Press.

Macafee, Caroline. 1983. *Glasgow.* (Varieties of English Around the World.) Amsterdam: Benjamins.

McCafferty, Kevin. 2003. 'Innovation in language contact *Be after* V-*ing* as a future gram in Irish English, 1670 to the present'. *Diachronica* 21(1):113–60.

McClure, J. Derrick. 1994. 'English in Scotland'. *English in Britain and Overseas: Origins and Development* (The Cambridge History of the English Language, Vol. 5), ed. by R. Burchfield, pp. 23–93. Cambridge: Cambridge University Press.

Majewicz, Elżbieta. 1984. 'Celtic influences upon English and English influences upon Celtic languages'. *Studia Anglica Posnaniensia* 27:45–50.

Montgomery, Michael. 2000. 'The Celtic element in American English'. *Celtie Englishes II*, ed. by H. L. C. Tristram, pp. 231–64. Heidelberg: Winter.

Moody, Theodore W. and Francis X. Martin (eds). 1994 [1967]. *The Course of Irish History.* Cork: Mercier.

Nevalainen, Terttu. 1997. 'Ongoing work on the *Corpus of Early English Correspondence*'. *Tracing the Trail of Time: Proceedings of the Conference on Diachronic Corpora, Toronto, May 1995*, ed. by R. Hickey, M. Kytö, I. Lancashire and M. Rissanen, pp. 81–90. Amsterdam: Rodopi.

Nevalainen, Terttu and Helena Raumolin-Brunberg. 2003. *Historical Socio-linguistics. Language Change in Tudor and Stuart England.* Longman Linguistics Library. London: Longman.

Ó Sé, Diarmuid. 2004. 'The "after" perfect and related constructions in Gaelic dialects'. *Ériu* 54:179–248.

Palmer, Patricia. 2000. *Language and Conquest in Early Modern Ireland.* Cambridge: University Press.

Raumolin-Brunberg, Helena. 1997. 'Incorporating sociolinguistic information into a diachronic corpus of English'. *Tracing the Trail of Time: Proceedings of the Conference on Diachronic Corpora, Toronto, May 1995*, ed. by R. Hickey, M. Kytö, I. Lancashire and M. Rissanen, pp. 105–18. Amsterdam: Rodopi.

Romani, Roberto. 1997. 'British views on Irish national character, 1800–1846: an intellectual history'. *History of European Ideas* 23(5/6):193–219.

Sand, Andrea. 2000. 'From mimicry to hybridity: can the study of the Celtic Englishes benefit from post-colonial theory?' *Celtic Englishes II*, ed. by H. L. C. Tristram, pp. 40–56. Heidelberg: Winter.

Synge, John Millington. 1992 [1899]. *The Aran Islands*, ed. by Tim Robinson. London: Penguin.

Thomason, Sarah G. and Terence Kaufman. 1988. *Language Contact, Creolization, and Genetic Linguistics*. Berkeley/Los Angeles/London: University of California Press.

Todd, Loreto. 1989. *The Language of Irish Literature*. London: Macmillan.

Trudgill, Peter. 1986. *Dialects in Contact*. Oxford: Blackwell.

Vallancey, Charles. 1788. 'Memoir of the language, manners, and customs of an Anglo-Saxon colony settled in the baronies of Forth and Bargie, in the County of Wexford, Ireland, in 1167, 1168, 1169'. *Transactions of the Royal Irish Academy* 2:19–41.

Zettersten, Arne. 1967. *The Virtues of Herbs in the Loscombe Manuscript: A Contribution to Anglo-Irish Language and Literature*. Lund: Gleerup.

6
The Manuscript-Based Diachronic Corpus of Scottish Correspondence

Anneli Meurman-Solin

1 Introduction

The compilation of the Corpus of Scottish Correspondence (CSC) was motivated by my awareness that royal, official and family letters were a data source with unique properties in research seeking the reconstruction of both past language use and social as well as cultural practices. Correspondence is a unique source in the sense that it offers both linguists and historians a wide range of informants representing different degrees of linguistic and stylistic literacy and different social ranks and mobility. A number of other factors influenced the decision-making process in the creation of the CSC. Since three geographical areas are well represented in the Corpus of Early English Correspondence (CEEC; see Raumolin-Brunberg and Nevalainen, this volume), namely East Anglia, London and the North of England,[1] the focus on Scotland seemed very relevant. Tracing the diachronic developments and diffusion of numerous linguistic features in the history of English requires directly comparable data originating from the various areas of Scotland.

The most important triggering factors were, however, related to my involvement in theoretically and methodologically similar work at the Institute for Historical Dialectology (IHD), University of Edinburgh, where two projects are concerned with reconstruction of the diatopic–diachronic patterns of the medieval Anglic vernaculars of England and Scotland: A Linguistic Atlas of Early Middle English (LAEME, being compiled by Margaret Laing; see Laing, 1993), covering the period circa 1150 to 1300, and A Linguistic Atlas of Older Scots (LAOS, being compiled by Keith Williamson), phase 1, circa 1380 to 1500. The basic methodology in these projects derives from that used to create A Linguistic Atlas of Late Medieval English (LALME; McIntosh *et al.*,

1986). The databases of linguistic material are lexico-grammatically tagged corpora of full diplomatically edited texts, rather than questionnaire-delimited sets of isolated word forms (Williamson, 1992–93). Further, the 'fit technique', a method of interpolating texts of unknown provenance into a dialect continuum, has been computerized (Williamson, 2000; Laing and Williamson, 2004). I would like to acknowledge the important influence that research at the IHD has exerted on my approach to philological computing (Meurman-Solin, 2001a). The contract signed by the universities of Edinburgh and Helsinki, which permits the use of software developed by Williamson, has been pivotal in creating the system of tagging for the CSC texts.

Like the texts in the Edinburgh databases, those in the CSC are based on diplomatic transcripts of the original manuscripts, which ensures authenticity as well as the inclusion of a much wider range of letters than those edited previously, primarily because of their historical significance. The general approach is viewed as linguistic archaeology because of the focus on applying new technology to the reconstruction of text languages extant in authentic historical documents, providing detailed inventories of linguistic specimens and describing and interpreting them with reference to time, space and social milieu (see also Lass, 2004).

2 Representativeness

Three sets of criteria have been used to structure the text selection process. First, it has been considered important to stress the primacy of criteria ensuring diachronic and diatopic representativeness, so that the corpus will permit the creation of a diachronic linguistic atlas and provide data for historical dialectology. The second set of criteria positions the texts on a continuum depending on their validity as evidence with respect to particular research questions, this assessment justifying the use of concepts such as 'primary witness' or 'anchor text'. The third set consists of variables relevant in the framework of historical sociolinguistics and historical stylistics and pragmatics. The CSC is a database which is being continually expanded as the transcription, digitization and tagging process proceeds, with revised and expanded versions being distributed biennially. The first tagged version comprising approximately 500,000 words of running text and will be published as a web-based resource in 2007, with a user's guide and software for data retrieval and presentation.

Since the CSC is exclusively based on diplomatically transcribed manuscripts, a further important feature as regards diachronic repre-

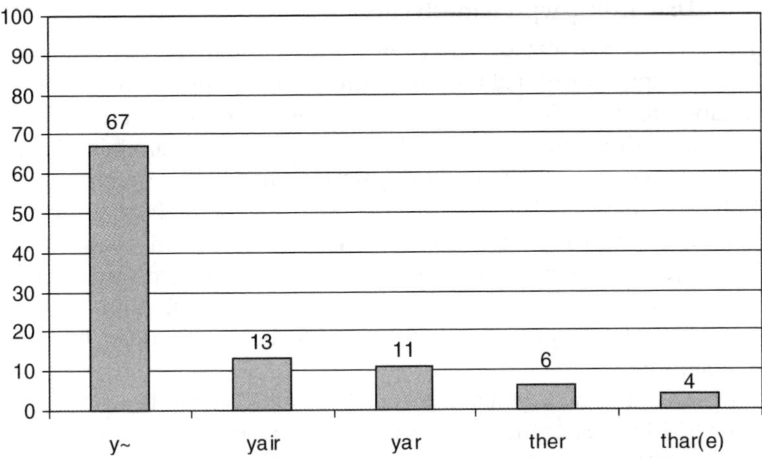

Figure 6.1 Percentages of variants of THERE in the correspondence of Mary of Lorraine, 1542–60

sentativeness is that, in this corpus, the superimposed 'diachrony' reflected in changes of editorial principles and practices over time does not distort the evidence. For example, normalization resulting from tacitly expanding contracted forms, which are quite frequent in letters, will change the data into the editor's artefact (see Lass, 1997, p. 95). Figure 6.1 shows that contracted forms of high-frequency words such as the adverb *there* form a large proportion of all the recorded occurrences (67 per cent), in the earlier letters in particular.

In editions, even though the full form replacing the contracted one may not have been attested in the text itself, a particular variant may have been selected to expand a contracted form, assuming there is knowledge of which form is a standard one in a given text or at a given time.

Since the digitized text is in upper case, the part represented by a flourish in the manuscript in contracted forms of words can be distinguished by providing the expansion in lower case. Contracted forms have been expanded resorting to emic representations, which obviously do not provide evidence equivalent to the full forms.[2] Change over time and space is not reflected in how contracted forms are expanded, the same expansion being given consistently throughout the corpus. Which form has been selected to represent a flourish is in no way related to the relative frequencies of attested variant forms.

2.1 Diachronic representativeness

The very earliest Scottish letters extant in the archives date from circa 1400. Despite continued browsing through the family archives kept in libraries, record offices or private hands, the size of the corpus comprising fifteenth-century letters will remain small. The number of autograph letters in particular will remain low. In fact a certain degree of imbalance between the quantity and quality of pre-Reformation evidence and data from later periods will remain a problem, the situation being quite different as regards early legal and administrative documents and literary texts. These form the core of the first phase of the Edinburgh Corpus of Older Scots (ECOS) being compiled by Keith Williamson.

Beside letters by Archibald, Earl of Angus, and Gavin Douglas dating from 1515 to 1521, the most valuable data in the first half of the sixteenth century have been extracted from SP2 in the National Archives of Scotland (NAS), which contains letters written by geographically diverse correspondents to Mary of Lorraine, Queen Dowager (widow of James V). A significant proportion of these letters are autograph and, since they date from a relatively short period (1542–60), they provide useful evidence for a synchronic study of diatopic and diastratic variation (Meurman-Solin, 2000b, 2001b and 2004b). However, the fact that such representativeness cannot be achieved evenly in data structured into periods of twenty years, the practice adopted in the CEEC, will reduce the validity of findings as regards developments over time in pre-1560 texts.

There is no lack of sources in the genre of correspondence in the later periods. The CSC is designed to be diachronically representative up to 1800, while Marina Dossena, University of Bergamo, covers the nineteenth century in her corpus of correspondence chiefly containing Scottish business letters and letters written by emigrants (Dossena, 2004).

2.2 Diatopic representativeness

For a text to be a primary witness or an anchor text, it should be unambiguously localizable on internal non-linguistic information, its history being recoverable reliably, including sufficient information about its writer. Diatopic representativeness can only be achieved by constructing a corpus in which there is an equal or at least largely comparable amount of data originating from each locality on a relatively densely gridded map. As regards quantity, the size of the sample in each locality is approximately 10,000 words of running text in the CSC, but in most areas the samples are much larger.

In considering the relatively large degree of linguistic heterogeneity between genres, the validity of evidence extracted from texts representing the same locality but different genres may vary depending on the type of research question. Comparability can usually be achieved only if the genres the localized texts represent are relatively evenly spread across Scotland. In the case of Scots, three types of text (charters, local records and letters) are especially relevant sources for diatopically valid information.

In the compilation process, the historical (pre-1975) counties of Scotland provided the first set of grids, ensuring a balanced geographical coverage. These are quite well represented in the present version: Ross and Cromartie, Moray, Grampian, Angus, Perthshire, Fife, Lothian, Borders, Lanarkshire, Strathclyde, Ayrshire, Argyllshire, and Dumfries and Galloway. Neither the Orkney and Shetland Islands nor the Western Isles have been included. There is a separate databank in which information about both the geographical origin of the writer, tracing his or her geographical mobility, and the place of writing of each letter has been recorded.

As stated in section 2.1, there are major gaps preventing the achievement of representativeness in a database of letters, if this is assessed by the variable of time. As regards the assessment of diatopic representativeness, there may be differences in how evenly different types of letters are spread across Scotland in the various time periods. A better balance can be created by including letters still kept in private hands. The general assumption is that letters representing a particular geographical area may sometimes be linguistically too heterogeneous to permit the interpretation of the findings with reference to dialectal preferences.

As I have discussed in my earlier research (Meurman-Solin, 2004c), the reification of the Scottish variety and its comparative description as part of a hierarchized system of varieties has tended to divert our attention from the more challenging task, that of providing a comprehensive description of variation and change in the various areas of Scotland. However, drawing on manuscript evidence, diatopically representative data make it possible to examine the history of Scots without reference to standardization (or anglicization; see Devitt, 1989) or indeed a preconceived language system. In the present emphatically data-driven approach, a comprehensive description can be presented more traditionally by illustrating the attested patterns of continued variation, or by resorting to ways made possible by new technology. The coordinates based on the Ordnance Survey maps will allow the production of digital maps, permitting the presentation of data extracted from the CSC in the format of a linguistic atlas. Since the CSC and the ECOS apply the same system of coordinates, they can be used as a combined data source.

2.3 Diastratic representativeness

My earlier corpus-based research (Meurman-Solin, 1999, 2000a, 2000b and 2001b) suggests that 'distance' as a social, economic and cultural construct, rather than as a concept defined purely geographically, is a significant conditioning factor in variation and change attested in the history of Scots. The informants in the CSC have thus been described with reference to their gender, age, social rank, social mobility and education, among other things. An attempt has also been made to reconstruct the informants' social networks, including the geographical spread of such networking. However, in the case of numerous women and younger sons in particular, this is only possible to the extent such information is provided by their exchange of letters. The databank of language-external variables is being built using standard reference works such as the *Scottish Peerage* and muniments of some of the most renowned Scottish families collected and edited by Sir William Fraser, as well as resorting to the continuously improving catalogues of the libraries and archives in Scotland. New information is also deposited in the bank, drawing on more recent historical and sociological as well as genealogical research. Approximately 20 per cent of the informants in the present version of the CSC are female. The age range is relatively representative except for very young informants, Patrick Waus's letters written to his parents at school age (circa 1540) being an exception.[3]

Since some of the language-external data in the information bank are inevitably hypothetical knowledge, they are kept separate from linguistic material. As discussed in Meurman-Solin (2001a, 2003 and 2004a), new users of corpora which have been carefully structured by language-external variables such as genre may sometimes apply such variables as interpretative tools rather uncritically. The decision to keep language-external information in a separate database will hopefully make them more cautious and motivate them to redefine these variables in accordance with their theoretical and methodological approach and their particular research question.

My earlier studies drawing on corpora of Older Scots have shown that, in general, no straightforward correlation between linguistic variation and the sociolinguistically relevant conditioning factors can be recorded. The spread of the relative pronoun WHO in sixteenth-century Scots reflects developments in how it is used as a reference signal, not only in noun phrase structures but also as a sentence-level constituent. Since the early instances have also been attested quite frequently in formulas (typically the final formula '[as knows] god who keep/preserve [the addressee of the letter] eternally'), the history of WHO in Scots must also be related to the spread of stylistic literacy (Meurman-Solin, 2000c). Early Scottish women's writing skills have been illustrated in Meurman-Solin (2001b), social milieu rather than formal education explaining the higher degree of stylistic literacy of some of the female informants. Meurman-Solin and Nurmi (2004) examine the use of circumstantial adverbial clauses introduced by *seeing* and *considering*. These topic-forming clauses are skilfully used by numerous letter-writers for providing background information of various kinds (see also Meurman-Solin and Pahta, 2006). Meurman-Solin (2002) shows that the progressive is more frequent in two specific environments in which its use can be shown to be conditioned by text type: narratives and speech-based texts, depositions of witnesses in trial proceedings being examples of the latter. Thus the frequencies and distributions of particular linguistic features can be related to various discourse properties.

Diastratic variation can be referred to as complementing our understanding of the spread of linguistic features, but the primary goal of my work at present is to create variationist typologies of linguistic systems drawing on microscopically detailed inventories of data. In this approach membership of a variationist typology is strictly limited to items that have been attested as genuine alternatives in a pattern of variation at a particular level of analysis: structural, syntactic or related to communicative or text-structuring functions, for instance.

3 Digitization principles

The Corpus of Scottish Correspondence consists exclusively of diplomatically transcribed and digitized original manuscripts of letters.[4] The early-seventeenth-century manuscript shown in Figure 6.2 illustrates the document type the majority of the letters in the CSC represent.

The majority of the manuscripts used for the present version of the CSC are deposited in the National Archives of Scotland and the National Library of Scotland. Expanding the corpus will necessitate getting permission to use documents kept in private hands as well. The transcription has usually been produced by using a xerox copy of the original. Sometimes it may be necessary to check this transcription

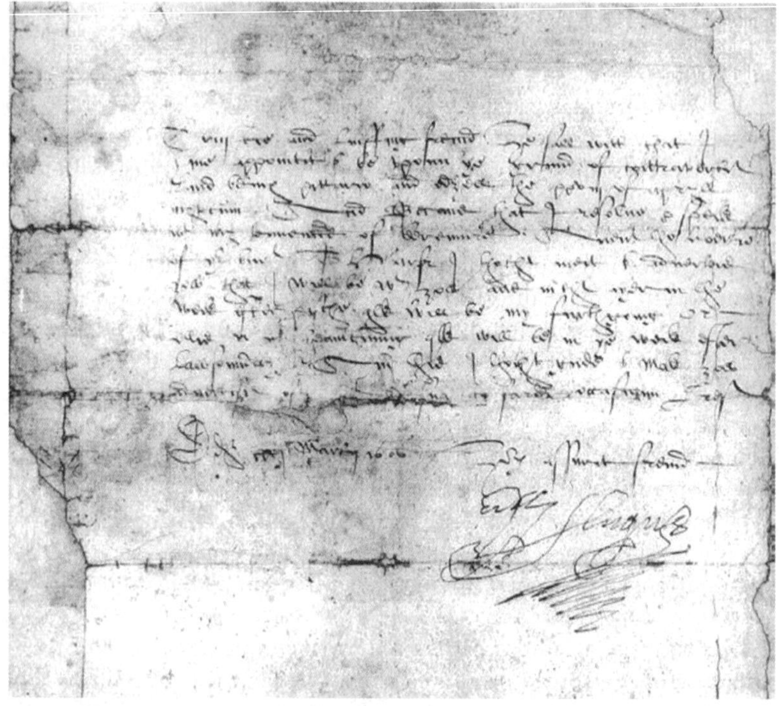

Published by the kind permission of the Trustees of Sir David Ogilvy of Inverquharity, Bt.

Figure 6.2 William Douglas, 10th Earl of Angus to Sir John Ogilvy of Inverquharity, 1606 (NAS GD205/1/34)

against the original: there may be an unclear word or passage which has remained unclear in the copy because of the paleness of the ink or a partly torn margin, for instance. When the process of transcribing began, manuscripts with seals could not be copied because of damage caused by the heat generated by the copying equipment. These manuscripts, as well as numerous others which were too pale or damaged to be legible in a copy, were transcribed *in situ*. As rechecking has been possible at various stages of their digitization and tagging, the transcripts of manuscripts available as copies in the CSC archive in Helsinki may have been checked several times, whereas those created *in situ* have usually been checked only once.

Detailed information about the digitization principles in the CSC will be provided in the corpus manual (Meurman-Solin, forthcoming), but a brief summary of the general practices may be useful in this context. Non-linguistic features such as change of hand, marked character shapes, number of folio, line break, punctuation of various kinds, paragraph structure, spacing, insertion, cancellation and position in margin or before or after the body of the letter have been indicated. Type of damage in the original is commented on in the transcription by inserting comments such as '{*partly torn*}', '{*blurred*}' or '{*ink blot*}'. Comments on marked character shape and idiosyncratic features of a particular hand, especially if these cause ambiguity or may affect the linguistic analysis, have been positioned in curly brackets before the document itself in each file.[5] A character is considered marked if it reflects irregularity of a kind that cannot be interpreted with reference to a consistent pattern in the choice of character shapes in a particular hand. Ambiguous character shapes are followed by a question mark, while two question marks are used to indicate that a character is illegible. A comment giving the reason for using question marks in a particular word may be positioned in curly brackets after that word.[6] When more than one reading is possible, a comment suggesting alternative readings is added whenever possible.

4 Basic and elaborated tagging

The theoretical approach to the tagging of the CSC data can be defined with reference to a set of principles guiding the reconstruction of past language use. First, the tagging is designed to reflect a profoundly variationist perspective. The shape of Scots over time, place and social milieu is assumed to reflect continued variation and variability, resulting in a high degree of language-internal heterogeneity, further increased by contact with numerous other languages and language varieties. A sophisticated tagging system seems an essential requirement in identifying and analysing such complex patterns of variation and tracing multidirectional processes of change, assessing their relative intensity over time and space.

Second, the system has been tailored to meet the challenge of tracing developments over a long time span. This requires that the source of an item or a collocate is kept transparent over time even though a later grammaticalization or re-analysis, for instance, would permit recategorization. Thus *according to* is tagged '$accord/vpsp-pr>pr' and '$to/pr<vpsp-pr', *seeing* (*that*) '$see/vpsp-cj{c}' and '$that/cj<' and *exceedingly* '$exceed/vpsp-aj-av' and '$-ly/xs-vpsp-aj-av', indicating that the ultimate source of all these is a present participle. Tags providing information about potential rather than established membership of categorial space are intended to ensure that comprehensive inventories can be created for examining the full scale of variation.

The third factor stressed in the theoretical approach is the inherent fuzziness and polyfunctionality recorded in language use when this is examined by drawing on representative large-scale corpora. The tagging principles have been influenced by the discussion of notional or conceptual properties, elaborated tags making the interrelatedness of the members of a particular notional category explicit (Anderson, 1997; Jackendoff, 2002). Even though the conventional categorization into parts of speech is applied to the tags, tags indicate fuzziness and polyfunctionality by referring to the coordinates of a cline rather than insisting on membership of a single category. Concepts such as 'nouniness' and 'adverbhood' reflect this approach. *Right honourable* as a term of address is tagged '$right/av, $honour/aj-n{ho}-voc' and '$-able/xs-aj-n{ho}-voc' (with '{ho}' commenting on the honorific function and 'voc' being an abbreviation of vocative). The tag type with two core category names combined by a hyphen (here aj-n) permits searches concerned with fuzziness or polyfunctionality. This practice can be illustrated by *conform to*, '$conform/aj-pr>pr' and '$to/pr<aj-pr', and *as soon as*, '$as/av>cj $soon/av-cj $as/cj<av' (for further information on multi-unit core properties, see Meurman-Solin, forthcoming).

Another essential ingredient in the theoretical approach is that zero realizations are included in variationist paradigms. There is a wide range of zero realization types, the tagging principles varying accordingly. Ellipted items, including features carefully discussed in grammars such as *that*-deletion, are indicated by comments such as '{zero v}', '{zero aux}', '{zero that}', and '{zero S}', while in the relative system both a comment and a tag introduced by a zero are used: '{zero rel}' followed by '$/0RO{y1}', for instance. Since the explicit marking of semantic relations at various levels is a salient feature in early letters, zero marking being much less frequent in the historical data examined than in similar registers in present-day English (Meurman-Solin, 2004a), comments are also used to indicate the absence of logical connectors.

It is noteworthy that in principle the term zero realization can be considered misleading, since it may not always be possible to verify empirically that something has been omitted. However, in the present approach a zero realization is indicated when a variational pattern comprising explicitly expressed variants and those left implicit has been repeatedly attested in the data.

A further aspect of the present approach is that the tagged texts will provide information about the non-linguistic features of the original manuscripts whenever such information may affect the analysis and interpretation of the linguistic features. Comments on these features (on the concept of visual prosody, see Meurman-Solin forthcoming) are perhaps used more sparingly than may be desirable, considering that the original manuscripts cannot be consulted easily and the keepers of the documents have not yet launched a project to make them available as part of their online digital archives.

The CSC is being tagged lexico-grammatically using software developed by Williamson, who describes the basic tagging system as being agnostic with respect to schools of modern formal syntactic theory, first providing annotation at the level of word and morpheme but permitting further elaboration beyond that level to higher-order syntactic and discourse units. Thus elaboration motivated by particular research questions may cause semantic, etymological, phonological or more detailed syntactic information to be added to some set of tags. The aim of developing the tagging systems, expressed broadly, is to discover the 'shape' of the text language we are investigating, rather than to impose on them categorial and other preconceived notions from modern varieties or from formal theory (Meurman-Solin and Williamson, 2004).

Motivated by a theoretical and methodological interest in reconstructing the system of connectives in particular, the tagging system adopted in the CSC represents the elaborated type as compared with practices applied in the linguistic atlas projects in Edinburgh (for an example of elaborated tagging at the IHD, see Laing, 2002). Since in variationist descriptions preconceived syntactic categories cannot be viewed as forming a valid basis for selecting items for a particular pattern of variation, tags in the CSC provide information about item-specific or collocate-specific structural features as well as indicate what semantic potential for re-analysis particular items or collocates have in a particular context. In tracing developments over time, space and social milieu in idiolects representing very different degrees of linguistic and stylistic literacy, it is necessary to record semantic potential rather than interpret a particular process of change, such as grammaticalization, straightforwardly as completed. In other words, if we choose a category label resorting to generalization in order to fix an item as a member of a class, we will fail to reflect categorial fuzziness and polyfunctionality. Yet fuzziness and polyfunctionality may suggest ongoing change which can only be traced by being sensitive to continued variation within paradigms. Fuzziness and polyfunctionality may also be inherent to a particular feature, so that, instead of reordering, specialization or change in relative frequencies, the perceived instability will prevail. As remarked in Meurman-Solin (2004a, p. 187):

> The rationale of not providing information about syntactic properties in the tags is that these are interpreted as secondary while structural and semantic properties are considered primary. In other words, the core function of structural and semantic information is descriptive – descriptive on the micro-level – while that of syntactic information is interpretative – interpretative on the macro-level, that is, aiming at the identification of grammatical rules and constraints.

The tags also provide information about relations between structural units at various levels of language use, including textual features.

Thus, semantic criteria are used in reconstructing the system of connectives so that all features creating relations between clausal structures or larger units of text have been included in the inventories to be analysed in great detail. Inventories recording patterns of variation also contain reduced and zero realizations of links. As summarized in Meurman-Solin (2004a), the following features are subjected to elaborated tagging:

1. Conjunctions (including single-word items and conjunctive phrases) reflecting varying degrees of grammaticalization and varying degrees of integration and subordination
2. Polyfunctional text-structuring elements, for example *and, but, for* and *so*
3. Connective adverbials (in correlative and non-correlative constructions)
4. Relative structures with a connective function
5. Non-finite and verbless adverbial clauses
6. Desententialization (resulting from the nominalization of adverbial clauses)
7. Grammaticalization of superordinate verbs with subordinative potential (for example, causative and optative verbs)
8. Inverted word order indicating subordination
9. Zero realization
10. Non-linguistic text-structuring devices indicating type of connection (manuscript layout, paragraph structure, punctuation, particular character shapes, spacing, and so on).

Similarly, the system of relative structures is tagged, paying attention to the following features:

(a) antecedent, number, definiteness, animacy, word order, nominal vs pronominal realization, premodification (for example, *such ... that*), coordinate structure, sentence, fixedness, nominal relative
(b) structural features (for example, prepositional structures and the attributive use)
(c) textual features (for example, relative pronouns as sentence-level constituents)
(d) zero realizations
(e) clause type.

The chief motivating factor for elaboration is to identify all the potential members of patterns of variation, describe them as accurately as possible, and so discover the shape of the system of a particular feature drawing on such data.[7] The rationale is that the tags should permit tracing variation and change over time, space and social milieu, so that varying realizations of a particular linguistic feature attested in data covering a long time span and representing geographically extensive and socially complex areas can be grouped together using software tailored for searches by a single tag component or a set of components. An appropriate degree of elaboration can be selected. The tagging process can also be made economical by considering a particular property a default feature of a particular linguistic structure. As regards type of antecedent, 'number' and 'animacy' are specified as part of the basic tag, while the distinction between generic and specific reference and the position of the antecedent in respect to the relative element are subjected to elaboration. A quantitative analysis of the data suggested that the adjacent position of the antecedent can be treated as a default property, so that only non-adjacency is explicitly expressed in the elaborated tag. Similarly, a nominal realization of the antecedent has been considered a default property. Instead of pragmatic considerations such as relative frequencies, decisions of this kind may also be based on earlier research. Since the earliest occurrences of WHO in Older Scots texts occur in formulaic expressions (Meurman-Solin, 2000c), it has been relevant to indicate this in fixed final formulas in letters by the component '{f}' in the tag:

> as knawiss god **quha** mot haue zour grace In keping et*er*nalye (1543 Elizabeth Keith, Countess of Huntly, Correspondence of Mary of Lorraine, NAS MS SP2, 1:17)
>
> $who/**RN{+h1}{f}**_QUHA

Elaborated tags make the interrelatedness of the members of a particular notional category explicit. By using semantic criteria rather than those defined by modern syntactic theory, it is possible to identify all the members of a particular pattern of variation and create a variationist typology of a linguistic feature. Definiteness was listed above as one of the features of the antecedent to be subjected to elaboration. Let us consider such variants as *who* (*that*), *who(so)ever, any man/person who, a person who* and *he/they who,* all attested in the sense 'anybody who', expressing generic reference. In the CSC tagging system items such as these are related to each other by adding a semantic component to the tags: '{g1}' to indicate generic reference to a nominal unit in the singular and '{g2}' to a unit in the plural. The following example extracted from the Helsinki Corpus of Older Scots (Meurman-Solin, 1995: http://helmer.aksis.uib.no/-icame/hc-oscot/biblio.htm) illustrates the tagging practice:

> **Thay that** ar quiet and fals flatterers **Thay that** ar doubel tu*n*git **the quhilk** sais ane thi*n*g now/a*n*d sine ane oder thing **thay quhilk** bakbitis thair nichtburs be hind thair bak /... (HCOS 1533 Gau:17)

$/P23N{g2}>R_*THAY
$that/**RN{g2}<P**_THAT

$/P23N{g2}>R_*THAY
$that/**RN{g2}<P>R**_THAT

$/T>R_THE
$which/**RN{g2}{non-ad}<T<R**_QUHILK

$/P23N{g2}>R_*THAY
$which/**RN{g2}<P**_QUHILK

The pair '>R' and '<R' are used to indicate a sequence of relative structures sharing the same antecedent, which has been left unrepeated.

Another example illustrating this approach is the tagging of *thereof, hereof, whereof, of that, of this* and *of it.* The following tags are used to permit searching for these items as part of the same variational pattern:

$thereof/Dat>pr $of/pr<Dat
$hereof/Dis>pr $of/pr<Dis
$whereof/RO>pr $of/pr<RO
$of/pr>Dat-n $/Dat-n<pr
$of/pr>Dis-n $/Dis-n<pr
$of/pr>P13OI $/P13OI<pr

Similarly, *herewith* in the context *They agree with this* (involving '>pr' and '<v', *agree with* being a prepositional verb) is tagged differently from the adverbial use, as in *I will send the document herewith*, the distinctive practices permitting the grouping of all prepositional verbs, irrespective of variation resulting from their varying types of complementation and degree of fixedness:

$/P23N
$agree/vps23<P+>pr
$herewith/Dis>pr $with/pr<Dis>v

$/P11N
$will/vm
$send/vi
$/T
$document/n
$herewith/Dis-av>pr $with/pr<Dis-av

There are also other high-frequency features which have been grouped together, so that, for example, all realizations of negation have 'neg' as the first element in the tag:

$nor/neg-cj{ts}_NOR[8]
{\}
{inversion>}
$do/vps11>P+>vi{neg}_DOE $/vps11>P+>vi{neg}_0
$/P11N_j
$think/vi<v_THINKE
{zero that}
$/P13NM_HE
$have{n}/vps13<P+_HATH
$any/pn_*ANY

In the following example, the scope of negation is the nominalized structure and, in contrast with 'neg<v', this is indicated by the tag 'neg>vn' (the comment '{rc}' for 'reduced clause' signals the nominalization):

$which/RN{sent}_WHICH
$be{n}/vpt13<R+_WAS
$part/n-av_PART+LY $-ly/xs-n-av_+LY
$/T_THE
$cause/n>pr-cj_CAUSE

$of/pr-cj<n_OF
$/P11G+C_MY
$/neg>vn_NOT
{\}
$come/vn{rc}_COM+ING $/vn{rc}_+ING
$/P02G_YOUR
$way/n-av_WAY

In making decisions about what structural and discourse features should be explicitly indicated in the tags, one of the principles is that features that cannot be searched simply by a basic tag, a string of such tags, or a particular lexeme can be subjected to more elaborate tagging as long as this does not lead to providing a syntactic analysis. A case in point is the appositive structure, which consists of juxtaposed nominal structures, often representing different degrees of structural complexity. In the system applied to the CSC, these can be searched both by a comment and a component in the tag of the second unit of an appositive structure. For example, in *my ladie your bedfellow*, a comment '{appositive}' follows the word *ladie*, and *bedfellow* is tagged '$bed/n>n-k' and '$fellow/n-k{app}<n', '-k' being attached to the second element in a compound and the pair '>n' '<n' indicating that both units in this compound are nouns by word class.

As this example illustrates, some degree of redundancy is allowed to provide a range of search options. If an appositive structure is in subject position, the present practice is that the tag of the predicate verb will contain information about the structural characteristics of the latter unit, the tag being '$be{n}/vps13<n-k{app}+', with 'n-k{app}+' referring to *bedfellow* as a complex noun phrase in which *bed* modifies the head *fellow*. A decision of this kind facilitates searching and should not be interpreted as a linguistic analysis. The description of structural and contextual features provided by the tags only facilitates the creation of comprehensive inventories, but of course these will have to be submitted to detailed linguistic analysis and interpretation.

Another interesting case subjected to elaboration is variation on the continuum from direct to indirect discourse following speech act verbs such as *pray* in the following example:

{zero pre}
$/P02N_YOU
$shall/vm_SHALL

$receave/vi_REACEUE
CEUE
$herewith/Dis-av>pr_HERE\-WITH $with/pr<Dis-av_-WITH
$/A+C_*AN
$letter/n>pr_LETTER
$to/pr+C<n_TO
‘_jHON^KING
$which/RO{y1}_WHICH
$/P11N_j
$pray{cause}/vps11<P+{sa}_PRAY $/vps11<P+{sa}_0
$cause/v-imp_CAUSE
$deliver/vi{-im}-av>pr_DELI\UER
$to/pr+H<vi-av_TO
$/P13OM_HIM

The tags selected suggest that the verb *cause* has been interpreted as a directive (‘v-imp’ imperative), the structure being different from *I pray you cause*. I have also decided to add the component ‘{sa}’ to all speech act verbs to be able to examine the whole range of variational patterns in which they occur in the data. Moreover, since I have considered it relevant that all items sharing the causative function can be included in a single inventory, the comment ‘{cause}’ is added to the lexeme and the following infinitive is tagged ‘vi-av’, ‘{-im}’ indicating the absence of the infinitive marker.

As stated above, the elaboration of tags is particularly ambitious in the case of connectives, one of the central themes drawing on CSC data in my research. Information of the following kind is considered crucial. Both the source or origin and the potential use as a connective will be indicated irrespective of degree of grammaticalization reflected in a particular example; the function in information processing, topic-forming potential, for instance, as well as its use as a text-structuring device are also signalled by the tags. The following example illustrates the tagging of *in regard of* followed by a nominalization:

$in/pr-cj_IN
$regard/n{rc}-pr-cj>pr-cj_REGARD
$of/pr-cj<n-pr-cj_OF
$/T_THE
$long/aj_LONG
$lie{p}/vn{rc}-av>pr>pr_LY+ING $/vn{rc}-av>pr>pr_+ING
$of/pr<vn-av_OF

```
$/P13OI_IT
$in/pr<vn-av_IN
$/T_THE
$bark/n_BARK
```

The tag attached to *regard* indicates that by word class it is a noun, but it occurs in a prepositional phrase with a connective function ('pr-cj'). Since that phrase introduces a nominalization, the preposition *of* also has a connective function, the practice aiming at relating the tagging of the finite clause realization (cf. *in regard that it had lied long in the bark*) and this reduced realization to one another as members of the same variational paradigm. The tagging remains the same irrespective of the date of the text. This makes it possible to trace the history of the feature and relate it to that of other features which share the same or similar semantic and structural properties. For example, it is possible to group all connectives incorporating a noun together and provide inventories of both those introducing finite clauses and those occurring in nominalizations.

Zero realizations of connectives are tagged by adding comments such as '{zero pre}' or '{zero post}' depending on whether a link such as *and* or *but* does not occur at the beginning of the first clause of a complex sentence or at the beginning of any kind of sentence, or *then* and *so* at the beginning of the second. This has been considered relevant because of the high frequency of explicit links in contexts where there is usually no link in present-day English. To contrast the practice of introducing the following sentence by *but*, for instance, and a zero link, the comment '{zero pre}' has been added:

```
{zero pre}
$/P11N_j
$be{n}/vps11<P+_AM
$confident/aj>cj_CONFIDENT
$if/cj{med}_jF
{\}
$/P02N_YOU
$be{n}/vsjpt02<P+{cond}_WERE
$here/av_HERE
$/P02X<_YOUR-SELF $-self/xs-P_-SELF
{,}
$that/cj{non-ad}<aj_THAT
$/P02N_YOU
```

```
$would/vm_WOULD
$condescend/vi>pr_CONDESCENDE
$to/pr+V<vi_TO
{\}
$/P13O1>pn-aj_IT
$all/pn-aj<P_ALL
```

The tag of *that* indicates that the nominal *that*-clause functions as a complement of the adjective *confident.*

5 Work in progress

The CSC is a protean corpus in the sense that it will be continuously expanded, and new knowledge will be deposited in the database containing information about language-external factors. It can also be flexibly reshaped and the tags revised and re-elaborated easily. The plan is to make the database available, so that the texts, a user's guide, software, case studies and an introduction explaining the theoretical and methodological approach will be part of the online resource of the product. At a more general level, expertise gained in compiling manuscript-based corpora will benefit the various digitization projects launched by national archives as well as the development of text annotation systems in a wide range of text languages.

Notes

1. The Court has been defined as a fourth area, more social than geographical.
2. Thus, the fact that 'yo~' (~ here indicating a flourish in a variant of 'your'), 'y~' ('there') and 'ans~' ('answer') have been expanded 'YOur', 'Yar' and 'ANSer' cannot be interpreted as evidence of the variants 'your', 'yar' and 'anser'.
3. The fate of the Waus Correspondence is unknown; according to the NAS, these letters may have been destroyed in the fire at Barnbarroch House in 1941, and are therefore only available in a late nineteenth-century edition (Vans Agnew, 1882).
4. Bundles of family documents frequently also contain contemporary or later copies of letters, but these have not been included in the CSC.
5. For example, to make the user of the material aware of some ambiguity, <t> without a horizontal stroke, the resemblance between <a> and <o> or <u> and <v> in particular environments in a particular hand may be commented on.
6. Typically, these comments refer to a character being unclear because of an ink blot or a partly torn fold or margin.
7. The principles of elaborated tagging are discussed in more detail in Meurman-Solin and Williamson (2004).

8. A connective is tagged 'cj', '{ts}' indicating that *nor* has been used as a text-structuring device.

References

Anderson, J. M. 1997. *A Notional Theory of Syntactic Categories.* Cambridge: Cambridge University Press.

Devitt, A. J. 1989. *Standardizing Written English: Diffusion in the Case of Scotland 1520–1659.* Cambridge: Cambridge University Press.

Dossena, M. 2004. 'Towards a corpus of nineteenth-century Scottish correspondence'. *Linguistica e Filologia* 18:195–214.

Jackendoff, R. 2002. *Foundations of Language: Brain, Meaning, Grammar, Evolution.* Oxford: Oxford University Press.

Laing, M. 1993. *Catalogue of Sources for a Linguistic Atlas of Early Medieval English.* Cambridge: D. S. Brewer.

Laing, M. 2002. 'Corpus-provoked questions about negation in early Middle English'. *Language Sciences* 24:297–321.

Laing, M. and K. Williamson. 2004. 'The archaeology of Middle English texts'. *Categorization in the History of English,* ed. by C. Kay and J. Smith, pp. 85–145. Amsterdam/Philadelphia: John Benjamins.

Lass, R. 1997. *Historical Linguistics and Language Change.* Cambridge: Cambridge University Press.

Lass, R. 2004. 'Ut custodiant litteras: editions, corpora and witnesshood'. *Methods and Data in English Historical Dialectology,* ed. by M. Dossena and R. Lass, pp. 21–48. Bern: Peter Lang.

McIntosh, A., M. L. Samuels and M. Benskin, with M. Laing and K. Williamson. 1986. *A Linguistic Atlas of Late Medieval English.* Aberdeen: Aberdeen University Press.

Meurman-Solin, A. 1999. 'Letters as a source of data for reconstructing early spoken Scots'. *Writing in Nonstandard English,* ed. by I. Taavitsainen, G. Melchers and P. Pahta, pp. 305–22. Amsterdam/Philadelphia: John Benjamins.

Meurman-Solin, A. 2000a. 'Change from above or from below? Mapping the *loci* of linguistic change in the history of Scottish English'. *The Development of Standard English, 1300–1800: Theories, Descriptions, Conflicts,* ed. by L. Wright, pp. 155–70. Cambridge: Cambridge University Press.

Meurman-Solin, A. 2000b. 'On the conditioning of geographical and social distance in language variation and change in Renaissance Scots'. *The History of English in a Social Context: A Contribution to Historical Sociolinguistics,* ed. by D. Kastovsky and A. Mettinger, pp. 227–55. Berlin: Mouton de Gruyter.

Meurman-Solin, A. 2000c. 'Geographical, socio-spatial and systemic distance in the spread of the relative *who* in Scots'. *Generative Theory and Corpus Studies: A Dialogue from 10ICEHL,* ed. by R. Bermúdez-Otero, D. Denison, R. M. Hogg & C. B. McCully, pp. 417–38. Berlin: Mouton de Gruyter.

Meurman-Solin, A. 2001a. 'Structured text corpora in the study of language variation and change'. *Literary and Linguistic Computing* 16(1):5–27.

Meurman-Solin, A. 2001b. 'Women as informants in the reconstruction of geographically and socioculturally conditioned language variation and change in 16th and 17th Century Scots'. *Scottish Language* 20:20–46.

Meurman-Solin, A. 2002. 'The progressive in early Scots'. *English Historical Syntax and Morphology. Selected Papers from 11ICEHL*, ed. by T. Fanego, M. J. López-Couso and J. Pérez-Guerra, pp. 203–29. Amsterdam: John Benjamins.

Meurman-Solin, A. 2003. 'Corpus-based study of Older Scots grammar and lexis'. *The Edinburgh Companion to Scots*, ed. by J. Corbett, D. McClure and J. Stuart-Smith, pp. 170–96. Edinburgh: Edinburgh University Press.

Meurman-Solin, A. 2004a. 'Towards a variationist typology of clausal connectives. Methodological considerations based on the Corpus of Scottish Correspondence'. *Methods and Data in English Historical Dialectology*, ed. by M. Dossena and R. Lass, pp. 171–97. Bern: Peter Lang.

Meurman-Solin, A. 2004b. 'Data and methods in Scottish historical linguistics'. *The History of English and the Dynamics of Power*, ed. by E. Barisone, M. L. Maggioni and P. Tornaghi, pp. 25–42. Alessandria: Edizioni dell'Orso.

Meurman-Solin, A. 2004c. 'From inventory to typology in English historical dialectology'. *New Perspectives on English Historical Linguistics: Selected Papers from 12 ICEHL, Glasgow, 21–26 August 2002*. Vol. 1: *Syntax and Morphology*, ed. by C. Kay, S. Horobin and J. Smith, pp. 121–51. Amsterdam/Philadelpia: John Benjamins.

Meurman-Solin, A. (forthcoming). *Introduction and Manual to the* Corpus of Scottish Correspondence. An online user's guide with auxiliary data sources, software and case studies.

Meurman-Solin, A. and A. Nurmi. 2004. 'Circumstantial adverbials and stylistic literacy in the evolution of epistolary discourse'. *Language Variation in Europe. Papers from ICLaVE 2*, ed. by Britt-Louise Gunnarsson, Lena Bergström, Gerd Eklund, Staffan Fridell, Lise H. Hansen, Angela Karstadt, Bengt Nordberg, Eva Sundgren and Mats Thelander, pp. 302–14. Uppsala: Universitetstryckeriet.

Meurman-Solin, A. and P. Pahta. 2006. 'Circumstantial adverbials in discourse: a synchronic and a diachronic perspective'. *The Changing Face of Corpus Linguistics*, ed. by A. Renouf and A. Kehoe, pp. 117–41. Amsterdam and New York: Rodopi.

Meurman-Solin, A. and K. Williamson. 2004. 'Tagging for the shape of a system: the case of relative pronouns'. Paper presented at the 25th Conference on the International Computer Archive of Modern and Medieval English, University of Verona, May 2004.

Vans Agnew, R. (ed.). 1882. *Correspondence of Sir Patrick Waus of Barnbarroch, Knight, 1540–1597*. Edinburgh.

Williamson, K. 1992–93. 'A computer-aided method for making a linguistic atlas of Older Scots'. *Scottish Language* 11–12:138–73.

Williamson, K. 2000. 'Changing spaces: linguistic relationships and the dialect continuum'. *Placing Middle English in Context*, ed. by I. Taavitsainen, T. Nevalainen, P. Pahta and M. Rissanen, pp. 141–79. Berlin and New York: Mouton de Gruyter.

Websites

Meurman-Solin, A. 1995 (comp.) *Helsinki Corpus of Older Scots*, 1450–1700. Helsinki: Department of English, in *ICAME Collection of English Language Corpora* (CD-Rom), Second Edition (1999), Knut Hofland, Anne Lindebjerg, Jørn Thunestvedt, comps. The HIT Centre, University of Bergen, Norway. http://helmer.aksis.uib.no/icame/hc-oscot/biblio.htm

7
Historical Sociolinguistics: The Corpus of Early English Correspondence

Helena Raumolin-Brunberg and Terttu Nevalainen

1 Background

The Corpus of Early English Correspondence (CEEC) was compiled within the Sociolinguistics and Language History research project, which was funded by the Academy of Finland and the University of Helsinki in 1993–97. After that date, the researchers concerned with this project formed the core of the Historical Sociolinguistics team in the Research Unit for Variation and Change in English (VARIENG) at the University of Helsinki, which was chosen as one of the national Centres of Excellence by the Academy of Finland for 2000–05 and 2006–11. During this period the CEEC has been enlarged, and work with grammatical annotation and methodological development will continue.

The general aim of the research project was to test the applicability of sociolinguistic methods to historical data, work which could not be carried out without a corpus designed specifically for this purpose. The team originally identified the following five requirements for the data to be used: (1) the size of the corpus should be sufficient for research on morphological variation and change, (2) information on the social background of the writers and their audiences should be readily accessible, (3) the language used should represent private writing and relate closely to the spoken idiom, (4) there ought to be easy access to the material, which should be available or made easily available in a computerized form, and (5) the corpus should cover a period of time long enough for diachronic comparisons (Nevalainen and Raumolin-Brunberg, 1996a, p. 39). The chronological range from Late Middle to Early Modern English was chosen in view of our research interests and experience.

The team decided to focus on personal letters, because they fulfil the requirements better than most other text types. Correspondence is available from the 1410s onwards, the amount of data increasing with time. The people who wrote and received letters are relatively easy to identify. Previous research has shown that the language of correspondence often resembles spoken registers more closely than most other types of writing (see Biber, 1995, pp. 283–300).

In retrospect, the original five requirements have kept their validity during the more than ten years of project work. The linguistic phenomena to be studied have been expanded to areas other than morphology, such as syntax, pragmatic phraseology and grammaticalized lexemes.

The letters were predominantly digitized from edited letter collections by scanning. Some edited material, such as the Johnson letters from 1542 to 1553, were not available in printed form and, consequently, their computerization involved the more laborious method of keying in the text. The members of the team also edited some letters to be included in the corpus (see Keränen, 1998; Nevala, 2001).

The CEEC corpora today consist of the five units listed below. The first two corpora have been completed, the CEEC representing the original corpus, and the CEECS the texts that were not under copyright restrictions in 1998. The Supplement contains additional material which was not available before 1998 or does not fulfil the criteria used, for example by having modernized spelling. The CEECE and CEEC Supplement are still incomplete, and the figures concerning their sizes are estimates (Laitinen, 2002, Kaislaniemi, 2006). The tagging and parsing of the PCEEC has been conducted as a joint project between the universities of York and Helsinki (see Taylor, this volume).

1. Corpus of Early English Correspondence (CEEC), 1998 version, *c*.1410–1681, 2.7 million words, 96 letter collections, 778 informants
2. Corpus of Early English Correspondence Sampler (CEECS), *c*.1410–1681, 450,000 words, 23 letter collections, 194 informants
3. Corpus of Early English Correspondence Supplement (CEEC Supplement), *c*.1410–1681, *c*.435,000 words, 18 letter collections, *c*.90 informants (in progress)
4. Corpus of Early English Correspondence Extension (CEECE), 1681–1800, *c*.2.1 million words, *c*.75 letter collections, *c*.310 informants (in progress)
5. Parsed Corpus of Early English Correspondence (PCEEC), *c*.1410–1681, *c*.2.2 million words, 84 collections, 666 informants.

Only two corpora have been released for general use i.e. the CEECS in 1998 and the PCEEC in 2006. The CEEC, its supplement and the CEECE can be used at the VARIENG Research Unit in Helsinki both by the members of the compiling teams and by visitors who have been granted a permission to use it.

The compilation of these corpora has been teamwork from beginning to end. All members have participated in the selection of material, including library visits in Finland and abroad, while the junior members have been responsible for the scanning, coding and proofreading. Arja Nurmi has been responsible for the PCEEC parts-of-speech annotation. The teams have consisted of the following members:

- CEEC, CEECS, PCEEC: Terttu Nevalainen (leader), Jukka Keränen, Minna Nevala (née Aunio), Arja Nurmi, Minna Palander-Collin and Helena Raumolin-Brunberg
- CEECE and the Supplement: Terttu Nevalainen (leader), Samuli Kaislaniemi, Mikko Laitinen, Minna Nevala, Arja Nurmi, Minna Palander-Collin, Helena Raumolin-Brunberg, Anni Sairio (née Vuorinen) and Tuuli Tahko.

In the following discussion we shall focus particularly on issues that turned out to be problematic in the creation of the CEEC. These include the use of edited letter collections, socio-regional representativeness, and the encoding of extralinguistic information. It is important to bear in mind that most of the relevant decisions were made in the first part of the 1990s with the technological facilities available at that time. Our later research has shown that the system that was developed was practical and is still applicable to the more recent sister corpora of the CEEC.

2 General guidelines

The guidelines for the compilation and sampling of the CEEC naturally go back to the aims of the Sociolinguistics and Language History project. The purpose was to create a versatile corpus which would constitute material for various types of research in historical sociolinguistics and would have good socio-regional and quantitative coverage of informants and linguistic data. These general guidelines have remained valid even in the later expansion of the corpus.

2.1 Time span

The period covered by the CEEC ranges from the 1410s to 1681. Several factors influenced the decision to settle on this period. The early decades of the fifteenth century provide the first letters written in English in any large quantities and therefore served as a natural point of departure. Fixing the cut-off point was more difficult. The need to guarantee a sufficient number of successive generations of letter-writers required coverage of the seventeenth century. As one potentially important factor was the possible connection between the Civil War and the rate of language change, the CEEC was extended until the last decades of the seventeenth century.

Research carried out on the CEEC (see, for example, Nevalainen and Raumolin-Brunberg, 2003) strongly suggested that the corpus should be extended to 1800. The findings indicated that some grammatical innovations, such as the introduction of *its*, only started to spread in the seventeenth century. There is considerable interest in monitoring these changes through the following century. The eighteenth century also offers more material by women and provides new types of external conditioning, such as the influence of prescriptive grammars.

2.2 Choice of informants

In order to fulfil the requirements of the best social coverage possible, the corpus team systematically looked for data from both sexes, young and old, and all sections of the social hierarchy. It was clear from the outset that several hundred informants were needed to provide sufficient amounts of data for all the cells that the correlative analyses would require, especially when the linguistic variable was not particularly frequent. Several synchronic sociolinguistic studies of present-day English are based on interviews with 50 to 100 informants (Labov, 2001, p. 39), but we needed more, as the CEEC was to be used for real-time diachronic research covering about 270 years.

The sampling models for guaranteeing adequate socio-regional representativeness were acquired from the writings of well-known social historians, such as Laslett (1983) and Wrightson (1982, 1991, 1994). In dealing with extralinguistic data and their subsequent analysis, our general policy was to rely on social historians to make sure that our classifications and explanations were based on contemporary viewpoints and social realities (see for example, Nevalainen and Raumolin-Brunberg, 1996b, 2003).

It was relatively easy to find letters by noblemen and gentlemen as well as professionals such as lawyers and clergymen, but gaining access to the ranks below the gentry was a real challenge. Throughout the 270-year period the CEEC covers, especially its first half, the rate of full literacy, that is, both reading and writing, was very low among the lower social strata. According to Reay (1998, p. 40), only 15–20 per cent of labourers used signatures instead of marks in various documents in 1580–1700, while the gentry and professionals were 100 per cent literate at the same time. The study of signatures as opposed to marks is the standard method of assessing the level of literacy. Since reading and writing were taught in succession as separate skills, the proportion of signatures constitutes the minimum estimate of those being able to read.

This socially stratified pattern of literacy was reflected in the availability of material. There were so many letters by higher-ranking informants that their inclusion in the corpus could be limited by regional criteria, for instance, whereas all data by non-gentry informants were welcomed.

Full literacy was also rare among women. According to Cressy (1980, pp. 119–21), the overall literacy of women was still low in the middle of the seventeenth century, as only around 5 per cent of women used a signature instead of a mark. The scarcity of women's letters led to the decision to include all available material by women, even if some was not autograph. Tables 7.1 and 7.2 give the figures concerning the gender and social division of the CEEC informants.

Table 7.1 Informants: gender

	Men	**Women**	**Women's share**	**Total**
Number of informants	610	168	26%	778
Running words	2.26 million	0.45 million	17%	2.71 million
Number of letters	4,973	1,066	18%	6,039

Table 7.2 Informants: social status (percentages)

	Men	**Women**	**Total**
Royalty	2	6	3
Nobility	12	23	15
Gentry	35	56	39
Clergy	16	6	14
Professionals	14	4	11
Merchants	10	2	8
Other non-gentry	11	3	10
Total	100	100	100

Table 7.3 Informants: regional division (percentages)

	Men	Women	Total
The Court	9	5	8
London	15	8	14
East Anglia	17	17	17
North	14	9	12
Other areas	45	61	49
Total	100	100	100

Not surprisingly, full regional coverage was not a possible goal. Most speakers of rural dialects belonged to the illiterate majority of the population. In the choice of material, our practical solution was to concentrate whenever possible on four broad areas: London, East Anglia, the North (the counties north of Lincolnshire) and the Court. The areas are self-explanatory except for the Court, by which we mean the royal family and its courtiers as well as diplomats and high administrative officers, many of whom lived in Westminster. All these areas were relatively well-represented from the fifteenth to the seventeenth century, offering a fair amount of diachronic continuity, sometimes even within one and the same family, such as the East Anglian Pastons and Bacons. These regional priorities provided an opportunity to study the supralocalization of linguistic innovations. The regional division of informants is given in Table 7.3.

Somewhat surprisingly, when compiling the CEECE we also encountered serious problems in finding lower-ranking informants from the eighteenth century. While full literacy was much more widespread then than in the previous century (Cressy, 1980, p. 177), and hence there are letters written by all ranks, it seems that the letters of non-gentry informants, despite being preserved in various archives, have not been edited and published in printed collections to the same extent as from those of the previous centuries. The eighteenth century also witnessed a new type of letter-writers, people active in literary circles. Their correspondence has inspired research into the language of these well-known social networks.[1]

2.3 Sampling and quantity of data

As the above discussion indicates, the Corpus of Early English Correspondence consists of judgement samples selected on the basis of extralinguistic criteria. The aim was to cover as broad a range of the language as was reasonably possible under the circumstances. However, with an uneven diachronic coverage of the various social strata, we could at best only aim at what Leech (1993, p. 13) calls a *balanced* corpus.[2]

Apart from social representativeness, the quantitative coverage of the corpus was an important issue. Not only did we try to secure enough data from the different social strata, but the contribution of individual informants also had to be sufficient. Whenever possible, a minimum of ten letters per writer was selected. However, occasionally writers of fewer letters would be valuable informants, especially when they came from the lower ranks or were women. In these cases linguistic material provided by several people could be pooled for the study of social stratification or regional usage. In some fortunate cases it was possible to secure letters by the same writer over long periods of time, up to 50 years or more in the case of John Holles and Elizabeth, Queen of Bohemia in the CEEC, as well as Lady Mary Wortley Montagu and Roger Newdigate in the CEECE. In these cases, enough material was selected to cover the entire letter-writing career as evenly as possible.

2.4 Authenticity

The primary material of the CEEC corpora consists of letters available in edited collections. A few manuscripts were also edited by the team members and included in the corpus. The use of edited letters means that we had no control over the philological decisions taken by the editors of the letter collections. Nevertheless, the authenticity of the data was given the highest priority in the compilation process.

The authenticity of a letter involves three separate issues: (1) authorship of the original, that is, whether it was actually written by the person in whose name it was composed or whether it was the work of a secretary or scribe, (2) the extent to which the details of the writer's social background can be identified, and (3) editorial policy as regards the original, for instance with respect to spelling. A decision was made to include information on all these aspects of authenticity in the coding scheme of the corpus, and to provide each letter with a qualitative specification. The four codes used were as follows:

A = autograph letter in a good original-spelling edition; writer's social background recoverable

B = autograph letter in a good original-spelling edition; part of the writer's background information missing

C = non-autograph letter (secretarial work or copy) in a good original-spelling edition; writer's social background recoverable

D = doubtful or uncertain authorship; problems with the edition, the writer's background information, or both.

In retrospect, it might have been wise to divide the C letters into two groups, those written by secretaries and those edited from copies, as these represent different types of authenticity (see section 2.4.1 below). The large majority of the letters were encoded either as A or C. Some problematic material with D coding was included but later checked against the originals, after which an appropriate new coding could be given.

2.4.1 *Authorship*

The authorship of the letters was not always unambiguous. The ideal case was a carefully edited collection of autograph letters which were actually delivered to their intended recipients and written personally by people whose social background details were known. Collections like this exist, but not in very large numbers. Cases in point are the letters of the Barrington family (1628–32) (Searle, 1983) and the letters by Dorothy Osborne to her future husband, Sir William Temple (1652–57) (Moore Smith, 1959[1928]).

There are many collections in which the majority of letters, although not all, are based on autograph sources. A typical instance is a collection pertaining to the individual who was the recipient of the autograph letters but, as far as his or her own writing is concerned, the only material that remains is a collection of drafts or a letter-book of copies. This is the case with the family letters of the diarist Samuel Pepys (1663–80) (Heath, 1955), for instance. Copies of letters sent by Pepys are found in a letter-book written in a secretary's hand, which is interspersed by corrections in Pepys's own writing.

One step removed, there are entire collections of letters edited from copies, such as *The Letters of John Holles, 1587–1637*, which were edited by P. R. Seddon (1975) from four letter-books copied by the eldest son of John Holles at various times. Going further still, the letters written by the members of the Plumpton family from Yorkshire (1480–1550) were edited in 1839 from early seventeenth-century copies (Stapleton, 1968[1839]).

As in the case of Pepys, it was customary for people in high administrative offices and of the highest ranks to employ secretaries. This was more or less the rule for royal letters, at least the non-private ones. At the other end of the social scale, the lower and middle sections of society and women in particular had to rely on secretarial help because of their inability to write. A decision had to be made on how to deal with non-autograph letters in general and drafts and copies in particular. It was relatively easy to decide how to deal with drafts and copies that were written by the sender personally. They were treated like authentic letters; in any case they were autograph and could have been delivered to the recipient. The letter-book copies in a secretary's hand but corrected by the sender were also given high priority. As far as uncorrected secretarial letters are concerned, there is no way of knowing whether they were dictated or written in accordance with some general instructions from the sender. They cannot be considered really representative of the sender's language. However, during the course of the compilation process it became clear that there are periods and social ranks which would fall beyond our reach if all copies were ignored. Consequently, some of them were included in the corpus, with a specific code indicating that they were copies (see section 2.4 above).

2.4.2 Editions

In order to preserve authorial authenticity, only original-spelling editions were used. This means that some modernized but otherwise excellent collections were excluded from the CEEC proper, but these were placed in the CEEC Supplement. These letters would not serve as reliable material for grammatical research, let alone phonology, but do provide good data for sociopragmatic studies. Although modern-spelling editions were excluded, minor changes were accepted, such as the modernization of capitalization and punctuation and the expansion of abbreviations.

The actual editorial quality of the collections varies considerably. Some have been made for historians by historians without any philological training, while others combine outstanding historical and linguistic expertise. The earliest editions date from the first half of the nineteenth century, and the latest from the early 2000s. Few collections have been re-edited, although the editions might be inadequately documented and cover only a small selection of the material available. Recent publications usually give extensive accounts of the editorial principles used, while some of the older ones hardly provide any information at all. A minority of the editions also fail to give any account of the autograph status of the material. All doubtful cases of authorship, whether due to editorial oversight or lack of the necessary background information, were recorded in the coding scheme. In addition, the corpus team checked suspicious editions against the original letters, and made spot checks on many others to establish their reliability.

2.5 Copyright

The use of edited collections meant that most of the CEEC material was under copyright restrictions. The regulations in the European Union protect copyright until 70 years have elapsed from the death of the copyright holder. Most of the editions were done in the twentieth century and the editors, or the publishers in some cases, consequently still held the copyrights in the 1990s.

The compilation work was carried out without attention to possible problems in copyright clearance, since it was known that the corpus could be used as private research material without restrictions. However, copyright clearance would have been needed for the release for general use. At the completion of the CEEC, the corpus team felt obliged to release as much material as possible quickly, which led to the creation of the CEEC Sampler, a corpus of 450,000 words, containing all collections free of copyright restrictions (for details, see Nurmi, 1998). This corpus has a relatively even chronological coverage of the full CEEC period *c.*1410–1680, and is especially suited to studies of high-frequency phenomena. (For the comparison between the CEEC and the CEECS, see Nurmi, 2002a.)

The relatively laborious copyright clearance process was started when new funding for corpus work was made available in the Research Unit for Variation and Change in English in 2000. The acquisition of copyright clearance not only meant contacting well-established publishers but also tracing the copyright holders of books whose publishers had disappeared from the market. Some publishers, such as local record societies, meet very rarely, and it took a considerable time to receive their answers. Luckily, the vast majority of copyright holders allowed the inclusion of their material in the corpus without fees. After this process, the tagging and parsing of approximately 2.2 million words of letters could begin with the goal of releasing the Parsed Corpus of Early English Correspondence (PCEEC) for public use in 2006. The size of this corpus, created in cooperation between the universities of York and Helsinki, is largely dictated by the available resources.

3 Formats and storage methods

The CEEC corpora consist of text files in two different formats. Both formats, the collection-based one and that based on personal files, vary in file size. The largest collections include the Paston Letters from Norfolk (1425–1519?) of approximately 240,000 words (Davis, 1978), and the Johnson Letters from London (1542–53) of nearly 200,000 words (Winchester, 1953). The smallest collections amount to a few thousand words, for example Henry VIII's love letters to Anne Boleyn (Stemmler, 1988). (For the collections, see Nevalainen and Raumolin-Brunberg, 2003, Appendix III.) The two versions so far released for general use, the Corpus of Early English Correspondence Sampler (CEECS) and the Parsed Corpus of Early English Correspondence (PCEEC), are given in the collection format, and the other CEEC corpora also exist as collections.

The personal file format consists of a large number of relatively small files, each covering all the letters written by a single informant. These files give access to individual usage and, seen against the background information of the sender database (see section 4.3 below), serve as ideal data for sociolinguistic research. However, it was necessary to make some modifications to the principle of storing the letters of each individual in separate files. Since creating very small files did not seem feasible, a limit was placed at 2,000 running words. The letters by people providing fewer than 2,000 words of data were stored in chronologically divided collection files. Both the CEEC and the CEECE are available in this personal-file format.

Apart from the Research Unit for Variation, Contacts and Change in English (VARIENG) in Helsinki, in which all the CEEC corpora are stored, the CEECS is preserved in the Oxford Text Archive (OTA) and the International Corpus Archive for Modern and Medieval English (ICAME) in Bergen, Norway. Both server versions and CD-ROMs exist and can be acquired from these bodies, together with the manual (Nurmi, 1998) in an electronic format. The PCEEC is deposited at the Oxford Text Archive.

4 Structure

Apart from the running text, the CEEC corpora contain some text-internal codes. Moreover, grammatical annotation has recently been encoded to a large part of the CEEC. The text-external background information on the CEEC and CEECE informants has been stored in separate databases.

4.1 Text-internal coding

As regards text-internal coding, the Corpus of Early English Correspondence follows the principles of the Helsinki Corpus of English Texts (HC). A detailed description of the conventions is given in the manual to the HC (Kytö, 1996, pp. 18–40). These codings include 'foreign language' (\ ..... \), 'emendation' [{ ..... {], 'editor's comment' [\ ..... \], 'our comment' [^ ..... ^] and 'heading' [} ..... }]. Old letters such as 'thorn' and 'yogh', which are occasionally found in Middle English letters, are coded with a plus sign preceding a letter, for instance 'thorn' is +t and 'yogh' +g. Superscripts are marked with an = sign on both sides of the letters printed in superscript, as in Ma=tie= for Matie. The CEEC coding differs from the Helsinki Corpus to the extent that the line divisions which appear in the printed letter collections are not encoded. The printed letters do not necessarily follow the line divisions in the original letters, and there is no reason to repeat the decisions made by the editors.

4.2 Corpus annotation

Apart from the corpus-internal coding described above, information has been inserted on every letter. One of the Cocoa-format parameters (see section 4.3 below), the 'text identifier', has been used to show the values of a number of letter-specific variables. These vary between the collection-based and personal file-based formats, including properties such as authenticity, writer, year of writing, relationship of the recipient to the writer, and source and page number in the source collection. This information, which can be displayed in connection with every occurrence of the linguistic features under examination, has proved helpful in analysis of the findings.

As mentioned above, the grammatical annotation of the CEEC was carried out in cooperation between the universities of York and Helsinki. Although advanced computer programs have been developed for automatic parsing for present-day written English, historical data have particular problems which have turned out to be quite difficult to deal with. The unstable spelling systems pose immediate problems for handling texts created in the past, and even subtle grammatical differences may play havoc with an analysis based on present-day English.

The program chosen for the tagging and parsing of the CEEC, the Penn Treebank, has proved its strength in the parsed versions of the Helsinki Corpus of English Texts (HC). All three sections of the HC, with some additions, have been parsed by using the Treebank, resulting in the York–Toronto–Helsinki Parsed Corpus of Old English Prose (see Taylor, this volume), the Penn–Helsinki Parsed Corpus of Middle English II, and the Penn–Helsinki Parsed Corpus of Early Modern English.

The annotation system provides part-of-speech tagging and syntactic parsing. Automatic processes are supplemented by manual corrections. The parsing system uses a limited tree representation in the form of labelled parenthesis. The main goal of the annotation is not to provide grammatical analysis but facilitate automatic searching for syntactic constructions. Hence, while it is not required of the user to agree with the grammatical analysis, the annotated corpus can be used for research in any syntactic framework. (For details, see Taylor, this volume.)

4.3 Letter- and writer-specific information

It was clear from the beginning of the corpus work that sufficient background information was indispensable for sociolinguistic analysis. To meet the immediate needs of recording who wrote which letter to whom, a form for each letter was completed. This form contains the basic social information about the sender of the letter and its recipient, including name and lifespan, date of writing, social status and occupation, education, domicile and migration history. Information is also given on the relationship between the sender and the recipient, as well as the content and the authenticity of the letter. Further comments could also be added to the forms. These letter forms comprise the basic database of the CEEC, CEECE and CEEC Supplement.

There were alternative ways to computerize these files. At the time the decision was made, the Text Encoding Initiative (TEI), a coordinating body for the encoding of language corpora, had suggested two different ways of presenting participant information (Figure 7.1). While both represent a text header, alternative 1 is of a freer type, while the second alternative is more structured.

The CEEC could also have followed the model that had been created for the Helsinki Corpus of English Texts, namely a 25-parameter text header in the Cocoa format (Kytö, 1996, pp. 40–56). These parameters contain information which would not be useful in a single-genre corpus, but some of the variables such as 'sex', 'age' and 'social rank of author' certainly could have been. It was apparent that neither this format nor the TEI model really corresponded to the requirements of the CEEC users. There was a need to create a file on the informants which could allow searches of the data within given parameter values or combinations of them. The solution involving text headers would have required the encoding of parameter values for over 6,000 letters, leading to a corpus with a large number of interruptions. In addition, the technical problems in making searches on the basis of the cocoa-format headers needed to be resolved. Our decision was to create a separate sender database (see also Raumolin-Brunberg, 1997).

```
Alternative1
<participant id=P1 sex = F age= 'mid'>
        <p> Female informant, well-educated, born in Shropshire, UK,
        12 Jan 1950, of unknown occupation. Speaks French fluently.
        Socioeconomic status B2 in the PEP classification scheme. </p>
</participant>


Alternative2
<participant id=P1 sex = F age= 'mid'>
        <birth date = '1950-01-12'>
                <date> 12 jan 1950</date/>
                <place> Shropshire, UK </place>
        <firstLang> English </firstLang
        <langKnown> French </langKnown>
        <residence> Long term resident of Hull </residence>
        <education> Unknown </occupation>
        <socecstatus source=PEP code=B2>
</participant>
```

Figure 7.1 Participant coding (TEI)

Source: Johansson (1994, p. 208).

Table 7.4 lists the extralinguistic variables encoded in the sender database. The dBASE program makes use of different types of data, including characters and numerical and logical data. Most of the parameter values are exclusive, but some also allow combinations of values, and there are three fields (nos 24–26) that represent open files, where any amount of information can be stored. With the help of this database, searches, indexing and counts can be made by using different combinations of parameter values. It is possible, for instance, to find all people with university education who wrote at least ten letters between 1590 and 1620. The following gives a brief description of the variables used.

Table 7.4 Sender database: the parameters

1. Last name
2 First name
3. Title
4. Year of birth
5. Year of death
6. First letter
7. Last letter
8. Sex
9. Rank
10. Father's rank
11. Social mobility
12. Place of birth
13. Main domicile
14. Migrant
15. Education
16. Religion
17. Number of letters
18. Number of recipients
19. Kind of recipients
20. Number of words
21. Letter contents
22. Letter quality
23. Collection
24. Career
25. Migration history
26. Extra
27. Complete

The parameter 'name' comprises two fields, since surname and given name are coded separately for the creation of correct alphabetical indices. 'Title' is there to identify the person, for example the Duke of Norfolk or the Bishop of Norwich. 'Year of birth' allows us to calculate the age of the writer at a specified point in his or her lifetime. 'Year of death' is less important, but it is known for more writers than their birth year, and allows us to place the person in the correct chronological context. 'First letter' and 'last letter' give the time span of writing. 'Sex' does not need further clarification. 'Rank' describes the social stratum the writer belongs to: nobility, gentry, merchants and so on. If the person's social status changes in his or her lifetime, the highest social position is given here. On this principle one and the same person may have had different social positions in the database.

'Father's rank' and 'social mobility' are both there to indicate the person's social mobility. 'Father's rank' characterizes intergenerational social mobility, but 'social mobility' can also show intragenerational mobility, that is, a situation where someone is raised to higher status during their lifetime, such as a gentleman elevated to the nobility. Geographical issues appear under 'place of birth', 'main domicile' and 'migrant', providing information for the study of supralocalization and dialectal variation. 'Education' contains information on schooling, such as university education or apprenticeship.

Among the numerical fields, 'number of letters' is self-explanatory. 'Number of recipients' is important for studies of register or stylistic variation. 'Kind of recipients' gives information about the relationships between the sender and the recipients. This code is used to distinguish family members from strangers, and so on. 'Number of words' needs no explanation. 'Letter contents' gives a general idea of what type of letters the person wrote, for instance private, official, business or news. 'Letter quality' gives the authenticity classification described in section 2.4 above (A, B, C, D). 'Collection' indicates the short title of the letter collection or collections from which we have taken that person's letters.

Then follow three so-called memo fields, open files with no limits to the quantity of text. 'Career' gives the details of a person's career, 'migration history' information on where that person lived and moved, and 'extra' includes any other comment we might want to make. It has mostly been used to describe kinship relations. Finally, 'complete' was added to ease the filling-in process: the value 'yes' was given when the file had been completed and no additions were expected.

Table 7.5 illustrates the database by showing the record of one informant, Philip Gawdy, who was born in 1562 and died in 1617. The letters included in the corpus date from between 1579 and 1616. He was of male sex (M) and represented the lower gentry (GL), which was also his father's rank. His social mobility was nil (N). The place of birth was Norfolk (F), but his main domicile was London (L), where he had migrated (YL, 'yes London'). He was educated at the Inns of Court (HI, 'high, Inns of Court') and an Anglican by religion (A). The corpus contains 42 letters by him, addressed to five different recipients, including nuclear family (FN) and non-nuclear family (FO, 'family other'). The size of Gawdy's contribution is 23,493 words, of mixed contents (M), including news (N) and private matters (P). The letters have been edited from autograph letters, hence qualifying as A. The short title of

Table 7.5 DBASE record: Philip Gawdy

LNAME	GAWDY
FNAME	PHILIP
TITLE	
YBIRTH	1562
YDEATH	1617
FLETT	1579
LLETT	1616
SEX	M
RANK	GL
FRANK	GL
SOCMOB	N
PBIRTH	F
DOM	L
MIG	YL
EDUC	HI
REL	A
NLETT	42
NREC	5
KREC	FN0
NWORDS	23493
LETTCONT	MNP
LETTQUAL	A
COL	GAWDY
CAREER	'YOUNGER SON OF A YOUNGER SON'
MIGHIST	MOVED FROM WEST HARLING, NORFOLK, TO LONDON
EXTRA	SON OF BASSINGBOURNE GAWDY SENIOR
COMPLETE	Y

the collection is GAWDY. The open file under 'career' says 'younger son of younger son', and the 'mighist' file contains a comment on his move from Norfolk to London. In a recent project, the letter- and correspondent-based databases have been linked to the letter texts and a new user-friendly search system has been created.

5 Distribution and end-user issues

The CEEC corpora are distributed on a non-commercial basis for research purposes. As mentioned above, the CEECS and the PCEEC are available in the Oxford Text Archive (OTA, http://ota.ahds.ac.uk) The International Corpus Archive for Modern and Medieval English (ICAME, http:// helmer.aksis.uib.no/icame) has included the CEECS in its corpus CD-ROM together with other corpora, which is available for a small fee. The manuals are available in an electronic format.

The CEEC corpora can be used with the standard tools, such as WordCruncher, (see Kytö, 1996, p. 65–7), TACT (developed by Ian Lancashire and his colleagues), WordSmith (developed by Mike Scott) and Corpus Presenter (Hickey, 2003). The tagged and parsed version, PCEEC, can be employed with the search engine called CorpusSearch, developed for the purpose at the University of Pennsylvania. This program uses queries created by the corpus user (for further information, see Taylor, this volume).

Those who employ the CEEC corpora need to sign a user declaration and are expected to acknowledge their data sources.

6 Research on the CEEC

The compilation of the CEEC, which lasted five years, was partly guided by the results of the pilot studies that were carried out during the corpus work. In other words, the principles of data acquisition were continually tested in different ways. Seeing that variables such as social status and gender proved to be relevant to language change was a spur for the continuing work of compilation. Our pilot studies in Nevalainen and Raumolin-Brunberg (1996b) also dealt with interactional sociolinguistics, using politeness theory to shed light on the development of address forms. These pilot studies were instrumental in helping us locate sections of society that had been inadequately covered by the corpus.

The pilot studies also showed that the information collected in the sender database formed a valuable source for the analysis of extralinguistic factors. However, we realized already at this early stage that the use of the sender database required a great deal of historical background reading by its users. In order to avoid naive interpretations, the database users had to have a fairly good command of the sociohistorical realities of Early Modern England. Although this is one of the reasons for not making the entire database publicly available, the facts concerning the writer's identity have been placed in the 'text identifier' line as a header to every letter, as mentioned in section 4.2.

As of 2006 the CEEC has provided data for over 100 hundred publications. Three doctoral dissertations based on it, *A Social History of Periphrastic* DO (Nurmi, 1999), *Grammaticalization and Social Embedding: I* THINK *and* METHINKS *in Middle and Early Modern English* (Palander-Collin, 1999) and *Address in Early English Correspondence: Its Forms and Socio-Pragmatic Functions* (Nevala, 2004) illustrate the versatility of the corpus. The CEEC has offered material for novel analyses of previously thoroughly studied grammatical changes like the periphrastic *do* as well as research on grammaticalization and politeness in a socio-pragmatic framework.

Our monograph *Historical Sociolinguistics: Language Change in Tudor and Stuart England* (Nevalainen and Raumolin-Brunberg, 2003), offering the results of ten years of work on CEEC data, demonstrates how 14 morphosyntactic changes spread among the population of England. The volume reveals that external factors such as gender, region and social status played a significant role in the diffusion of these changes. On the whole, the CEEC has proved to be a useful tool for research in historical morphology and syntax especially.[3] In a joint project with the Helsinki Institute for Information Technology (HIIT), we have started to develop new computational methods for analysing real-time language change by using the CEEC as test material.

The sampler version, CEECS, has found its way to the hands of many historical linguists, who have often used it as one linguistic source among many (see, for example, Koivisto-Alanko and Rissanen, 2002; Kahlas-Tarkka and Kilpiö, 2002; and Heikkinen and Tissari, 2002). No doubt the Parsed Corpus of Early English Correspondence will provide material for more sophisticated studies of historical syntax.

Notes

1. Articles on networks in eighteenth-century correspondence, such as Bax (2000, 2002), Fitzmaurice (2000) and Tieken-Boon van Ostade (1996, 2000a, 2000b), are based on material collected by the researchers for these particular studies. The CEECE will provide excellent material for the continuation of their work.
2. The term 'balanced corpus', often used to refer to a balance of genres, text types and styles, has been employed here in a slightly different sense. The balance in our corpus, which comprises one genre only, has been sought as regards social representativeness in terms of social rank, gender, geography and age, and in terms of type of correspondence, based on the contents of the letters, such as news, love, family matters and business. Furthermore, we have aimed at balance by looking for different relationships between the writers, in other words, fathers, sons, mothers, daughters, lovers, friends writing to each other. (See also Kennedy, 1998, pp. 62–3; Meyer, 2002, pp. xi–xvi.)
3. Most of the publications based on the CEEC have appeared in journals and conference proceedings. In recent articles, the members of the Historical Sociolinguistics team have dealt with the following topics: sociolinguistic patterns of language change (Nevalainen, 2000, 2002b, 2002c, 2003b, 2006 a; Nevalainen and Raumolin-Brunberg, 2000, 2002; Nurmi, 2002b, 2003a, 2003b; Raumolin-Brunberg, 2000, 2005b), letter-writing (Nevalainen, 2001, 2002a, 2004; Nevala and Palander-Collin, 2005), corpus linguistics (Nurmi,

2002a), standardization of English (Nevalainen, 2003a), history of vernacular universals (Nevalainen, 2006b), stable variation in history (Raumolin-Brunberg, 2002), patterns of interaction in a historical perspective (Palander-Collin, 2002), eighteenth-century social networks (Sairio, 2005), code-switching (Nurmi, and Pahta, 2004), language change in adulthood (Raumolin-Brunberg, 2005), indefinite pronouns and their anaphora (Laitinen, 2004).

References

Letter collections

Davis, N. (ed.). 1971, 1976. *Paston Letters and Papers of the Fifteenth Century*. Parts I and II. Oxford: Clarendon Press.

Halsband, R. (ed.). 1965–67. *The Complete Letters of Lady Mary Wortley Montagu*. Facsimile. Oxford: Clarendon Press.

Heath, H. T. (ed.). 1955. *The Letters of Samuel Pepys and His Family Circle*. Oxford: Clarendon Press.

Jeayes, I. H. (ed.). 1906. *Letters of Philip Gawdy of West Harling, Norfolk, and of London to Various Members of his Family 1579–1616*. London: Roxburghe Club.

Moore Smith, G. C. (ed.). 1959 [1928]. *The Letters of Dorothy Osborne to William Temple*. Oxford: Clarendon Press.

Nevalainen, T. (ed.) 'Letters of Elizabeth, Queen of Bohemia'. Unpublished. Edited from State Papers 81, Public Record Office.

Searle, A. (ed.). 1983. *Barrington Family Letters, 1628–1632*. Camden Fourth Series, 28. London: Royal Historical Society.

Seddon, P. R. (ed.). 1975. *Letters of John Holles, 1587–1637*, Vol. I. Thoroton Society Record Series, 31. Nottingham: Thoroton Society.

Stapleton, T. (ed.). 1968 [1839]. *Plumpton Correspondence. A Series of Letters, Chiefly Domestick, Written in the Reigns of Edward IV, Richard III, Henry VII, and Henry VIII*. Camden Original Series, 4. New York: AMS Press.

Stemmler, T. H. (ed.). 1988. *Die Liebesbriefe Heinrichs VIII. an Anna Boleyn* [The love letters of Henry VIII to Anne Boleyn]. Zürich: Belser Verlag.

Wendland, A. (ed.). 1902. *Briefe der Elizabeth Stuart, Königin von Böhmen, an Ihren Sohn, den Kurfürsten Carl Ludwig von der Pfalz. 1650–1662* [Letters of Elizabeth Stuart, Queen of Bohemia, to her son the Electoral Prince Carl Ludwig von der Pfalz, 1650–1662]. Bibliothek des Litterarischen Vereins in Stuttgart, 228. Tübingen: Der Litterarische Verein in Stuttgart.

White, A. W. A. (ed.). 1995. *The Correspondence of Sir Roger Newdigate of Arbury, Warwickshire*. Dugdale Society, vol. 37. Hertford: The Society.

Winchester, B. (ed.). 1953. 'The Johnson Letters, 1542–1552'. Unpublished PhD dissertation, University of London.

Studies

Bax, R. 2000. 'A network strength scale for the study of eighteenth-century English'. *European Journal of English Studies* 4(3):277–89.

Bax, R. 2002. 'Linguistic accommodation: the correspondence between Samuel Johnson and Hester Lynch Thrale'. *Sounds, Words, Texts and Change: Selected Papers from 11 ICEHL, Santiago de Compostela, 7–11 September 2000*, ed. by

T. Fanego, B. Méndez-Naya and E. Seoane, pp. 9–23. Amsterdam/Philadelphia: Benjamins.

Biber, D. 1995. *Dimensions of Register Variation*. Cambridge: Cambridge University Press.

Cressy, D. 1980. *Literacy and Social Order: Reading and Writing in Tudor and Stuart England*. Cambridge: Cambridge University Press.

Fitzmaurice, S. 2000. '*The Spectator*, the politics of social networks, and language standardisation in eighteenth-century England'. *The Development of Standard English, 1300–1800: Theories, Descriptions, Conflicts*, ed. by L. Wright, pp. 195–218. Cambridge: Cambridge University Press.

Heikkinen, K. and H. Tissari. 2002. '*Gefeah* and *geblissa* or happy birthday! On Old English *bliss* and Modern English *happy*'. *Variation Past and Present: VARIENG Studies on English for Terttu Nevalainen*, ed. by H. Raumolin-Brunberg, M. Nevala, A.Nurmi and M. Rissanen, pp. 59–76. Mémoires de la Société Néophilologique de Helsinki, 61. Helsinki: Société Néophilologique.

Hickey, R. 2003. *Corpus Presenter: Software Language Analysis with a Manual and a Corpus of Irish English as a Sample Data*. Amsterdam: Benjamins.

Johansson, S. 1994. 'Some aspects of the recommendations of the Text Encoding Initiative, with special reference to t*he encoding of language corpora'. Corpora across the Centuries: Proceedings from the First International Colloquium on English Diachronic* Corpora, ed. by M. Kytö, M. Rissanen and S. Wright, pp. 203–12. Amsterdam and Atlanta, Ca: Rodopi.

Kahlas-Tarkka, L. and M. Kilpiö. 2002. 'The preposition *anent* "concerning": development and grammaticalisation'. *Variation Past and Present: VARIENG Studies on English for Terttu Nevalainen*, ed. by H. Raumolin-Brunberg, M. Nevala, A. Nurmi and M. Rissanen, pp. 33–58. Mémoires de la Société Néophilologique de Helsinki, 61. Helsinki: Société Néophilologique.

Kaislaniemi, Samuli. 2006. *The Corpus of Early English Correspondence Extension, Supplement and Databases*. Poster presented at the 27th ICAME Conference, Helsinki, 2006.

Kennedy, Graeme. 1998. *An Introduction to Corpus Linguistics*. London and New York: Longman.

Keränen, J. 1998. 'Forgeries and one-eyed bulls: editorial questions in corpus work'. *Neuphilologische Mitteilungen* 99(2):217–26.

Koivisto-Alanko, P. and M. Rissanen. 2002. '*We give you to wit*: semantics and grammaticalisation of the verb *wit* in the history of English'. *Variation Past and Present: VARIENG Studies on English for Terttu Nevalainen*, ed. by H. Raumolin-Brunberg, M. Nevala, A. Nurmi and M. Rissanen, pp. 13–32. Mémoires de la Société Néophilologique de Helsinki, 61. Helsinki: Société Néophilologique.

Kytö, M. 1996. *Manual to the Diachronic Part of the Helsinki Corpus of English Texts: Coding Conventions and Lists of Source Texts*, 3rd edn. Helsinki: University of Helsinki, Department of English.

Labov, W. 2001. *Principles of Linguistic Change. Volume 2: Social Factors*. Oxford and Cambridge, Mass.: Blackwell.

Laitinen, M. 2002. 'Extending the *Corpus of Early English Correspondence* to the 18th century'. *Helsinki English Studies* 2: http://www.eng.helsinki/hes/

Laitinen, M. 2004. 'Indefinite pronominal anaphora in English correspondence between 1500 and 1800'. *New Perspectives on English Historical Linguistics*.

Volume I: Syntax and Morphology, ed. by C. Kay, S. Horobin and J. Smith, pp. 65–81. Amsterdam: John Benjamins.

Laslett, P. 1983. *The World We Have Lost – Further Explored*. London: Routledge.

Leech, G. 1993. '100 million words of English'. *English Today* 9(1):9–15.

Meyer, C. 2002. *English Corpus Linguistics: An Introduction*. Cambridge: Cambridge University Press.

Nevala, M. 2001. '*With out any pregyduce or hindranc*: editing women's letters from 17th-century Norfolk'. *Neuphilologische Mitteilungen* 102(2):151–71.

Nevala, M. 2004. *Address in Early English Correspondence: Its Forms and Socio-Pragmatic Functions*. Mémoires de la Société Néophilologique de Helsinki, 64. Helsinki: Société Néophilologique.

Nevala, M. and M. Palander-Collin. 2005. 'Introduction: letters and letter writing'. *European Journal of English Studies* 9(1). Thematic issue on Letters and Letter Writing, ed. by M. Palander-Collin and M. Nevala, pp. 1–7.

Nevalainen, T. 2000. 'Gender differences in the evolution of Standard English: evidence from the *Corpus of Early English Correspondence*'. *Journal of English Linguistics* 28(1):38–59.

Nevalainen, T. 2001. 'Continental conventions in early English correspondence'. *Towards a History of English as a History of Genres*, ed. by H.-J. Diller and M. Görlach, pp. 203–24. Heidelberg: Universitätsverlag C. Winter.

Nevalainen, T. 2002a. 'English newsletters in the 17th century'. *Text Types and Corpora: Studies in Honour of Udo Fries*, ed. by A. Fischer, G. Tottie and H. M. Lehmann, pp. 67–76. Tübingen: Gunter Narr Verlag.

Nevalainen, T. 2002b. 'Language and woman's place in earlier English'. *Journal of English Linguistics* 30(2):181–99.

Nevalainen, T. 2002c. 'Women's writings as evidence for linguistic continuity and change in Early Modern English'. *Alternative Histories of English*, ed. by R. Watts and P. Trudgill, pp. 191–209. London: Routledge/Taylor & Francis.

Nevalainen, T. 2003a. 'English'. *Germanic Standardizations: Past to Present*, ed. by A. Deumert and W. Vandenbussche, pp. 127–56. Impact: Studies in Language and Society 18. Amsterdam and Philadelphia: Benjamins.

Nevalainen T. 2003b. 'Sociolinguistic perspectives on Tudor English'. *'Nothing but Papers My Lord': Studies in Early Modern English Language and Literature, SEDERI XIII*, ed. by J. L. Bueno Alonso, J. Figueroa Dorrego, D. González Álvarez, J. Pérez Guerra and M. Urdiales Shaw, pp. 123–40. Vigo: Universidade de Vigo, Servicio de Publicacións.

Nevalainen, T. 2004. 'Letter writing: introduction'. *Journal of Historical Pragmatics* 5(2). Special Issue on Letter Writing, pp. 181–91.

Nevalainen, T. (2006a). 'Historical sociolinguistics and language change'. In A. van Kemenade and B. Los. (eds) *The Handbook of the History of English*. Malden, MA: Blackwell Publishing, pp. 558–88.

Nevalainen, T. (2006b). 'Vernacular universals? The case of plural *was* in Early Modern English'. In T. Nevalainen, J. Klemola and M. Laitinen (eds) *Types of Variation: Diachronic, Dialectal and Typological Interfaces* (Studies in Language Companion Series 76). Amsterdam/Philadelphia: Benjamins, pp. 351–69.

Nevalainen, T. and H. Raumolin-Brunberg. 1996a. 'The Corpus of Early English Correspondence'. *Sociolinguistics and Language History: Studies Based on the Corpus of Early English Correspondence*, ed. by T. Nevalainen and H. Raumolin-Brunberg, pp. 39–54. Amsterdam and Atlanta, Ga: Rodopi.

Nevalainen, T. and H. Raumolin-Brunberg (eds). 1996b. *Sociolinguistics and Language History: Studies Based on the Corpus of Early English Correspondence*. Amsterdam and Atlanta, Ga: Rodopi.

Nevalainen, T. and H. Raumolin-Brunberg. 2000. 'The changing role of London on the linguistic map of Tudor and Stuart England'. *The History of English in a Social Context. A Contribution to Historical Sociolinguistics*, ed. by D. Kastovsky and A. Mettinger, pp. 279–337. Berlin and New York: Mouton de Gruyter.

Nevalainen, T. and H. Raumolin-Brunberg. 2002. 'The rise of the relative *who* in Early Modern English'. *Relativisation on the North Sea Littoral*, ed. by P. Poussa, pp. 109–21. LINCOM Studies in Language Typology, 7. München: LINCOM EUROPA.

Nevalainen, T. and H. Raumolin-Brunberg. 2003. *Historical Sociolinguistics: Language Change in Tudor and Stuart England*. Longman Linguistics Library. London: Longman.

Nurmi, A. 1998. *Manual for the Corpus of Early English Correspondence Sampler CEECS*. Department of English, University of Helsinki: http://helmer.aksis.uib.no/ icame/manuals/ceecs/INDEX:HTM

Nurmi, A. 1999. *A Social History of Periphrastic* DO. Mémoires de la Société Néophilologique de Helsinki, 56. Helsinki: Société Néophilologique.

Nurmi, A. 2002a. 'Does size matter? The *Corpus of Early English Correspondence* and its sampler'. *Variation Past and Present: VARIENG Studies on English for Terttu Nevalainen*, ed. by H. Raumolin-Brunberg, M. Nevala, A. Nurmi and M. Rissanen, pp. 173–84. Mémoires de la Société Néophilologique de Helsinki, 61. Helsinki: Société Néophilologique.

Nurmi, A. 2002b. 'WILL/WOULD and SHALL/SHOULD in the sixteenth century: a sociolinguistic study'. *Modality in Late Middle English and Early Modern English: Semantic Shifts and Pragmatic Interpretations*, ed. by D. Hart and M. Lima, pp. 31–43. Napoli: Cuen.

Nurmi, A. 2003a. '*Youe shall see I will conclude in it*: sociolinguistic variation of WILL/WOULD and SHALL/SHOULD in the sixteenth century'. *English Modality in Context. Diachronic Perspectives*, ed. by D. Hart, pp. 89–107. Bern: Peter Lang.

Nurmi, A. 2003b. 'The role of gender in the use of MUST in Early Modern English'. *Extending the Scope of Corpus-based Research: New Applications, New Challenges*, ed. by S. Granger and S. Petch-Tyson, pp. 111–20. Amsterdam and Atlanta, Ga: Rodopi.

Nurmi, A. and P. Pahta. 2004. 'Social stratification and patterns of code-switching in early English letters'. *Multilingua* 23:417–56.

Palander-Collin, M. 1999. *Grammaticalization and social embedding: I* THINK *and* METHINKS *in Middle and Early Modern English*. Mémoires de la Société Néophilologique de Helsinki, 55. Helsinki: Société Néophilologique.

Palander-Collin, M. 2002. 'Tracing patterns of interaction in historical data'. *Variation Past and Present: VARIENG Studies on English for Terttu Nevalainen*, ed. by H. Raumolin-Brunberg, M. Nevala, A. Nurmi and M. Rissanen, pp. 117–34. Mémoires de la Société Néophilologique de Helsinki, 61. Helsinki: Société Néophilologique.

Raumolin-Brunberg, H. 1997. 'Incorporating sociolinguistic information into a diachronic corpus of English'. *Tracing the Trail of Time: Proceedings of the Diachronic Corpora Workshop, Toronto, May 1995*, ed. by R. Hickey, M. Kytö,

I. Lancashire and M. Rissanen, pp. 105–17. Amsterdam and Atlanta, Ga: Rodopi.

Raumolin-Brunberg, H. 2000. 'WHICH and THE WHICH in Late Middle English: free variants?' *Placing Middle English in Context*, ed. by I. Taavitsainen, T. Nevalainen, P. Pahta and M. Rissanen, pp. 209–25. Berlin and New York: Mouton de Gruyter.

Raumolin-Brunberg, H. 2002. 'Stable variation and historical linguistics'. *Variation Past and Present: VARIENG Studies on English for Terttu Nevalainen*, ed. by H. Raumolin-Brunberg, M. Nevala, A. Nurmi and M. Rissanen, pp. 101–16. Mémoires de la Société Néophilologique de Helsinki, 61. Helsinki: Société Néophilologique.

Raumolin-Brunberg, H. 2005a. 'Language change in adulthood: historical letters as evidence'. *European Journal of English Studies* 9(1). Thematic issue on Letters and Letter Writing, ed. by M. Palander-Collin and M. Nevala, pp. 37–51.

Raumolin-Brunberg, H. 2005b. 'The diffusion of subject you: a case study in historical sociolinguistic'. *Language Variation and Change* 17:55–73.

Reay, B. 1998. *Popular Cultures in England 1550–1750*. London and New York: Longman.

Sairio, A. 2005. '"Sam of Streatham Park": a linguistic study of Dr. Johnson's membership in the Thrale family'. *European Journal of English Studies* 9(1). Thematic issue on Letters and Letter Writing, ed. by M. Palander-Collin and M. Nevala, pp. 21–35.

Tieken-Boon van Ostade, I. 1996. 'Social network theory and eighteenth-century English: the case of Boswell'. *English Historical Linguistics 1994*, ed. by D. Britton, pp. 327–37. Amsterdam and Philadelphia: Benjamins.

Tieken-Boon van Ostade, I. 2000a. 'Social network analysis and the history of English'. *European Journal of English Studies* 4(3):211–16.

Tieken-Boon van Ostade, I. 2000b. 'Social network analysis and the language of Sarah Fielding'. *European Journal of English Studies* 4(3):291–301.

Wrightson, K. 1982. *English Society 1580–1680*. London: Unwin Hyman.

Wrightson, K. 1991. 'Estates, degrees, and sorts: changing perceptions of society in Tudor and Stuart England'. *Language, History and Class*, ed. by P. J. Corfield, pp. 30–52. Oxford: Blackwell.

Wrightson, K. 1994. '"Sorts of people" in Tudor and Stuart England'. *The Middling Sort of People: Culture, Society and Politics in England 1550–1800*, ed. by J. Barry and C. Brooks, pp. 28–51. London: Macmillan.

Websites

International Corpus Archive for Modern and Medieval English (ICAME), Bergen, Norway: http://helmer.aksis.uib.no/icame

Oxford Text Archive (OTA): http://ota.ahds.ac.uk

8

Revealing Alternatives: Online Comparative Translations of Interlinked Chinese Historical Texts

Naomi Standen and Francis Jones

1 Introduction

This chapter describes a project which will create and store in a database English translations for a set of five interlinked histories written in China between 974 and 1344 CE. The finished database is intended to provide the most comprehensive body of historical translations yet produced for China's imperial period. Once completed, it will form an invaluable resource for historians, whether they are examining the period which the histories describe, or exploring wider frontier-studies issues.

But how does this project relate to the other database projects described in this volume; in particular, how far is it a sociolinguistic venture? Ours is not the only database of historical texts. For example, Raumolin-Brunberg and Nevalainen, and Meurman-Solin deal with correspondence (early English and Scottish respectively), while Taylor addresses Old English prose. However, the usefulness of these databases rests upon their grammatical or syntactic tagging, and the prime user appears to be the linguist. At first sight, our database, by contrast, appears to be designed not for the linguist to analyse the texts, but for the historian to consider views of the events they describe: an aim seemingly reinforced by our decision to provide modern English translations rather than the medieval Chinese originals. But designing our database is not merely a question of editorial and technical decision-making; and translating, like all linguistic communication, has sociolinguistic significance. The overriding purpose of the database, in fact, is not to translate simply for the purpose of increasing access to those who do not read Classical Chinese. In product terms, we use translation as an analytical tool to highlight the evolving relationships between terms and concepts in the Chinese originals, and to reveal the multiplicity of alternative voices in a particular set of texts. And in process terms, we aim to track the linguistic socio-ethnography of our own interpretative processes as translator-historians within a framework of cross-border and post-colonial power relations. The interlinked nature of the texts, therefore, and the fact that they are being translated and thus opened up to interpretation, is what makes our history database project into a multidisciplinary research venture. The design process draws on insights from historiography (that is, how historians create and communicate representations of the past), historical usages of Classical Chinese and translation theory. It will thus enable us to address crucial practical and theoretical concerns that lie on the interface of history and translation studies: an interface virtually unresearched by either discipline (*pace* Aksoy, 2002).

In this chapter, we outline the key theoretical and practical issues raised by this project. We first describe the historical context, role and nature of the source texts (that is, the texts to be translated), focusing on the complex relationships between the narratives which they present. These relationships, we argue, are best explored in the framework of a database of comparative translations informed by insights from historical analysis and translation studies. Within a context of how these two disciplines model the processes of textual interpretation, we discuss the challenges presented by the texts. We subsequently argue that the potential solutions to these challenges lie in a database design which retains an openness to the multiple readings of events generated by the various source texts and their translations. We finally describe how these solutions will be incorporated in the database structure itself.

2 The database project: issues and aims

2.1 Historical background

The Five Dynasties (907–60 CE) was a complex and confusing interregnal period between the major dynasties of Tang (618–907) and Song (960–1276). As such, it formed the central portion of an immense transition occurring in China between about 750 and 1050, which radically transformed political and military institutions, social and gender relations, economic structures and connections, ideology and religious ideas, technology and culture. A crucial feature of the Five Dynasties period was the establishment, in the lands lying north of the notional line of the Great Wall of China (the Wall itself did not exist at the time), of a rival dynasty led by a non-Chinese pastoralist people called the Khitan. This dynasty, known as the Liao (907–1125), was the strongest power in the region during the Five Dynasties, and remained at least the equal of the Song empire that followed. Because the Liao came to control the populations living on a small portion of territory south of the Great Wall line and subsequently fought chronically with the Song, they are regarded as the first of China's 'conquest dynasties'. The conquest dynasties are those founded by ruling groups considered to be of non-Chinese ethnicity, originating in the lands north of the Great Wall line, and practising pastoral nomadism to various degrees, the most famous of these grouts being the Mongols, whose Yuan dynasty (1260–1368) ruled the whole of China as part of a world empire.

2.2 The source texts

The Chinese-language source texts which will be translated for the database are a linked set of histories for the Five Dynasties period. The works, compiled over a 350-year span between 974 and 1344, are:

- Xue Juzheng *et al.*, *Old History of the Five Dynasties*, 974 (dynastic history)
- Ouyang Xiu, *New History of the Five Dynasties*, 1077 (replaced *Old History* as the official dynastic history)
- Sima Guang *et al.*, *Comprehensive Mirror for Aid in Government*, 1084 (universal history covering 403 BCE–959 CE)
- Ye Longli, *Record of the Khitan State*, probably 1247 (private history using official sources)
- Toghto, Ouyang Xuan *et al.*, *Liao History*, 1344 (dynastic history).

The *Comprehensive Mirror*, unusually, is a universal history organized on purely chronological lines closely resembling chronicles from medieval Europe (Standen, 1996). The other four texts, however, follow the more common 'annals–biographies' form, usually consisting of three sections:

- Annals: condensed from daily records of court activities focused on the actions of the emperor
- Treatises: coherent accounts of particular institutions (for instance, finance laws, regulations and methods; or the organization of the

bureaucracy), written at time of compilation by members of the History Office from records kept by the dynasty in question

- Biographies: coherent accounts of a single life compiled chiefly from eulogies written by a relative or friend of the deceased, selected as exemplars from among the ruling classes.

The composite nature of these texts raises a number of issues for historical analysis. The annals and biographies, in particular, cover much of the same ground, but since the ultimate sources are quite different, they variously repeat information, perpetrate omissions and contradict each other. This makes histories on the annals–biographies model inherently open to alternative readings (Hardy, 1994; Moloughney, 2002). The *Mirror* provides a contrast by combining annalistic and biographical material to create a unified narrative, but nevertheless working methods shared with most other official history projects create the possibility that even this text does not reflect an entirely consistent viewpoint.

Although Ouyang Xiu and Ye Longli essentially worked alone, sole authorship like this was unusual. Official history projects usually involved editorial teams that could number up to a couple of dozen people. The exact division of labour is unclear for the histories considered here, but while project directors like Sima Guang probably read and approved a great deal of the final draft of their texts, much of that work was also delegated to their chief assistants (Wang, 1958; M. Chan, 1974–75; H. Chan, 1981; Twitchett, 1992). Hence, although compilers edited extensively, their normal working methods meant that they could not (and probably did not intend to) produce works speaking in one voice alone (Hardy, 1994).

The different voices within single works are worthy of notice, but more interesting here is the development of new viewpoints over time. Each of the later works in the set of texts listed above borrows heavily from its predecessors. Entire segments from earlier sources are reproduced without citation as part of later works, producing sets of 'interlinked passages', all recounting the same incident. A set of interlinked passages might include accounts from the annals sections of three different texts, one or more versions found in the biographies of one or more of the texts, and the unified narrative from the *Comprehensive Mirror* (see Figure 8.1 for an example). It is not unusual to find half a dozen versions of the same event scattered across different sections of, say, four out of the five texts.

It is widely believed that interlinked passages such as these were produced by copying verbatim from the earlier to the later works, and that

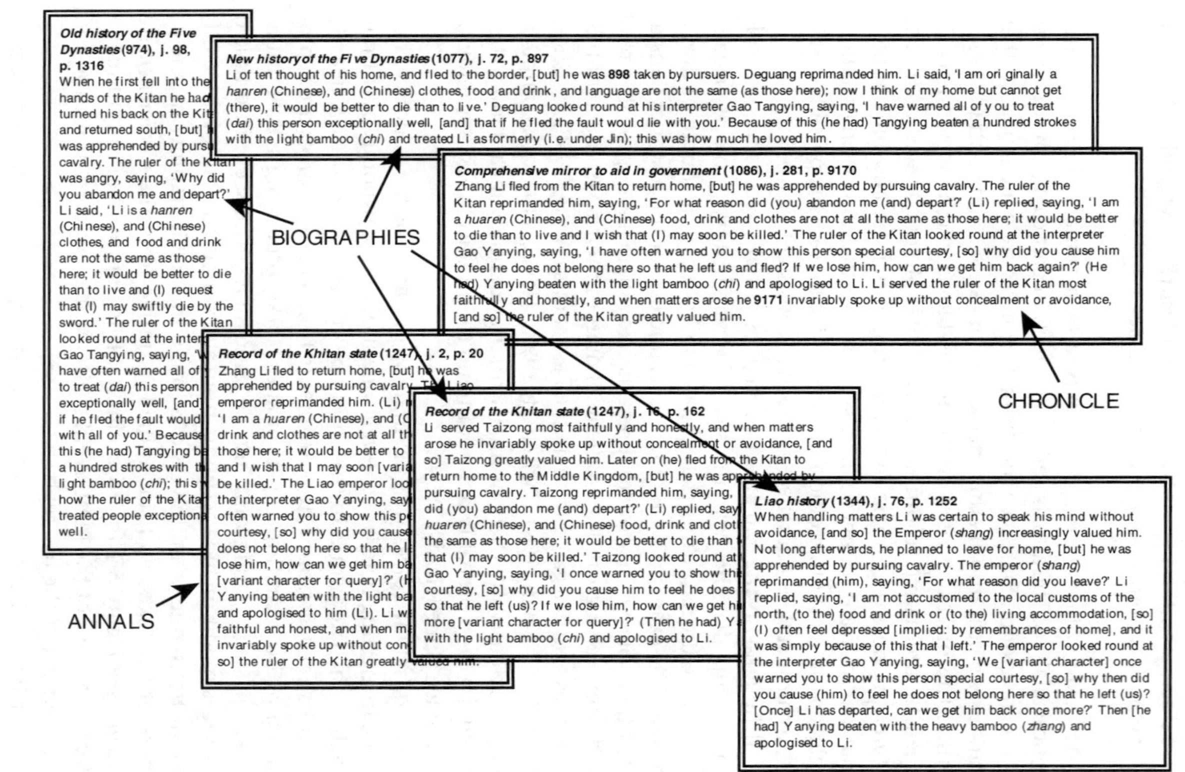

Figure 8.1 Six interlinked passages translated comparatively

they are therefore identical but for 'slight variations' in wording (see Durrant, 2001, for a recent statement of the general principle). In fact the situation is rather more complicated, because although there is indeed a great deal of word-for-word reproduction, the 'slight variations' are by no means always insignificant. On the contrary, careful comparison of interlinked passages indicates that many changes are the result of active editorial choices made by compilers following more or less explicit agendas that varied from one writer to another, and which were pursued within different contexts as time passed and circumstances changed. A straightforward example is the designation of rulers, as illustrated in Figure 8.1. The *Old History* speaks of 'the ruler of the Khitan' (*Qidan zhu*), a term that acknowledges his leadership within his own regime but does not permit him the superior designation of 'emperor'. For these compilers there could be only one emperor at any time and they naturally reserved the term for their own rulers and their avowed predecessors. Ouyang Xiu, unusually, completely rewrote the *Old History* to make it more didactic, and he uses the Liao ruler's personal name, Deguang, indicating a reluctance to accept his status as a ruler. Sima Guang's *Mirror* reproduced a great deal of the *Old History* while also drawing on over three hundred additional sources, including Ouyang Xiu's *New History* (see Ouyang Xiv, 2004). (The relationships between the texts are illustrated in Figure 8.2.) Sima uses much of the *Old History*'s exact wording, including 'the ruler of the Khitan', but elsewhere makes greater or lesser changes in wording for his own purposes. The *Record of the Khitan State* copies most of its account directly from the *Mirror*, but abridges heavily and sometimes makes dramatic changes, not all of which can be attributed simply to the carelessness of the compiler. In this example the *Record* alters the designation to 'the Liao emperor' (*Liao di*) and 'Taizong'. Taizong is Deguang's 'temple name', awarded after death and often used in official histories. Both usages imply the legitimacy and even superiority of this ruler, but on other occasions the *Record* uses terms to be expected of a writer apparently located at the Southern Song court. These conflicting usages have contributed to a considerable debate about the purpose, dating and authenticity of the *Record* (Yu, 1980, pp. 270–3; Li, 1981; Chen *et al.*, 1983, pp. 284–5), which, however, does not recognize the potential for multivocality in this type of history. The *Liao History* draws from all the earlier surviving sources as well as several lost works. Its changes reflect the concerns of the Mongol court within which it was produced, and so it refers to 'the emperor' (*shang*).

When it comes to presenting these texts to the modern reader, it is relatively easy to generalize about the broad approaches of the different

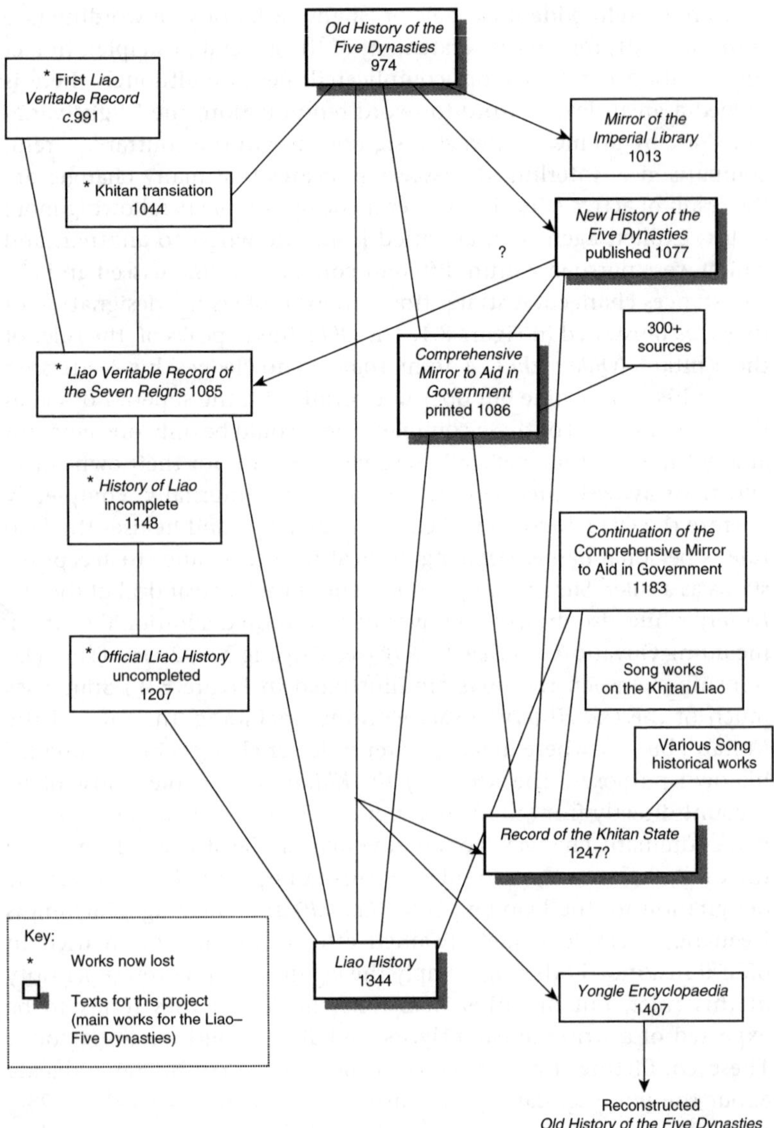

Figure 8.2 Intertextual relationships of sources for the Liao and Five Dynasties
Source: Adapted from Denis Twitchett, personal communication.

texts without detailed comparison of individual passages (e.g. Ouyang Xiu, 2004; Wittfogel and Feng, 1949), but this risks interpreting the sources as if each simply has one consistent viewpoint throughout. But if one were to a make careful comparison of interlinked passages, this would not merely locate nuances in a general approach, but may also give evidence for quite new interpretations of historical events. 'Slight variations' between different versions often turn out to be purposeful editorial interventions that can alter the emphasis of a passage by omission or addition, or by changes to even a single character (cf. Bredehoft, 2001, on similar effects in different manuscripts of the *Anglo-Saxon Chronicle*). In extreme cases, rewriting can completely change the personnel involved in a particular incident, or convert a military defeat into a victory. For instance, the example in Figure 8.1 has been used to raise issues about changing notions of ethnic identity in the tenth century by paying attention to the striking alteration of one phrase in one text. The *Old History*, *Mirror* and *Record* all offer virtually identical wording of the passage including Zhang Li's statement that he is a Chinese (*hanren* or *huaren*), and so much unaccustomed to nomadic ways that he would rather be dead. Ouyang Xiu adds a further brief phrase to otherwise identical wording. The same passage also appears in the *Liao History*, except that here, Zhang Li's words (but no others) are completely rewritten in order to omit his statement of Chinese identity. This supports an argument that the Mongols were acutely conscious of ethnic identity, but can also lead us to reflect on how Zhang Li's declaration of 'Chineseness' was understood by the earlier writers (Standen, 2007).

2.3 The translational database and the project

A comparative approach, therefore, is crucial to the analysis of texts such as these, as in Garmonsway's translation of the *Anglo-Saxon Chronicle* (1953), which formed the initial inspiration for our project. In Garmonsway's *Chronicle*, all the surviving manuscripts are translated together and set out so that all versions of a particular event can be seen (usually) on a single opening of the volume. However, the nature of the Chinese dynastic histories, and the peculiarities of the period in question and the texts recording it, force us beyond the straightforward linear alignment that was appropriate for the *Anglo-Saxon Chronicle*. Moreover, tracing the relevant passages across the several sections of five texts is extremely time-consuming, and comparative translation takes further time and great attention to detail. Thus, though working at this level of detail can prove very rewarding, it has been impossible for individual scholars to apply comparative methods systematically to more than a small amount of historical material (for instance, Pulleyblank, 1976, on An Lushan's rebellion of 755–63; Standen, 1994, 2007).

In the present project, therefore, it was felt that a computer-based comparative database would dramatically improve access to interlinked passages and allow more sophisticated and nuanced work with these texts than is currently practicable. The nature of the texts and the way in which we wanted to analyse them, however, meant that we had to devise innovative ways of incorporating cross-text links into the database, enabling searches, for example, not only by text string, but also by semantic notions such as person and event, as we describe below.

The project plans to work at the interface of history and translation studies: two disciplines which share a common concern with the interpretation of text, but whose potential synergy is under-explored. If funded, the project will have several important research implications:

- Examining the tenth-century Liao–Five Dynasties relationship will contribute both to our knowledge of a key period in imperial Chinese history and to the wider field of comparative frontier studies.
- By permitting systematic comparison of multiple narratives in a particular set of texts, the database will demonstrate the analytical value of historical translation, and will dramatically enhance access for specialists and comparativists.
- Developing a methodology for comparative translation as an analytical tool will enable sophisticated exploration of other closely linked sets of translated texts (for example, the various translations and adaptations generated by a single literary source text).
- Exploring how historians' and translation scholars' approaches to textual analysis can enrich each other will enable us to establish a sophisticated model of history translation, with spin-off benefits for both underlying disciplines.
- The database itself will provide a potential design model for other databases looking at filiated texts.

The processes of database development are also important to the project: observation of historical translating and decision-making as it happens will provide an explicit and rigorous self-reflexive perspective on research and methodological decisions.

The following sections discuss the key theoretical and practical issues which have informed the design of this project, and the resulting design solutions. For reasons of space, however, the present chapter will not discuss how the project aims to track the *processes* of database development.

3 Ideology, history and translation

The theory base of this project combines insights from historiography and from translation studies. Both disciplines describe communication through language, and both share the assumption that communication involves interpretation. Historians do not describe 'what happened', but give their own reading of data (eye-witness reports, annals, and so on): data which are themselves narrative interpretations of primary events. Nor can a translator ever be a pane of glass, since no two languages have the same grammatical, lexical and attitudinal resources in even the narrowest of subject domains. Hence translators, too, give their own reading of the textual and paratextual evidence in their source text. As historians and translators, therefore, we participate in a web of interpretation of the original historical events, as shown in Figure 8.3.

3.1 Terminology and attitudes: the barbarian Other

To focus first on the historiographical aspects of the web shown in Figure 8.3, this database and the process of its generation both force and enable us to explore a set of historical concerns within the wider

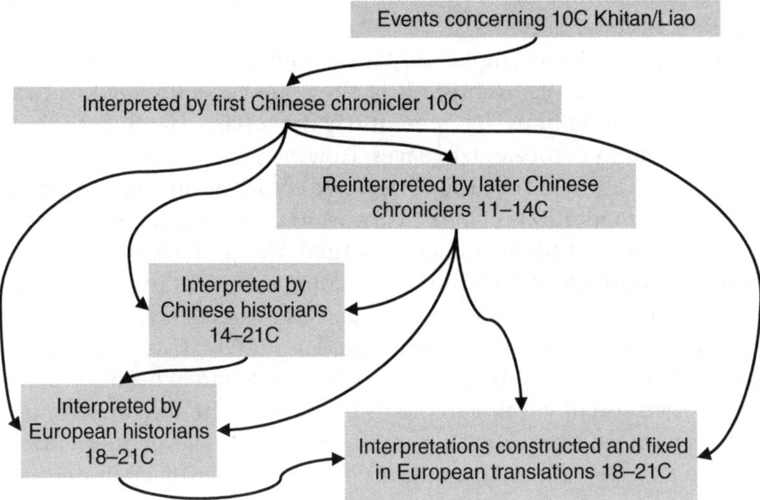

Figure 8.3 History/translation as interpretation

field of frontier studies: in particular, the issue of how Sinocentric assumptions in the Classical Chinese source texts are routinely reinforced by Sinocentric assumptions on the part of historians writing in both East Asian and European languages. The texts contain accounts of Liao–Five Dynasties relations which are largely written by the Liao's southern neighbours, not by the Liao themselves. (The chief exception for our purposes is the annals for the tenth century in the *Liao History*, which often bear no relation to anything in the earlier texts and, to that extent, can be regarded as independent.) The partial (in both senses) nature of the evidence provided by these texts is compounded by the fact that Chinese writing about their own history in modern times have often adopted a nationalistic viewpoint which regards the rule of any part of China by non-Chinese as a threat to Chinese culture and a denial of self-determination to 'the Chinese people'. This view builds on stereotypes of supposedly great antiquity that apparently set up a binary opposition between non-Chinese who are regarded as 'barbarians' and their Chinese counterparts who are correspondingly assumed to be civilized (see Pines, 2000). In this common formulation, the relationship is regarded as inherently confrontational, and is characterized as consisting of 'barbarian' attempts to gain a share of China's wealth by using nomadic military superiority to extort favourable trading relationships, or failing that to seize goods by force. Moreover, as most historians writing in European languages analyse relations across this frontier from within a China-studies framework, Sinocentric attitudes have frequently informed their interpretations to a greater or lesser degree.

The sources, for example, contain a wide range of words for the northern pastoralists. Almost all of these are generally held to carry negative connotations by present-day historians, writing both in Chinese and in European languages. However, it is not clear that all of these words always carried such negative connotations for contemporaries. The implications of a particular word could be different in different contexts, and could change over time. Hence the word *kou*, often taken to imply specifically nomadic raiding on sedentary farmers, can in fact refer to any raid on anyone regarded as an enemy, regardless of ethnic or economic orientation (Standen, 2003). Historians of the pastoral–sedentary relationship, however, have rarely been so careful about their use of vocabulary, and those who write in European languages have tended to choose terminology that, however unintentionally, reflects prevailing assumptions about an atavistic clash between civilization and barbarism (Beckwith, 1987).

Here, however, it is important to point out that, if we define ideology as a system of ideas that governs our actions and choices, a neutral, non-ideological stance is impossible. Any historical narrative is constructed by its interpreters in accordance with their own belief systems (White, 1987; Campbell, 1998, pp. 34–40; Jones, 2004). Thus even a non-Sinocentric view of cross-border relations in the Five Dynasties period is also a 'reading' of historical evidence, and has no intrinsically greater claim to objectivity, though it may perhaps be claimed that a reading based on respect for the Other's self-image is *ethically* superior to one that seeks to destroy the Other's self-image (Campbell, 1998, pp. 42–3).

3.2 Translation as closure

Designing the database has also forced and/or enabled us to explore how translation can fix and conceal the ideological subtexts inherent in any historical reading, and specifically in the Five Dynasties histories. This in turn has forced and/or enabled us to explore how translation might also *reveal* ideological subtexts and provide *alternative* readings.

'Translation', in Venuti's words, 'wields enormous power in constructing representations of foreign cultures' (1998, p. 67). Translation of any written text begins with reading, and reading inevitably involves interpretation, the creation of 'a reading'. In the interpretative chain of the tenth-century histories shown in Figure 8.3, the risk is that this reading may already simplify concepts which are contested, fluid and multifaceted. Moreover, translation conventionally ends in closure: a source-text item is normally converted into a single equivalent which is fixed in the written or spoken medium of the resulting target (that is, translated) text. Thus a term or text extract that is simply quoted in the source language can remain nuanced or open to alternative readings, as in the hypothetical phrase 'relations between Han and *fan* kingdoms'. But if the same term or text extract is translated, however, what all too often occurs is that it becomes invested with one particular reading, as in 'relations between Han and barbarian kingdoms'.

And, as this example shows, this closure may have an ideological dimension. *Fan*, in the first half of the tenth century, might well have simply meant 'foreign'; translating it as 'barbarian' means that for most English readers foreignness is automatically equated with a lack of civilization. While it may well be that certain words in Classical Chinese were intended by the writer to convey precisely these connotations, we cannot assume either that this will always be so, or that the writer's intended connotations are the same as those conveyed by the English word 'barbarian', with all the cultural and historical freight that it carries with it. This is compounded by the fact that two languages rarely have the same number of near-synonyms in any semantic field. Thus translations such as 'barbarian' and 'caitiff', and their equivalents in French and other European languages, are often used for a much wider range of Chinese terms.

Here we appear to have a classic case of a more powerful target (that is, translated-into) culture violating source-culture concepts (Venuti, 1998, p. 2). When Europhone analyses of cross-border relations use terms and passages translated from Chinese, however, the ideological forces at play go beyond Venuti's somewhat Manichean opposition between an ideologically pristine source text and an ideologically corrupting translation (see Lane-Mercier, 1997). As discussed earlier, the source texts in our project already encode a power imbalance (Sinocentric views of the 'lesser' pastoralist Liao), and thus the Eurocentric interpretations of the Inner Asian Other, as displayed in translated terms and texts, do not start from an ideological *tabula rasa*. In this case, the stereotyping effect of translation appears rooted in the fact that the two interpretations (the Sinocentric and the Eurocentric) have *common* ideological concerns. Translating *fan* as 'barbarian', therefore, taps both into Sinocentric attitudes towards the 'uncivilized' Other and into a deep well of fear among Europeans of the Inner Asian 'barbarians' in their own past, be they Huns, Mongols, or (at least in origin) Ottoman Turks.

The terminology commonly used in English translation, therefore, risks being affected by attitudes to the pastoralist barbarians at the border by which the urban/arable Subject, whether Chinese or Western, defines his or her own identity. This in turn effectively limits the range of questions that Anglophone historians can ask, and so ties understanding to a discourse rooted in modern ideas of the nation state, where ethnic boundaries are clear, and groups and polities are defined chiefly in terms of territory (Duara, 1995).

3.3 Translation as opening

Closure, however, and thus the selection of one reading and the ideological baggage it potentially carries, need not be inevitable. In the body of their text, for example, translators/historians may choose a translation equivalent which represents one interpretation ('foreigner', say); but other meanings ('barbarian', say), or the fact that meaning is fluid or indeterminate, may be recorded in footnotes, endnotes or a separate Introduction chapter. Alternatively, they may use a technique of expansion or explicitation (Klaudy, 1998) to work multiple meanings into the translated text itself: for example 'He was a foreigner or, as some might say, a barbarian'.

Moreover, the need to record readings of the source text as explicit equivalents on a target-text page or computer screen can be deliberately used to bring covert and implicit issues of interpretation and interpreter ideology into the open. Indeed, if one takes a critical approach to the selection of target vocabulary, translation can be seen as having important analytical value in its own right. In our case, if translators continually question *why* they are privileging one potential English equivalent for a Chinese term above another potential equivalent, they will often be performing primary historical analysis. Thus, by examining the relative merits of 'barbarian' versus 'foreigner' as a translation for *fan*, they will be analysing to what extent the chroniclers saw the Khitan as uncivilized or inferior: an act of analysis that might not have taken place without the need to translate the term. And explicit introspection and logging of why certain decisions were made can, by making the ideological ground rules clear to all, open a set of translated texts to alternative interpretations by other researchers.

This 'critical translation' approach, by which we constantly question our translation decisions and make the answers we find available to other database users, underlies our praxis in this project. This has two research benefits. On the one hand, our decision-making processes will form the basis for a valuable case study of translators' decision-making processes under 'extreme' conditions, among the latter being the exceptionally wide culture and time gap between medieval Chinese and modern-day Anglophone readers, the difficulty of often actually *knowing* what is meant by a certain term or reference, and the fact that interpretations are conditioned by a corpus of exegetic literature. Though previous studies into translation, ideology and culture have looked at textual products (see, for example, Tymoczko and Gentzler, 2002; Calzada Pérez, 2003), we know of none which looks at the processes of decision-making under such conditions. We would hypothesize, however, that translators on this project need to have a particularly sharp awareness of target readers' knowledge about the period and cultural background and of the ideological effects of their own translation actions, whilst being constrained by the need for standardization within and across the texts.

On the other hand, once the database is constructed, historian users will be able to confront issues of historical meaning and interpretation easily overlooked when working only in the original language. Historians writing in modern standard Chinese do not feel the need to translate their Classical Chinese sources, even though (in the People's Republic at least) only a tiny minority, even among university graduates, can read Classical Chinese with any facility. By contrast, historians writing about pre-modern China in European languages are routinely confronted with opportunities to consider exactly what a particular word means in a given context.

Considering this context-mediated meaning may even, on occasion, involve resisting the closure offered by dictionaries. Dictionaries, after all, are compiled by philologists who, as individuals in the real world, rely at least in part on intuition and implicit value-systems in order to judge how terms should be described or what translation equivalents should be assigned to them. Leaving the task of interpreting words in context to philologists, therefore, can lead historians to privilege particular interpretations or historical relationships, and not consider others that may have more explanatory power but which depend on reconsidering assumptions carried by the standard vocabulary used for translating particular words in Classical Chinese.

3.4 Terminology control and multiple meanings

Nevertheless, the fact remains that scholarly translations normally require standardized terminology. If in a scholarly article the word *fan*, for instance, were sometimes translated as 'barbarian' and at other times as 'foreigner', depending on the nuance that appeared to be operating in the historical source in question, the reader of the article would have no way of knowing that the underlying term was the same across the sources; a knowledge that might be crucial for the interpretation of the source data. The need for standardized terminology is particularly pressing in our database, where the presence of the same word across various source texts can be a key point of entry into different readings of the same incident. Moreover, standardized terminology will also inform the non-Chinese reader that, when a *different* word is used by two translated texts to describe the same event, this reflects a difference in source wording: a difference which may again be crucial for the present-day historian.

But isomorphism, that is, a one-to-one mapping of terms onto concepts, can be problematical even for concrete technical items (Nkwenti-Azeh, 1995). It is more problematical for human or abstract terms which have a large interpretative potential (such as *enemy*, say).

And it is all the more problematical when, as in our source texts, the concepts underlying the Chinese words are culturally specific, fluid across the different texts being studied, and disputed by scholars. A term found in a tenth-century text, say, does not necessarily mean the same thing or carry the same connotations as the same term found in a fourteenth-century text, even where the later text uses substantially the same wording as the earlier text. Furthermore, it is not necessarily the case that even two eleventh-century writers will mean the same thing by the same term. Conversely, a single term in Chinese may have more than one appropriate English translation, which may be easily and precisely determined by context, or may be more open to debate.

Our underlying approach to this issue is again a critical one: one of continually examining, testing and logging the links between key terms and concepts, and the relationships and boundaries between different terms/concepts, rather than merely taking them as pre-existing givens (Nkwenti-Azeh, 1995). But, however critical the approach to target terminology, there is always the fact that any translation choice privileges one interpretation over another. Hence our need for terminological control is opposed by our need to avoid closing down multiple meanings and to make the ambiguities and alternative possibilities located in this set of texts accessible to other researchers addressing questions of their own.

We are left, therefore, with two crucial questions. Close scholarly translations that cross-cite each other normally require standardized terminology, but how does one do this when the texts have been compiled over such a wide period of time – a period, furthermore, in which attitudes to issues such as 'foreigners' may well have changed significantly (Standen, 2007)? How can we, as historians or translators or both, simultaneously provide accurate and comparable translations and yet keep alive the multiple possibilities of meaning in these texts? Earlier, we proposed a comparative database as a solution to the problem of tracking the intertextual weft of our five histories. But if the database is to answer these crucial intellectual questions, its design needs to go beyond the conventional string-search and markup-based model, as we discuss in the following section.

4 Technical solutions

4.1 Approach and procedure

In the light of the considerations discussed so far, our design priority has been to create translations reflecting the relationships between the

Liao–Five Dynasties sources that would allow us to explore methods both of standardizing terminology and of retaining openness to 'multiple definition' (Richards, 1932, in Hermans, 2002).

Our underlying approach has been to turn the close relationship between the texts to advantage. By systematically placing interlinked source passages side by side, differences between the relevant texts can be highlighted. If we then translate those interlinked passages as a set, the effort to find ways of representing in translation the smallest differences in the wording of different source texts forces a much deeper engagement with the alternative possibilities located within those texts. The presentation of these tiny differences in translation by means of simultaneous display of interlinked passages can then alert the user of the translations to some of the alternative interpretations that may be possible. Though for each different term a selection still has to be made between the alternatives, the advantage is that now the choice is being made from a wider range of possibilities and in a much more conscious and considered manner. The issue then becomes a matter of technical solutions, allowing the user of the translations database to have continuous access to the other terminological possibilities.

4.2 Beyond the string search

We have argued that the scattered nature of the source texts (not to mention their large volume) makes a relational database the most practical method of providing easy access to all the interlinked passages on a particular subject. However, in order to locate all the passages recounting a particular incident without omission, it is not enough to rely on string-searching. If one were, say, interested in passages relating events in the life of a particular individual, it would not be enough merely to allow the database to retrieve all passages containing that person's name, since their name might not be mentioned in all the relevant interlinked passages. Furthermore, historical figures frequently have one or more alternative names and if one of these were used in one version of the passage, that passage would not be retrieved. In addition, alterations from one text to the next often result in certain names being omitted, added or changed, which would again produce an incomplete set of interlinked passages.

The project proposes to resolve this problem by manually building a data table that links all interlinked passages for a particular incident, regardless of what details are included or excluded. In other words, besides the main table containing all the translations of all the passages, the project team must also construct a much simpler table listing

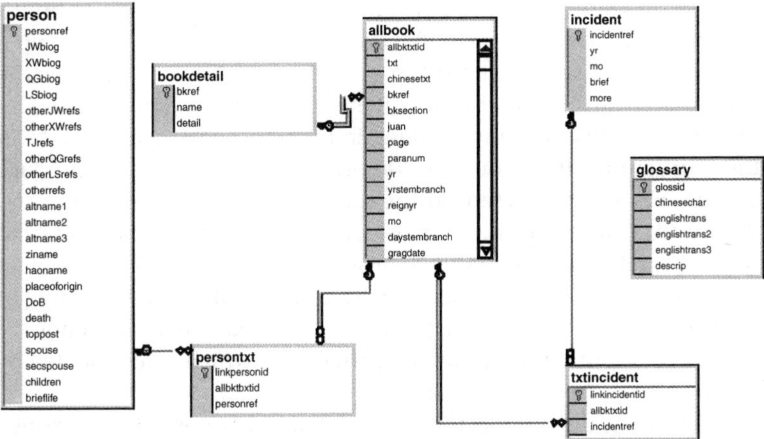

Figure 8.4 Chinese historical translations project: basic database design

incidents (this is the table called 'txtincident' in Figure 8.4). Hence, in the completed database a search on, say, 'investiture AND Shi Jingtang', will produce not only all passages containing those two strings, but also all interlinked passages that recount this particular event without mentioning the word 'investiture' and/or Shi Jingtang's name. Without this table, users would have to attempt to ensure comprehensiveness by using 'OR' searches, so increasing the number of hits to unmanageable proportions, and could still not be sure that they had indeed located all the interlinked passages.

Moreover, since there is such a heavy biographical content in all these texts (they are, in many ways, a collection of individual and group biographies organized broadly around a set of annals that is, in effect, the biographies of the emperors), it makes sense to construct manually a second data table capable of supplying all references to a particular person regardless of whether they are mentioned by name. In this case a search on a particular name would produce not only all passages containing that exact name, but also interlinked passages where the person is referred to by some other name or even not at all.

4.3 Terminology and the glossary

As discussed above, use of standardized terminology is essential, both to offer a reliable interpretation of the source texts (or, at the very least, one where the grounds of interpretation are open and explicit) and to facilitate effective string-searching for terms other than names. This, however, is counterbalanced by our wish to retain openness to multiple meanings. Designing the database so that the user can call up a comprehensive set of interlinked passages regardless of whether the exact search string is included will ensure the user's maximum exposure to alternative wordings existing in the source texts and reflected in the translations. It is, however, important to do more than reproduce alternatives already present in the source texts. The power of translation to fix a single meaning for a particular term is such that alternative interpretations/translations must also be made readily available if the user is not to be misled into a false certainty about the meaning of a particular word, phrase or passage. As argued above, the range of alternative meanings is often greater than that which is represented by different terms in the source texts.

Accordingly, our approach in the texts themselves is, where possible, to use a single standardized translation equivalent for each key source term. Therefore, as shown in Figure 8.5, 'person' (or 'people', since Chinese has no plurals) will be used (uncrossed arrow in Figure 8.5) as the only equivalent for *ren*, and the gendered alternative 'man' (or 'men') will not be used (crossed arrow). Multiple equivalents will sometimes be unavoidable: thus *gui* will be translated as 'pledge allegiance' and 'return', depending on context (see Figure 8.5). But although in certain cases it might seem possible to translate several Chinese terms by the same English term, this will be scrupulously avoided in our database (with the help of terminology-management software) in order to reflect the separation between source terms; a separation potentially crucial to the non-Chinese-reading user. Thus, though both *fan* and *hu* might have been translated as 'barbarian', 'barbarian' will be reserved as the equivalent for *hu*, and 'foreigner' will be used to translate *fan* throughout the database.

But whether a single or a multiple equivalent is chosen, any term where alternative meanings appear to be significant will be linked to

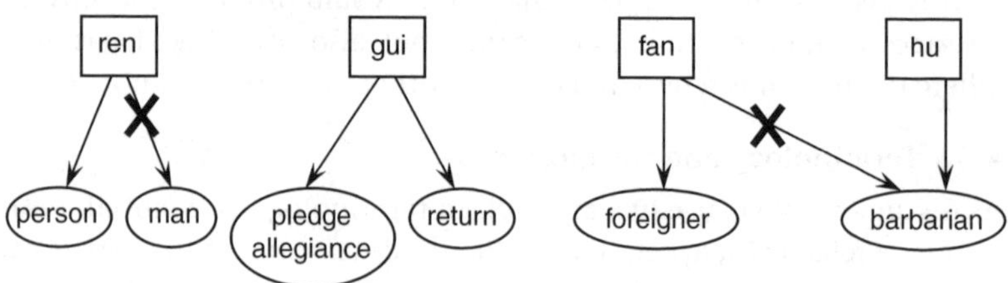

Figure 8.5 Relations between source and target terms

a glossary, which will chiefly document multiple English translations of a single Chinese word. Glossary entries will vary considerably in length. Thus *gui* might have a relatively short entry explaining its alternative meanings, and noting that in most circumstances it is easy to identify which meaning accords with the context. The word *hu* might have a much longer entry discussing the common translation of 'barbarian', unfreighted alternatives, observing changes in usage over time, and explaining the research team's choice of one or more standardized translations. Glossary entries will be continuously available to the user by simply clicking on a particular glossarized term in any retrieved passage. Clicking will bring up a pop-up box containing the relevant glossary entry. Users will thus be invited to consider further possibilities beyond those indicated in the translations themselves.

4.4 Markup

It will, of course, be desirable to be able to export marked-up text from the database, and to be able to search the database using categories indicated by markup. It is anticipated that markup (using XML) will be needed to indicate categories such as given and family names, place names, imperial edicts of various kinds, official titles, honorifics, substantive posts, military and other technical terminology, dates, astronomical phenomena and so on. Of course, markup categories can proliferate very rapidly, so it will be necessary to prioritize carefully, and to attempt to create a minimal list of categories of maximum helpfulness to users.

5 Creating the database

Clearly the process of creating this database will be highly complex, and work will have to be rigorously systematic if we are to maintain the desired comprehensiveness, accuracy and transparency. The database will be instantiated in a 'FiveDynasties' schema in SQL Server, and accessed via a web portal created with ASP.NET. Users will thus be able to use the database via most web browsers and will require no special software. We will use the standard published scholarly editions of all texts. The basic unit of work will be the text-month: that is, the annalistic and biographical material from all five texts that relates to one particular lunar month, though the amount of material can vary considerably from month to month. The *Comprehensive Mirror*'s chronological arrangement makes it a convenient 'spine' for the rest of the work;

this, however, is purely for practical purposes, and does not privilege the *Mirror* over the other texts. The stages of work will be as follows:

- Translate one month from the *Mirror*, together with the annalistic material from the other four texts that refers to the same period. Dating can sometimes be slightly different in the other texts, and in the case of the *Record of the Khitan State* can be consistently out by a year for long periods of recorded time. In such cases we will match incidents rather than dates.
- This will supply only a small part of the interlinked material; most of it is contained in the biographical sections of the four histories that follow the annals–biographies format. We will locate biographical material interlinking with the incidents found in the annals by listing personal names found in the annalistic material and then using published biographical indexes to track down other references to these people. Basic biographical information will be entered into the 'person' table.
- This will produce a large number of references, from which interlinking passages will be identified by inspection of the source texts. These passages will then be translated with reference to the annalistic material. Future phases of the project will add material unique to one location (including that in sources other than the five considered here), but in Phase 1 the focus will be on tackling the issues arising from the complex process of creating interlinked target texts.
- At this point in the work on each text-month the project team will meet to discuss and agree a list of incidents for that text-month. Also at this point, the team will check that no incident listed for this month is duplicated in work already completed. The agreed list will then be entered into the database's 'incident' table.
- Terminology-bank software will be used to maintain a standardized vocabulary and to assist the building of the glossary. However, the translation itself will all be manual: there will be no attempt to use machine translation. The team will further agree any additions or changes to the glossary and these will be written into the 'glossary' table straightaway.
- In the light of the foregoing decisions, the full set of translations will then be compared and amended to show even the smallest differences found in the source texts.
- Once the comparison of the translations is complete, the passages will be tagged in XML in accordance with the TEI schema and our own agreed policies.

- The finished translations will be entered into the main 'allbook' database table. For the *Mirror*, we will follow the paragraphing in the standard edition, creating one database record for each paragraph. The other texts frequently include a much wider range of material in a single paragraph and we will break down such paragraphs into coherent segments in accordance with date and subject matter. In these cases each segment will form a single database record. Apart from the text, each record will also contain fields giving citation details, date in contemporary and modern standard forms, and sequencing information (the latter permitting consecutive retrieval if desired).
- The 'txtincident' and 'persontxt' data tables will then be built manually to map the interlinking between passages. The 'txtincident' table will link passages on the basis of what incidents they record and the 'persontxt' table according to persons mentioned.
- Finally the newly entered data will be checked for accuracy and comprehensiveness.

6 Conclusion

At this early design stage, we have already shown the usefulness of a methodological synergy between the 'core' discipline of historical textual analysis on the one hand, and translation-studies approaches to textual transformation on the other. The combination of methods here is largely new and has been developed to address a complex set of historiographical and translation issues peculiar to a particular group of historical texts, but similar approaches may prove useful in other cases of complex intertextuality or difficult-to-align texts. Scholars working on the York–Helsinki corpus (see Taylor, this volume), for example, have already expressed an interest in using some of our methods.

In terms of furthering scholarly understanding, the strength of the design is that it not only provides opportunities for users to compare alternatives (which many XML-based databases already do) but it also actively confronts them with multiple readings. These would otherwise only be available to someone personally engaged in comparative translation, whereas our database will greatly increase comparative access to these texts, and not only to people who do not read Classical Chinese. Furthermore, the comparative method and simultaneous presentation of interlinked passages will radically increase the sophistication with which these materials can be used. Instead of narrowing down translation to one fixed representation and restricting historical interpretation to a single narrative, historians and translators will have ready opportunities to explore the multiple possibilities revealed by highlighting the intertextuality of these histories.

References

Aksoy, Berrin. 2002. 'Aspects of textuality in translating a history book from Turkish into English'. *Babel* 47(3):193–204.

Beckwith, Christopher I. 1987. 'The idea of the "barbarian" and the creation of fourth world nations in Asia'. Unpublished paper.

Bredehoft, Thomas A. 2001. *Textual Histories: Readings in the* Anglo-Saxon Chronicle. Toronto: University of Toronto Press.

Calzada Pérez, María (ed.). 2003. *Apropos of Ideology: Translation Studies on Ideology – Ideologies in Translation Studies*. Manchester: St Jerome.

Campbell, David. 1998. *National Deconstruction: Violence, Identity and Justice in Bosnia*. Minneapolis: University of Minnesota Press.

Chan, Hok-Lam. 1981. 'Chinese official historiography at the Yüan court: the composition of the Liao, Chin and Sung histories'. *China under Mongol Rule*, ed. by John D. Langlois, pp. 56–106. Princeton, NJ: Princeton University Press.

Chan, Ming K. 1974–75. 'The historiography of the *Tzu-chih t'ung-chien*: a survey'. *Monumenta Serica* 31:1–38.

Chen Gaohua, Chen Zhichao *et al.* (eds). 1983. *Zhongguo gudai shi shiliao xue* [Study of materials for the pre-modern history of China]. Beijing: Beijing chubanshe.

Duara, Prasenjit. 1995. *Rescuing History from the Nation: Questioning Narratives of Modern China*. Chicago: University of Chicago Press.

Durrant, Stephen. 2001. 'The literary features of historical writing'. *The Columbia History of Chinese Literature*, ed. by Victor H. Mair, pp. 493–510. New York: Columbia University Press.

Garmonsway, G. N. 1953. *The Anglo-Saxon Chronicle*. London: Dent.

Hardy, Grant. 1994. 'Can an ancient Chinese history contribute to modern Western theory? The multiple narratives of Ssu-ma Ch'ien'. *History and Theory* 33(1):20–38.

Hermans, Theo. 2002. 'Paradoxes and aporias in translation and translation studies'. *Translation Studies: Perspectives on an Emerging Discipline*, ed. by Alessandra Riccardi, pp. 10–23. Cambridge: Cambridge University Press.

Jones, Francis R. (2004). 'Ethics, aesthetics and decision: literary translating in the wars of the Yugoslav succession'. *Meta* 49(4):711–28.

Klaudy, Kinga. 1998. 'Explicitation'. *Routledge Encyclopaedia of Translation Studies*, ed. by Mona Baker, pp. 80–4. London: Routledge.

Lane-Mercier, Gillian. 1997. 'Translating the untranslatable: the translator's aesthetic, ideological and political responsibility'. *Target* 9(1):43–68.

Li Xihou. 1981. 'Ye Longli he *Qidan guo zhi*' [Ye Longli and the *Record of the Khitan State*]. *Qidan guo zhi* [*Record of the Khitan State*], pp. 282–7. Shanghai: Shanghai guji chubanshe.

Moloughney, Brian. 2002. 'Derivation, intertexuality and authority: narrative and the problem of historical coherence'. *East Asian History* 23:129–48.

Nkwenti-Azeh, Blaise. 1995. 'Terminology'. *An Encyclopaedia of Translation: Chinese–English, English–Chinese,* ed. by Sin-Wai Chan and David Pollard, pp. 610–27. Hong Kong: Chinese University Press.

Ouyang Xiu. 2004. *Historical Records of the Five Dynasties.* Translated by Richard L. Davis. New York: Columbia University Press.

Pines, Yuri. 2000. 'Beasts or humans: pre-imperial origins of [the] Sino-barbarian dichotomy'. Unpublished conference paper.

Pulleyblank, E. G. 1976. 'The An Lu-shan rebellion and the origins of chronic militarism in late T'ang China'. *Essays on T'ang Society: The Interplay of Social, Political and Economic Forces,* ed. by John Perry and Bardwell L. Smith, pp. 33–60. Leiden: E.J. Brill.

Standen, Naomi. 1994. 'Frontier crossings from North China to Liao, *c.*900–1005'. PhD thesis, Durham University.

Standen, Naomi. 1996. '*Sui generis* or universal definitions? Chinese historical works and "the medieval chronicle"'. Unpublished conference paper.

Standen, Naomi. 2003. 'Raiding and frontier society in the Five Dynasties'. *Political Frontiers, Ethnic Boundaries and Human Geographies in Chinese History,* ed. by Nicola Di Cosmo and Don Wyatt, pp. 160–91. London: Routledge.

Standen, Naomi. 2007. *Unbounded Loyalty: Frontier Crossings in Liao China.* Honolulu: University of Hawai'i.

Twitchett, Denis C. 1992. *The Writing of Official History under the T'ang.* Cambridge: Cambridge University Press.

Tymoczko, Maria and Edwin Gentzler (eds). 2002. *Translation and Power.* Amherst and Boston, Mass.: University of Massachusetts Press.

Venuti, Lawrence. 1998. *The Scandals of Translation.* London: Routledge.

Wang, Gungwu. 1958. 'The *Chiu Wu-tai shih* and history-writing during the Five Dynasties'. *Asia Major* 6(1):1–22.

White, Hayden. 1987. *The Content of the Form: Narrative Discourse and Historical Representation.* Baltimore, Md: Johns Hopkins Press.

Wittfogel, Karl A. and Feng Chia-sheng. 1949. *History of Chinese society: Liao (907–1125).* Philadelphia: American Philosophical Society.

Yu Jiaxi. 1980. *Siku tiyao bianzheng* [Analysis of the *Siku tiyao*], 4 vols. Beijing: Zhonghua shuju.

9
The York–Toronto–Helsinki Parsed Corpus of Old English Prose

Ann Taylor

1 Introduction

The York–Toronto–Helsinki Parsed Corpus of Old English Prose (YCOE) is a 1.5 million-word syntactically annotated corpus of Old English prose texts. It was produced at the University of York, UK, between 2000 and 2003, by Ann Taylor, Anthony Warner, Susan Pintzuk and Frank Beths, with a grant from the English Arts and Humanities Research Board (B/RG/AN5907/APN9528). The YCOE is part of the English Parsed Corpora Series. It was the third historical corpus to be completed in this format, and uses the same kind of annotation scheme as its sister corpora, the Penn–Helsinki Parsed Corpus of Middle English II (PPCME2), the York–Helsinki Parsed Corpus of Old English Poetry and the Penn–Helsinki Parsed Corpus of Early Modern English. Two other corpora in the series, the parsed version of the Corpus of Early English Correspondence and the Penn Parsed Corpus of Modern British English, are currently under construction (at the University of York, UK, in cooperation with the University of Helsinki, Finland, and the University of Pennsylvania, USA, respectively). In addition, Modern English is represented by the various Penn Treebank corpora, which include texts from the *Wall Street Journal* corpus and the Brown Corpus, as well as transcribed speech from the Switchboard Corpus. Each of the corpora (apart from the Old English Poetry corpus) includes over a million words.

The English Parsed Corpora Series differs from other historical corpora, such as the Helsinki Corpus and the Toronto Old English Corpus (both of which were used as the basis of some of the corpora in the series), in being syntactically annotated. Every word is labelled for part of speech, and the grammatical structure of each syntactic unit of the text (usually a sentence) is represented using a limited tree representation in the form of labelled parentheses.

2 Background

The corpus series was designed particularly with historical syntacticians in mind and, more particularly, those who use quantitative methods in their work. In the pre-electronic revolution days, there were two basic ways of approaching diachronic work in syntax. One approach was to base the study on the researcher's impressions of general patterns and on individual examples illustrating these patterns or exceptions to them (for example, Canale, 1978; Roberts, 1985; van Kemenade, 1987; even extensive multi-volume works like Mitchell, 1985, and Visser, 1963–73, have been done in this way). The problem with studies of this sort is that it is often impossible to determine whether the reported results are really representative of the language as a whole, and differences between texts often go unnoticed. The alternative methodology has been to search substantial text samples by hand, keeping count of the number of occurrences of the phenomenon under investigation, and carefully tracking variation (for example, Kohonen, 1978; Bean, 1983; Kroch, 1989; Pintzuk, 1999; Taylor, 1994). Because of the labour-intensive nature of this enterprise, however, studies using really large amounts of data were rarely carried out (the study of 'do' in Ellegård, 1953, being a notable exception). This method of data collection yields the right sort of data in theory, but in practice it is time-consuming, tedious, error-prone and inflexible, and the results cannot be reproduced by other investigators.

The creation of electronic text corpora was a big leap forward for data collection in historical studies, making many texts easily available in balanced collections and, even more importantly, searchable for the first time, and all historical linguists who study the English language owe a vote of thanks to the Helsinki and Toronto teams that produced these early corpora. As with most technological innovations, however, their limitations soon became clear. While lexical items and combinations of items can be searched for (as long as spelling is consistent, or all variants known), more abstract structures often could not. It is impossible, for instance, to find all clauses with a direct and an indirect object automatically from an electronic text corpus. Thus, while availability and to some extent speed of collection were improved, the other problems remained.

The next logical step for increased ease and accuracy of automatic searching is to introduce annotations into the text that encode grammatical information. Part-of-speech tagging is a first step in this process, but only adds limited word-related information. Full syntactic annotation includes, as well as information at word level, the organization of phrases and clauses, and can include functional information such as grammatical role and clause type, as well as some kinds of semantic relations. Full syntactic annotation, however, is difficult and time-consuming, and requires of the annotator considerable knowledge of the language being annotated, as well as linguistic sophistication. It is important to ask, therefore, in this age of budget shortfalls and intense competition for grant money, whether the work of annotation is, in fact, worth it. The answer, experience has shown, is clearly positive. The feasibility of corpus-based linguistic analysis depends first of all on the availability of sufficient data in accessible form; but, second, it must be convenient to retrieve accurately the relevant information from the corpus. While simple electronic text corpora fulfil the first requirement, for syntacticians, at least, only annotated corpora fulfil the second.

Many of the questions that interest linguists, and virtually all the questions that interest syntacticians, require structural information about language that is not accessible from word strings: information such as part of speech (noun, verb, adjective and so on) and grammatical function (subject, object, temporal adverb and so on). Beyond this, annotation also makes it possible to search for abstract constructions: for example, relative clauses, all occurrences of subject–auxiliary inversion, sentences which start with a temporal noun phrase (NP), like 'the day before yesterday', sentences in which there is both a direct and an indirect object, and so on. The value of an annotated corpus lies in the researcher being able to easily search for and classify sentences on the basis of similarities and differences in their structure, as well as the words they contain.

A standard example of the type of structure that is easily accessible in an annotated, but not a text, corpus is the relative clause. These clauses may be marked by a wh-word (*the hat* ***which*** *the man bought*), a complementizer, such as *that* (*the hat* ***that*** *the man bought*), or nothing (*the hat the man bought*). Searching text corpora for abstract constructions such as relative clauses results in two types of problems: low precision (getting unwanted data) and low recall (missing wanted data). In the case of relative clauses, as mentioned above, those with no marker would be missed completely (low recall). In addition, the lexical items used to signal relative clauses, wh-words and complementizers, are also present in other constructions, such as questions, that-clauses, noun phrases and so on; thus, much unwanted data would also be extracted (low precision). Even part of speech tagging will not solve this problem, because of the presence of these items, with the same part-of-speech, in other constructions. While low precision can be solved by the time-consuming process of culling the results by hand, low recall is unsolvable without going through the entire text manually, thus obviating the need for an electronic text in the first place.

A syntactically annotated corpus can solve the problems inherent in extracting data from paper or electronic texts. Retrieval of examples is quick and easy, and any type of structure can be searched for: data collection that used to take months or years now takes hours or days. The system is also very flexible. It is often the case that as an investigation progresses, the researcher's ideas about what data are relevant change. When collecting data by hand this means starting again, often at a huge cost in lost time. With a parsed corpus, any number of possible options can be explored very quickly and then either pursued or abandoned with little loss. Rare data are also more easily found in an annotated corpus. If some syntactic construction occurs only five or ten times in a million words, it is unlikely that it will be found by a hand search (or that the time invested in the search could be justified). That construction, however, may be crucial to deciding between two possible analyses. Thus, an annotated corpus is a permanent resource that can be used over and over again for any number of investigations. On this basis alone, it is worth the initial time investment required to create it.

For quantitative studies of the type often carried out in historical work, which seek to describe and explain variation and/or change over time and space, it is necessary to be able to track and compare frequencies of occurrence in different subsets of data; it is also necessary to have sufficient data available to be able to report significant results. Clearly, the smaller the amount of data the analysis is based on, the less likely it is that the results are really representative. On this score, annotated corpora can reduce or eliminate the problems associated with both impressionistic studies and hand-collected corpora, primarily by increasing the speed at which data collection can be done, which in turn often increases the size of the database and makes the results more representative. Obviously the amount of data that can be extracted from a corpus depends on the size of the corpus; but it is almost always more than can reasonably be extracted by hand. A recent diachronic study of verb–object order in Old and Middle English (Pintzuk and Taylor, 2006), for instance, is based on almost 10,000 tokens from approximately 90 texts. Automatic extraction can also be more accurate than hand collection since, unlike that of the hapless researcher, the computer's attention never lapses.

Finally, unlike results reported on the basis of personal, hand-made databases, those based on a publicly available parsed corpus are verifiable and reproducible by other researchers in a way never before possible. All work is open to scrutiny, thereby raising the overall quality of work in the field.

Corpora, and especially annotated corpora, do, of course, introduce problems of their own. First, the automatic collection of examples can divorce the researcher from the language itself, and the often intimate knowledge of the data developed by those reading through the texts and recording examples may be lost, with a concomitant loss of understanding. Second, it is crucial in using such tools that all results are checked in order to determine that the data extracted are really the data which are required. There is a strong temptation, which must be manfully resisted, to skip this relatively time-consuming step and simply trust the numbers. Corpora are tools and, like all tools, if badly used, they will produce bad results. Finally, there is the problem of errors in the annotation itself. As anyone who has tried to do this sort of work knows, it is impossible (without unlimited time, money and human resources) to eliminate all errors. The work is simply too complex. We have tried hard to eliminate systematic errors in our corpus, with the result that any remaining errors should be random. Given the amount of data that it is generally possible to extract from our corpus for anything except quite rare constructions, a small number of randomly distributed errors leading to the inclusion of irrelevant data or exclusion of relevant data will not appreciably affect the results.

2.1 Research applications

The corpus is most suited to studies of the sentential syntax of the various stages of English, either synchronic or diachronic. Like most corpus-builders, I suspect, we created the tool that would be of most use to us in our own work, which focuses on this area. However, the corpus will certainly be of use in any sort of syntactic study, as well as many morphological and lexical studies. Even in cases where we have not included the most minute level of syntactic or morphological detail required for a particular study, it will be possible to do much of the preliminary searching and sorting automatically, with the final necessary distinctions made by hand. Because the corpus files and the output files created by CorpusSearch, the search engine for the corpus (see section 5), are in ASCII (TXT) format, they can be edited by any word processor. This makes it easy to add more information by hand either to the corpus files themselves (probably not advisable) or to the output files of CorpusSearch. This information, if added in the appropriate way (see the discussion of coding in section 5), can then itself be searched by CorpusSearch. Thus, the corpus, together with its search engine, provides a very flexible way to collect and categorize data which can be applied to almost any type of study.

The Middle English corpus (PPCME and PPCME2) has been used to research such topics as the syntax of subjects (Haeberli, 2000), imperatives (Han, 1998, 2000), the verb-second constraint (Kroch *et al.*, 2000; Haeberli, 2002), verb–object order (Kroch and Taylor, 2000), null subjects (Williams, 2000), and the rise of the 'to' dative (McFadden, 2002). The more recently released Old English corpus (YCOE) has been used together with the PPCME2 in an investigation of verb–object order in Old and Middle English, with special focus on quantifiers (Pintzuk and Taylor, 2006), as well as the structure of the Determiner Phrase (DP) (Crisma, forthcoming) and topicalization (Silverstone, 2004). It is currently being used in investigations as diverse as verb projection raising, the position of the finite verb, negation, the syntax of adjective phrases, scrambling, the influence of translation from Latin on Old English syntax, and the effect of prose rhythm on verb–object order.

3 Methodology and representation

3.1 Contents

The York Old English Corpus contains a subset of the 3,037 texts in the Old English Corpus created for the *Dictionary of Old English*, edited by Antonette diPaolo Healey (http://www.doe.utoronto.ca/index.html). This dictionary was conceived by Angus Cameron as an historical dictionary in the tradition established by Sir James Murray for the *Oxford English Dictionary*. The corpus on which the dictionary is based is a complete record of surviving Old English between 600 and 1150 AD, except for some variant manuscripts of individual texts. In choosing texts to include in the YCOE, our aim was to include as many of the prose works of syntactic interest as possible. The highest priority for inclusion was length, since longer texts provide more data, often although not always, locatable in time and space. The other priority was to include texts containing extensive running prose, as opposed to lists, scribbles, notes, prayers, charms and so on (that is, Cameron

```
<tei.2 id="T03060">
<teiheader>
<filedesc>
<titlestmt>
<title type="st">&AE;LS (Sebastian)></title
<title type="ss">&AE;LS (Sebastian)</title></>titlestmt
<editionstmt><edition n='2'><date>January 2000</date></edition></editionstmt>
<extent>~31 KB, 150 citations</extent>
<publicationstmt><publisher>Dictionary of Old English</publisher>
<address><addrline>130 St. George St. Rm. 14285</addrline>
<addrline>University of Toronto</addrline>
<addrline>Toronto, Ontario</addrline>
<addrline>M5S 3H1</addrline>
<addrline>CANADA</addrline>
</address>
<idno>B1.3.6</idno>
<availability><p
We ask that you not copy and/or (re)distribute the corpus without the written consent of the
Dictionary of Old English. The individual scholar must take responsibility for clearing
copyright with the editors and publishers of the editions used in his/her own citations of the
material.</p></availability></publicationstmt>
<sourcedesc><bibl>Saint Sebastian:<author n="Skea  t 1881-1900">Skeat 188 1-1900</author>I,116-
46 <edition><title>&AE;lfric's Lives of Saints</title>, 4 vols., EETS 76, 82, 94, 114 (London)
[repr. in 2 vols. 1966]</edition>.</bibl></sourcedesc></filedesc>
<encodingdesc><refsdecl><p>
Citation is by line no. assigned by DOE, following the lineation of the
edition.</p></refsdecl></encodingdesc>
<profiledesc><textclass><catref target="P"></textclass></profiledesc>
<revisiondesc><change><date>January 2000</date>
<respstmt><name>DOE</name><resp>staff</resp></respstmt><item>
Updated the bibliographic information from the Healey-Venezky "List of Texts".
</item>
</change></revisiondesc></teiheader>
<text><body><p>
<s id="T03060000100" n="1"><foreign>XIII. KALENDAS FEBRUARII</foreign>.</s >
<s id="T03060000200" n="1"><foreign>PASSIO SANCTI SEBASTIANI MARTYRIS</foreign>.</s>
<s id="T03060000300" n="1"> Sebastianus hatte sum halig Godes &d;egn se w&ae;s lange on lare
on Mediolana byrig, and wear&d; on Criste gefullod mid fullum geleafan.</s>
<s id="T03060000400" n="4">He w&ae;s swi&d;e snotor wer and so&d;f&ae;st on spr&ae;ce,
rihtwis on dome and on r&ae;de foregleaw, getreowe on neode and strang fore&t;ingere, on
godnysse scinende and on eallum &t;eawum arwur&d;ful.</s>
<s id="T03060000500" n="8"> D&ae;ghwamlice he gef  ylde his drihtnes &t;enunge geornlice, ac he
bediglode swa &t;eah his d&ae;da &t;am casere Dioclitiane se w&ae;s deofles biggencga.</s>
```

Figure 9.1 The beginning of a file in the *DOE* Corpus (SGML format)

B.23–B.28). Of other material of less syntactic interest, either because of the short length of the texts (most documents) or the nature of much of the syntax (computus, scientific and medical material), we included a sample of the available texts. We also included in some cases more than one manuscript of a single work (Gregory's *Dialogues* C and H, *Anglo-Saxon Chronicle* A, C, D and E, the *Gospel of Nicodemus* A, C, D and E, and so on). In all cases, complete texts rather than samples were used. The corpus is divided into 100 files. In general each file contains a single work, although published collections, such as the Vercelli or Blickling homilies, have been kept together. Prologues and epilogues (such as Alfred's prologue to the *Cura Pastoralis*, Aelfric's prologue and epilogue to Genesis, and so on), however, are separated from their texts, as they represent a different genre of writing and often original as opposed to translated text.

3.2 Creation

As mentioned above, the electronic texts of the corpus were taken from the *Dictionary of Old English* (*DOE*) Corpus. The first step in compiling the corpus was, therefore, to convert the Toronto texts into a format that could be parsed. Because of the complexity of the parsing scheme, it is essential that as little non-text material is included in the parsed version as possible, and thus we had to remove or reduce much of the metatext data included in the Toronto version. This was done automatically using programs written in Perl. At the same time we converted the HTML representation of special characters (&*t*; thorn, &*d*; eth, &*ae*; ash, and so on) into the ASCII representations used by Helsinki (+*t*, +*d*, and +*a*) to maintain compatibility with earlier corpora, and tokenized the text for input to the tagger. This requires separating the punctuation and formatting the text with one token per line. The beginning of a Toronto text has the form in Figure 9.1. The text after conversion is given in Figure 9.2.

Three types of information are retained in the conversion: source information to allow a user to locate the text in the Toronto corpus and access the removed information <T03060_+ALS_(Sebastian)_B1.3.6>, token identifiers which include the Toronto reference number as well as some way of identifying the location of the token in the published text, in this case the line number <T03060000100,1>, and some HTML codes, such as <foreign>, which contain information about the text.

Following conversion of the text to an appropriate format, it is automatically part-of-speech tagged using the Brill tagger. This trainable

```
<T03060_+ALS_ [Sebastian]_B1.3.6>
<T03060000100,1> <foreign> XIII. KALENDAS FEBRUARII </foreign> .
<T03060000200,1> <foreign> PASSIO SANCTI SEBASTIANI MARTYRIS </foreign> .
<T03060000300,1> Sebastianus hatte sum halig Godes +degn se w+as lange on lare on Mediolana
byrig , and wear+d on Criste gefullod mid fullumgeleafan.
<T03060000400,4> He w+as swi+de snotor wer and so+df+ast on spr+ace , rihtwis on dome and on
r+ade foregleaw , getreowe on neode and strang fore+tingere , on godnysse scinende and on
eallum +teawum arwur+dful.
<T03060000500,8> D+aghwamlice he gefylde his drihtnes +tenunge geornlice , ac he bediglode swa
+teah his d+ada +tam casere Dioclitiane se w+as deofles biggencga .
```

Figure 9.2 The YCOE text following conversion from *DOE* text

tagger adds tags to the words of the texts following a forward slash, as in Figure 9.3 (the meaning of the tags can be found in section 4.1).

On Old English, the tagger achieves accuracy rates of approximately 80 to 85 per cent, thus requiring correction of 15 to 20 per cent of the tags. This correction is done using an interface developed by the Penn Treebank, which allows the corrector to move through the text one

```
<T03060_+ALS_ [Sebastian]_B1.3.6>
<T03060000100,1> <foreign> XIII./ADJ|N KALENDAS/FW FEBRUARII/FW </foreign> ./.
<T03060000200,1> <foreign> PASSIO/FW SANCTI/FW SEBASTIANI/FW MARTYRIS/FW </foreign>
./.
<T03060000300,1> Sebastianus/NR|N hatte/VBD sum/Q|N halig/ADJ|N Godes/NR|G
+degn/N|N se/D|N w+as/BEDI lange/ADV|T on/P lare/N|D on/P
Mediolana/N|G byrig/N|D ,/, and/CONJ wear+d/BEDI on/P Criste/NR|D gefullod/VBN
mid/P fullum/ADJ|D geleafan/N|D ./.
<T03060000400,4> He/PRO|N w+as/BEDI swi+de/ADV snotor/ADJ|N wer/N|N and/CONJ
so+df+ast/ADJ|N on/P spr+ace/N|D ,/, rihtwis/ADJ|N on/P dome/N|D and/CONJ on/P
r+ade/VBP foregleaw/N|N ,/, getreowe/VBPS on/P neode/N|D*/N and/CONJ strang/ADJ|N
fore+tingere/N|N ,/, on/P godnysse/N|D scinende/ADJ|N and/CONJ on/P eallum/Q|D
+teawum/N|D arwur+dful/ADJ|N ./.
<T03060000500,8> D+aghwamlice/P he/PRO|N gefylde/VBD his/PRO$ drihtnes/NR|G
+tenunge/N|A geornlice/ADV ,/, ac/CONJ he/PRO|N bediglode/VBN swa/P +teah/ADV
his/PRO$ d+ada/N|N +tam/D|D casere/N|D Dioclitiane/N|A se/D|N w+as/BEDI deofles/N|G
biggencga/N|N ./.
```

Figure 9.3 Text after automatic part-of-speech tagging

```
<T03060_+ALS_[Sebastian]_B1.3.6>
<T03060000100,1> <foreign> XIII./ADJ|N*/FW KALENDAS/FW FEBRUARII/FW </foreign>
./.*/,
<T03060000200,1> <foreign> PASSIO/FW SANCTI/FW SEBASTIANI/FW MARTYRIS/FW </foreign>
./.
<T03060000300,1> Sebastianus/NR|N hatte/VBD sum/Q|N halig/ADJ|N Godes/NR|G
+degn/N|N se/D|N w+as/BEDI lange/ADV|T on/P lare/N|D*/N on/P Mediolana/N|G*/NR|G
byrig/N|D ,/, and/CONJ wear+d/BEDI on/P Criste/NR|D gefullod/VBN mid/P fullum/ADJ|D
geleafan/N|D ./.
<T03060000400,4> He/PRO|N w+as/BEDI swi+de/ADV snotor/ADJ|N wer/N|N and/CONJ
so+df+ast/ADJ|N on/P spr+ace/N|D*/N ,/, rihtwis/ADJ|N on/P dome/N|D and/CONJ on/P
r+ade/VBP foregleaw/N|N*/ADJ|N ,/, getreowe/VBPS*/ADJ|N on/P neode/N|D*/N and/CONJ
strang/ADJ|N fore+tingere/N|N ,/, on/P godnysse/N|D*/N
scinende/ADJ|N*/VAG and/CONJ on/P eallum/Q|D +teawum/N|D arwur+dful/ADJ|N ./.
<T03060000500,8> D+aghwamlice/P*/ADV he/PRO|N gefylde/VBD his/PRO$ drihtnes/NR|G
+tenunge/N|A*/N geornlice/ADV ,/,*/. ac/CONJ he/PRO|N bediglode/VBN*/VBD swa/P*/ADV
+teah/ADV his/PRO$ d+ada/N|N*/N|A +tam/D|D casere/N|D Dioclitiane/N|A*/NR|D se/D|N
w+as/BEDI deofles/N|G biggencga/N|N ./.
```

Figure 9.4 Corrected part-of-speech file

word at a time by pressing the space bar. Incorrect tags are replaced simply by typing the correct tag and pressing the space bar. In the text, the correct tag is added to the original following an asterisk to allow error rates to be calculated. The incorrect tags are later removed at the post-processing stage. The text itself is protected and cannot be altered by the corrector. An experienced corrector can achieve rates of around 3,000 words an hour using this method. The corrected part-of-speech file is illustrated in Figure 9.4.

Following part-of-speech tagging the text is automatically parsed using a probabilistic parser developed by Michael Collins (1998). This parser produces output in the Penn Treebank format, as in Figure 9.5 (for details on the annotation system, see section 4.1).

Hand correction again follows, using a drag-and-drop interface also developed for the Penn Treebank. Using this interface, labels can be changed, new constituents bracketed and constituents moved, all using mouse and keyboard commands. The corrected file is then post-processed to produce the final form, as in Figure 9.6.

```
( (IP-MAT (CONJ ac)
          (NP-NOM (PRO|N he))
          (VBD bediglode)
          (ADVP (ADV swa))
          (ADVP (ADV +teah))
          (NP-ACC (PRO$ his) (N|A d+ada))
          (NP-DAT (D|D +tam) (N|D casere)
                  (NP-DAT (NR|D Dioclitiane)))
          (CP (WNP 0)
              (C 0)
              (IP-SUB (NP-NOM (D|N se))
                      (BEDI w+as)
                      (N P-GEN (N|G deofles) (N|N biggencga))))
          (. .)))
```

Figure 9.5 Output of automatic parsing phase

Following this stage, systematic error checking for malformed tokens and common errors is carried out using the search engine CorpusSearch (see section 5).

4 Structure

4.1 Annotation

The main feature of the corpus is that it is syntactically annotated. The main goal of the annotation is to facilitate automatic searching for syntactic constructions, not to give a correct linguistic analysis of each sentence: that is, the corpus is a tool, not the result of a research program. There is a slight theoretical bias in the annotation toward earlier versions of generative (X-bar) syntax in the choice of names for labels and some ways of representing relations (the use of traces, for instance). This follows partly from the history of these corpora as part of the Penn Treebank tradition, and partly from our conviction that this is a widely recognized system and, for parsing in tree format, a

```
( (IP-MAT (CONJ ac)
          (NP-NOM (PRO^N he))
          (VBD bediglode)
          (ADVP (ADV swa) (ADV +teah))
          (NP-ACC (PRO$ his) (N^A d+ada))
          (NP-DAT (D^D +tam) (N^D casere)
                  (NP-DAT-PRN (NR^D Dioclitiane))
                  (CP-REL (WNP-NOM-1 (D^N se))
                          (C 0)
                          (IP-SUB (NP-NOM *T*-1)
                                  (BEDI w+as)
                                  (NP-NOM-PRD (NP-GEN (N^G deofles))
                                              (N^N biggencga)))))
          (. .)) (ID coaelive,+ALS_[Sebastian]:8.1215))
```

Figure 9.6 Corrected parse in final form

very useful one. However, we have felt no compunction to remain true to any particular aspect or version of the theory, but have focused our efforts on creating a useful annotation system. Although we have tried within the bounds of time and money to annotate as much as possible, in as linguistically valid a way as possible, it cannot be stated too strongly that the annotation system may not reflect linguistic reality in any direct way.

All words, phrases and clausal structures in the corpus are labelled. The label is attached to the left parenthesis of the pair which delineate the extent of the constituent. The major part-of-speech categories (that is, word-level labels) are given in Figure 9.7, and phrase labels in Figure 9.8.

The initial part of a label is formal, that is, it identifies part of speech (such as N, ADJ) or type of phrase (NP, ADJP and so on); this is followed immediately by case for the appropriate categories. This part of the label may then be followed by one or more function labels. All IPs and CPs are identified by type. Therefore there is no simple IP or CP label in the corpus; they always have an extended label identifying them further. Outside of CP and IP, phrases may or may not have

N	common noun	PRO	pronoun
NR	proper noun	PRO$	possessive pronoun
		MAN	indefinite "man"
WPRO	wh-pronoun	WPRO	wh-adverb
WADJ	wh-adjective	WQ	WHETHER

ADJ, ADJR, ADJS	adjective, comparative adj., superlative .adj
Q, QR, QS	quantifier, comp. quant., sup. quant.
ADV, ADVR, ADVS	adverb, comparative adv., superlative .adv

CONJ	conjunction	RP(X)	adverbial particle
C	complementizer	FP	focus particle
D	determiner	FW	foreign word
P	preposition	INTJ	interjection
NEG	negation	NUM	number

labels beginning with:

BE	forms of the verb BE (e.g. BEPI, BEDI, etc.)
HV	the verb HAVE (HVPI, HVDI, etc.)
AX	auxiliary verbs (AXPI, AXDI, etc.)
MD	modal verbs (MDPI, MDDI, etc.)
VB	all other verbs (VBPI, VBDI, etc.)

Case and adverbial function labels added to word-labels

^N	nominative	^T	temporal
^A	accusative	^L	locative
^G	genitive	^D	directional
^I	instrumental		

Figure 9.7 YCOE part-of-speech tags

```
CP    complementizer phrase
IP    inflection phrase
PTP   participial phrase

NP     noun phrase             WNP        wh-NP
ADJP   adjective phrase        WADJP      wh-ADJP
QP     quantifier phrase       WQP        wh-QP
ADVP   adverb phrase           WADVP      wh-ADVP
PP     prepositional phrase    WPP        wh-PP

CONJP  conjunction phrase

As at word-level, phrases may be labelled for case.

-NOM   nominative            -GEN   genitive
-ACC   accusative            -DAT   dative
```

Figure 9.8 YCOE phrase labels

function labels. The lack of a function label on NPs, for instance, generally indicates that they are arguments. The function labels for clauses and phrases are given in Figure 9.9.

The texts in the corpus are divided into tokens. A token consists most basically of one main verb (or verb sequence) with all associated arguments and adjuncts. The majority of tokens therefore are matrix IPs (IP-MAT), that is, sentences, but they may also be CPs (for example, direct questions CP-QUE). Each token is enclosed in a 'wrapper', a pair of unlabelled parentheses. The wrapper contains minimally the parsed

IP-MAT	matrix IP
IP-SUB	subordinate IP (i.e., dominated by CP)
IP-SUB-CON	conjunct subordinate clause
IP-INF	complement infinitive
IP-INF-NCO	non-complement infinitive
IP-INF-ABS	infinitival absolute
IP-SMC	small clause
CP-ADV	adverbial clause
CP-CAR	clause-adjoined relative
CP-CLF	cleft
CP-CMP	comparative clause
CP-DEG	degree complement
CP-EOP	infinitival relative/purpose clause with gap
CP-FRL	free relative clause
CP-QUE	question
CP-REL	relative clause
CP-THT	that-complement
Functions added to phrase labels	
-ADT	adjunct
-DIR	directional
-EXT	extent
-LFD	left-dislocation
-LOC	locative
-PRD	predicate
-PRN	appositive or parenthetical
-RFL	reflexive
-RSP	resumptive
-SPE	direct speech
-SBJ	non-nominative subject
-TMP	temporal
-VOC	vocative

Figure 9.9 YCOE clause function labels

text, a unique ID node to identify the token, which includes the filename, the *Dictionary of Old English* (*DOE*) short title for the text, and some way of finding the token in the text (page and/or line number, for instance). The *DOE* identifiers are included in the text at the point that they occur in the original. Generally this coincides with the beginning of a token, in which case the identifier is included in the wrapper. Typical tokens are illustrated in Figure 9.10.

The annotation scheme uses a limited tree representation in the form of labelled parentheses. Each set of parentheses represents a constituent. The open parentheses have an associated label, identifying the constituent as either a phrase label (CP, IP, NP, ADJP and so on) or a word label (also called a part-of-speech, or POS, tag, such as N, ADJ). The initial part of the label provides formal information (that is, part of

```
( (CODE <T03010000800,25>)     ← Dictionary of Old English identifier
  (IP-MAT (NP-NOM (NUM^N An) (N^N woruldcynincg)) ← parsed text
          (HVPI h+af+d)
          (NP-ACC (NP (Q fela)
                      (NP-GEN (N^G +tegna)))
                  (CONJP (CONJ and)
                         (NP-ACC (ADJ^A mislice) (N^A wicneras))))
          (. ;)) (ID copreflives,+ALS_[Pref]:25.14)) ← ID node

( (CODE <T02190003900,283.79>)
  (CP-QUE (WADVP-1 (WADV Hwi))  ← CP-QUE token
          (IP-SUB (ADVP *T*-1)
                  (MDD wolde)
                  (NP-NOM (NR^N God))
                  (BE beon)
                  (VBN acenned)
                  (PP (P of)
                      (NP-DAT (VBN^D beweddodan) (N^D m+adene))))
          (. ?)) (ID cocathom1,+ACHom_I,_13:283.79.2423))
```

Figure 9.10 The form of tokens in the YCOE

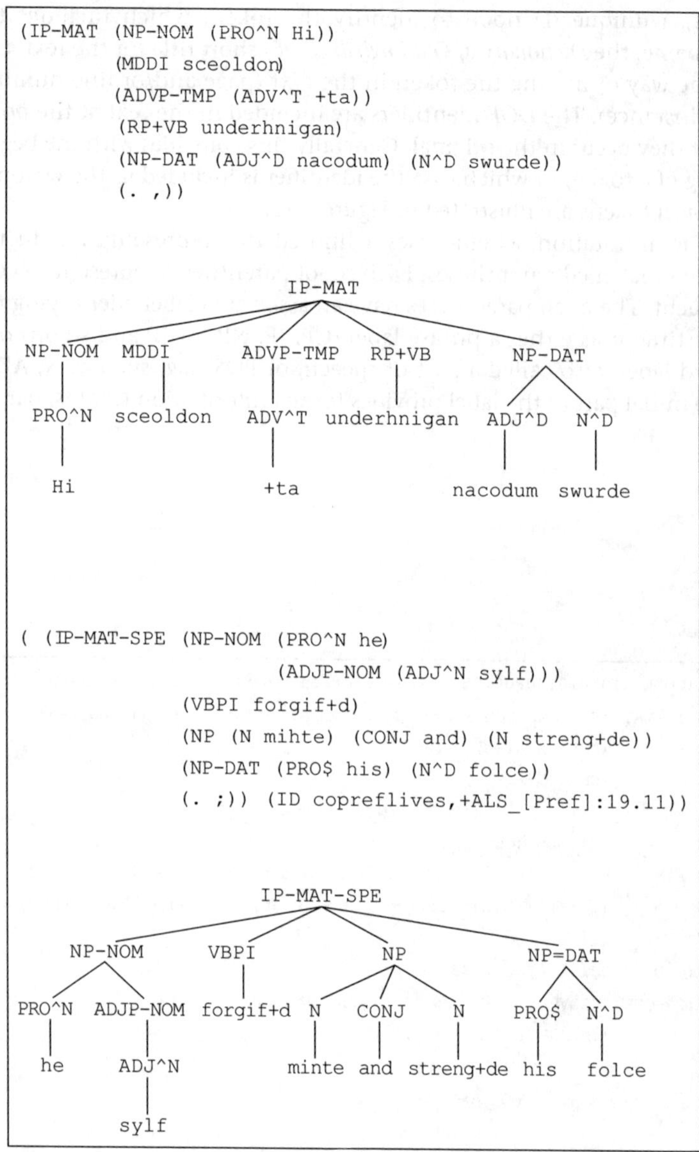

Figure 9.11 Simple tokens with their tree representations

speech or type of phrase), and for inflecting categories, case (NP-NOM = nominative NP, N^N = nominative noun, and so on) while further labels, if present, generally provide functional information (-LFD = left-dislocated, -PRD = predicate, and so on). The punctuation of the text is included in the corpus as a labelled item, but is normally ignored by CorpusSearch, along with other metalinguistic elements of the parse such as comments, when searching. Some examples of simple tokens and their associated tree representation are given in Figure 9.11.

As can be seen by these examples, the tree which is used to represent structure in the corpus is heavily underspecified: that is, the number of levels of structure included is quite limited and certain types of phrases are not included at all, with the result that the trees are multiple branching and quite flat. The most obvious example of this is the lack of a VP node. Within the IP, all verbs and arguments of the verb (both internal and external, that is, both subject and complements), as well as all adjuncts, are immediately dominated by the IP with no intervening phrasal node. This is not a theoretical, but rather a practical decision, since omitting the VP level eliminates the need to identify the boundaries of the VP, which is not an easy task in Old English, and vastly reduces the complexity of the parsing.

Phrases such as NP, PP, ADJP and so on are also relatively flat. Structure is only added when it serves to make a necessary distinction. Thus, as with clauses, the phrasal node immediately dominates the head category (for example, N, P, ADJ): that is, no intermediate bar-levels are indicated, as illustrated in Figure 9.12.

Because of the lack of intermediate bar levels, modifiers and complements are sisters of the head, as illustrated in Figure 9.13.

```
(NP-DAT (N^D anginne) )
(ADJP-NOM (ADJ^N hwilwendlic) )
(ADVP-TMP (ADV^T +afre) )
(ADVP (ADV so+dlice) )
```

Figure 9.12 Illustration of phrasal categories with no intermediate nodes

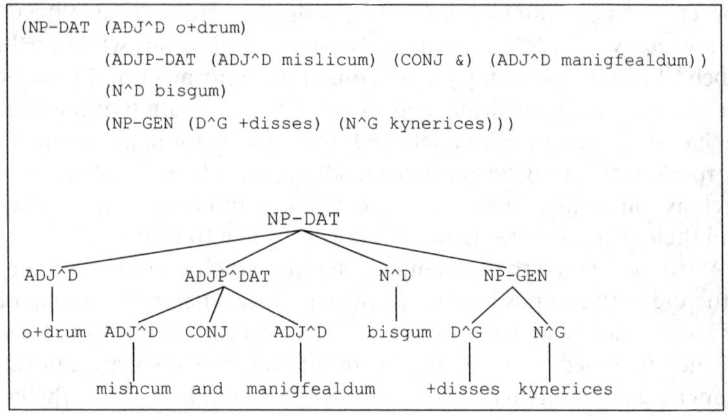

Figure 9.13 A phrase illustrating the sisterhood of heads, modifiers and adjuncts

4.2 Annotation principles

In developing an annotation scheme for any language, many decisions must be made: what sort of features to annotate; how much detail to include in the annotation; how to deal with formal or structural ambiguity; and how to prioritize in cases where linguistic accuracy conflicts with the needs of the user when searching. The first question, what sort of features to annotate, is largely a personal question which depends heavily on the interests of the creators and the users they anticipate. Even if it were possible to create a corpus with every conceivable linguistic feature annotated, such a corpus would probably be so unwieldy to use that it would not satisfy anyone. While care should be taken to include features that will make the corpus useful to as wide a range of people as possible, there is no point, for instance, in including detailed phonological annotation in a corpus designed for syntacticians. Morphology, on the other hand, might arguably be useful. For the Old English corpus, which was designed primarily for syntacticians, we made the decision to include some morphological information (case marking and verbal mood) but not all that it would be possible to include (we omitted, for instance, number).

The issue of how much detail to include in the annotation can be a difficult one. More detail allows more precise searching; on the other hand, it also complicates the system, making it harder to learn and making searches more difficult to formulate. For this reason we try not to include structure that is completely predictable. For instance, in the first example in Figure 9.14, the unmodified ADJ is not dominated by a

```
(NP (D the) (ADJ tall) (N girl))
(NP (D the)
    (ADJP (ADV very) (ADJ tall))
    (N girl))
```

Figure 9.14 Modified and unmodified adjectives

phrasal ADJP node, while in the second the modified ADJ is. This is because in the first example the boundaries of an ADJP, if included, and its relationship to the other members of the NP would be completely predictable, that is, they would be exactly the same as the boundaries and relationship of the ADJ. In the second example, on the other hand, this is not the case. Here the ADJP serves to indicate that the ADV and ADJ are sisters, and the ADJP is sister to the N.

Another case where less detailed annotation can be useful is in cases of indeterminacy. In Old English, the surface order of the VP is still in flux, and determining the boundaries of this node would be difficult and time-consuming, if not impossible, in many cases. For this reason we simply do not include the node. The result of this decision is that the verb (or verbs) and all its arguments, both subjects and complements, are sisters, directly dominated by the sentential node, IP. While this is not a good linguistic analysis, it solves the problem of the indeterminacy and, as a bonus, actually makes searching for different orders of sentential elements much easier than it would be in a more complicated system.

Another problematic area is ambiguity. If the annotator cannot accurately make a distinction, then it is difficult to include it in the annotation. There are two ways to deal with ambiguity. The first is to allocate large amounts of resources to resolving the ambiguity. This is the approach to take when the ambiguity occurs in an area central to the purpose of the corpus: for instance, morphological ambiguities should probably be resolved in a corpus which is primarily intended for morphological analysis. If it is not possible or desirable to allocate sufficient resources to resolving the ambiguity, there are two ways it can be avoided. The first is to divide the ambiguous items into two categories, one which includes clear cases which are not ambiguous, and

```
(N^D handum)     ← unambiguous dative in isolation
(N sige)         ← ambiguous nom ./acc./dat. in isolation
```

Figure 9.15 Case on lexical items: unambiguous vs ambiguous

one which contains everything else. This is appropriate when some of the items can be reliably identified in all cases. This is the approach we took with marking case. Case is a fully productive category in Old English, but some case endings are formally ambiguous, making it difficult to identify them in isolation. In some cases the ambiguity is easily resolved on the basis of neighbouring words, but in others it is not. Our approach, therefore, was to indicate case when it was formally clear, but not when it was ambiguous. Thus a noun like *handum* is unambiguously dative, and is always labelled dative. A noun like *sige*, on the other hand, could, in isolation, be nominative, accusative or dative. Thus, unless it is accompanied by an unambiguous determiner (such as *+tone*), it will not be labelled for case, as shown in Figure 9.15.

This means that some lexical items in the corpus that bear case (nouns, pronouns, adjectives and determiners) are labelled for case, and the user may rely on that information being correct. The rest of the case-bearing lexical items are simply not labelled. Thus, we have a number of clear unambiguous case categories, such as nominative and accusative, and one category, unlabelled, which includes all the ambiguous items.

The second way to resolve ambiguity is simply to have one category which includes all cases. This is the approach to take when none of the cases can be reliably assigned to a clear category. For example, the distinction between argument and adjunct PPs is notoriously difficult to make, and including such a distinction would result in many errors of categorization, almost certainly in both directions. The result would be two different categories, adjunct PP and argument PP, presented as clear categories, but both potentially contaminated by instances of the other, wrongly labelled. By not making the distinction, we simply have one category which is clearly understood to contain both types. Similarly, phrases headed by a participle without an overt subject may be adjunct participials (*she walked down the street, eating ice cream*) or reduced relatives (*the man standing on the roof was about to jump*). Distinguishing the types is often dependent on punctuation, however,

```
(CP-REL (WNP-ACC-1 (WPRO^A +tone))   ← structure of a relative clause
        (C 0)                            with empty complementizer
        (IP-SUB ...))                    position represented

(CP-QUE (WNP-ACC-1 (WPRO^A hw+at))   ← direct question with no
        (IP-SUB ...))                       complementizer position

(CP-QUE (IP-SUB ...))                ← yes/no question
(CP-ADV (IP-SUB ...))                ← V1 conditional
```

Figure 9.16 The annotation of verb-first clause types

as for example in '*The girl eating ice cream walked down the street*', which is interpreted as a reduced relative without punctuation separating the clause, or, with punctuation, '*The girl, eating ice cream, walked down the street*', as an adjunct participial. Since punctuation in early texts is often not reliable (or not used in the Modern English way), this distinction is unreliable, and we therefore do not make it. Instead we use a PTP label (participial phrase), which is purely formal, as a way of avoiding the problem.

Finally, there are constructions for which there is a standard analysis generally accepted by syntacticians which could be represented in the parsing system, but which would make searching more difficult. In these cases we give priority to ease of searching rather than linguistic validity. For instance, we represent the subject–verb inversion found in direct questions, yes/no questions and V1 conditionals by the lack of a complementizer position, an otherwise required element of every CP in our corpus, as illustrated in Figure 9.16. Since including the verb in the CP layer would cause various problems for parsing and searching, we simply represent this structure in a different, but easily recognizable, way.

Another example is adverbial clauses consisting of a preposition (subordinating conjunction) with a clausal complement (*before she came, if she goes*). Representing this directly in the parsing, as in the first example in Figure 9.17, however, makes it difficult to access the preposition when searching, since it is outside the CP node. For this reason we include the preposition inside the CP, as in the second example.[1]

```
(PP (P before)                    ← a reasonable linguistic analysis
    (CP-ADV (C 0)
            (IP-SUB she came))

(CP-ADV (P before)                ← an easily searchable structure
    (C 0)
    P-SUB she came))
```

Figure 9.17 The annotation of CP adverbials headed by prepositions

The preceding principles underpin the decisions we made in designing the annotation system for the YCOE. Some of them we adopted from the PPCME2 or Penn Treebank; others arose out of our experience using earlier corpora. The major problem with designing annotation systems is that you generally have to design the system before you have any experience of the data. Unfortunately, it is only when a significant amount of data has been parsed that flaws in the system show up, and at this point it may or may not be possible to go back and make changes. Basing a corpus on a previous one obviously can make designing the system easier, but can raise problems of its own. Sometimes a decision has to be made not to improve some aspect of the annotation system in order to maintain compatibility with other corpora which are intended to be used together. Thus, the two Early Modern English corpora, with a few exceptions, maintain strict conformity to the PPCME2, so that the three corpora will, in effect, form one larger corpus when complete. This is good for users in one way since searching the three corpora together will be possible. It is problematic in that lessons learned from parsing and using the PPCME2 and YCOE cannot be implemented.

5 Distribution and end-user issues

5.1 Availability

The corpus is deposited with the Oxford Text Archive (http://www.ota.ahds.ac.uk) and is available free for non-commercial use via FTP. Recipients of the corpus are required to sign an agreement stating they will not redistribute the corpus and will ensure that they are compliant with copyright law in their use of material from the corpus.

5.2 Documentation

The corpus is supplied with a full suite of documentation which can be viewed with a web browser. Reference manuals to part-of-speech tagging, syntactic parsing and CorpusSearch are included, as well as two 'Lite' manuals, one for the annotation and one for CorpusSearch. These manuals introduce in a simpler way the most important concepts which it is necessary for the beginner to understand in order to start to use the corpus effectively. In addition, information on each text, such as length, genre, manuscript, manuscript date, dialect and edition used, is included, to the extent that it is known. All the documentation is available on the YCOE website (http://www-users.york.ac.uk/~lang22/YCOE/YcoeHome.htm).

5.3 Searching the corpus

Although the corpus is in ASCII format and thus can be used on any platform and viewed and searched with any word-processing program, in order to utilize the annotations fully, a search program sensitive to structure is required. CorpusSearch is such a search program, conceived and designed by Ann Taylor and Anthony Kroch, and implemented by Beth Randall in Java.[2] CorpusSearch is not corpus-specific but will search any corpus in the correct format, including all the corpora in the English Parsed Corpora Series.

The most important and useful aspect of CorpusSearch, and the feature which distinguishes it from most other search programs of its type, is that it can search its own output. This feature makes it relatively slow in comparison to search programs that index the input before searching, but as the difference in time is small (taking minutes rather than seconds to conduct a large search), and newer computer processors are continually reducing the length of searches, the loss in time is easily made up for by the increase in usefulness, since searches can be carried out in steps, and data easily divided into subsets.

CorpusSearch takes as input a query file and an input file. The first contains the structure which is to be searched for and the second the file or files to search. It outputs a file which contains all tokens that match the query. It also prints a preface and a summary in each output file. The preface gives such information as the date, time, the name of the input and output files, and the query, as illustrated in Figure 9.18. Comments can also be included in the preface.

```
/*
PREFACE:  regular output file.
CorpusSearch copyright Beth Randall 2000.
Date:  Thu Mar 11 16:18:23 GMT 2004

command file:      vb-pro.q
output file:       vb-pro.out

node:     IP*
query:    ((NP-NOM iDominates PRO^*)
          AND (VB* precedes NP-NOM))
*/
```

Figure 9.18 The preface of a CorpusSearch output file

The summary, illustrated in Figure 9.19, repeats some of the information of the preface, but adds statistics on how many tokens were searched in each file used as input, as well how many matches ('hits' in CorpusSearch terminology) were found.

Searching with CorpusSearch requires the user first to define a node, that is, the constituent within which to search (such as IP, CP, NP) and then to define a tree structure using primarily the two relations *precedes* and *dominates*. For instance, to search for a pronominal subject following the verb, we first define the node, which in this case would be IP, since the structure we are looking for is sentential. Then we define the structure as (in plain English) 'the subject dominates a pronoun, and the verb precedes the subject'. In 'CorpusSearch-ese' this appears as shown in Figure 9.20 (the asterisk is a wild card).

```
/*
SUMMARY:  regular output file.

command file:      vb-pro.q
output file:       vb-pro.out

source files, hits/tokens/total
  coadrian.o34.psd       1/1/114
  coaelhom.o3.psd        121/119/4186
  coaelive.o3.psd        223/222/7969
  coalcuin.psd           31/30/402
  coalex.o23.psd         97/97/531
  coapollo.o3.psd        53/51/593
  coaugust.psd           0/0/4
grand total hits :  526
grand total tokens containing hits:  520
grand total tokens searched:  13799
*/
```

Figure 9.19 The summary of a CorpusSearch output file

All matching structures, such as the one in Figure 9.21, are extracted from the corpus (or subpart of the corpus as defined by the user) and printed to a file. CorpusSearch always prints the full text of the token first, between the markers /~* and *~/; it then prints what is known as the vector, between /* and */. The vector indicates which nodes CorpusSearch has identified as matching the various parts of the query. Following the vector is the parsed token that matches the query. The numbers on the open parentheses are added by CorpusSearch to help

```
node: IP  *
query: ((NP-NOM iDominates PRO^*)
       AND (VB* precedes NP-NOM))
```

Figure 9.20 A CorpusSearch query

```
/~*
+Da andwyrde he him +tus,
(coaelive,+ALS_[Christmas]:11.9)
*~/
/*
2 IP-MAT: 6 NP-NOM, 7 PRO^N he, 5 VBD andwyrde
*/
(NODE (2 IP-MAT (3 ADVP-TMP (4 ADV^T +Da))
                (5 VBD andwyrde)
                (6 NP-NOM (7 PRO^N he))
                (8 NP-DAT (9 PRO^D him))
                (10 ADVP (11 ADV +tus))
                (12 . ,))
      (ID coaelive,+ALS_[Christmas]:11.9))
```

Figure 9.21 Part of a CorpusSearch output file

match the vector to the token and can be turned off with a simple command.

CorpusSearch also includes many other search functions in addition to those illustrated here, and highly customizable output, making it a very flexible search program. There are online reference manuals available for both CorpusSearch 1.1 (on the YCOE website: http://www-users.york.ac.uk/~lang22/YCOE/doc/corpussearch/CSRefToc.htm), and CorpusSearch 2 (http://corpussearch.sourceforge.net/CS-manual/Contents.html).

CorpusSearch (version 1.1 and above) also contains a coding function. This allows the user to code all the tokens in a file according to any aspect of their structure, instead of extracting all tokens that match a certain structure. The structures to code are defined in the same way as queries using the same basic functions. An example of a coding file is given in Figure 9.22. This file codes column 1 for whether the clause is main (IP-MAT) or subordinate (IP-SUB). Column 2 codes for whether the verb is present (VBP*) or past (VBD*).

Our sample output token in Figure 9.21 is then coded, as in Figure 9.23. The coding string is contained in a node labelled CODING, with the columns separated by colons. The clause is matrix, so column 1 is coded *m*, while the verb is past, so column 2 is coded *d*.

```
node: IP*

1: {  m: (IP-MAT* iDominates NP-NOM )
      s: (IP-SUB* iDominates NP-NOM )
}

2: {  p: (IP* iDominates VBP*)
      d: (IP* iDominates VBD*)
}
```

Figure 9.22 A CorpusSearch coding file

```
/~ *
+Da andwyrde he him +tus,
(coaelive,+ALS_[Christmas]:11.9)
*~/

(0 NODE (0 CODING m:d)
        (1 IP-MAT (2 ADVP-TMP (3 ADV^T +Da))
                  (4 VBD andwyrde)
                  (5 NP-NOM (6 PRO^N he))
                  (7 NP-DAT (8 PRO^D him))
                  (9 ADVP (10 ADV +tus))
                  (11 . ,) )
        (12 ID coaelive,+ALS_[Christmas]:11.9)))
```

Figure 9.23 Part of a CorpusSearch coded file

Coding was originally introduced as a way of producing coding strings that can be used as input to statistical programs such as Varbrul, Datadesk and SPSS for further data manipulation. Its usefulness as part of the searching process itself was an unanticipated bonus. Since CorpusSearch will search on the coding strings it produces, data which are coded can be sorted and analysed very easily. Coding also makes it possible to combine structural information, automatically coded by CorpusSearch, with information that is not available in the annotations, such as, for instance, pragmatic or prosodic information. This is done simply by adding coding columns by hand to an output file. CorpusSearch will then search these columns in the same way as columns it produced itself. Since coding strings are passed on by CorpusSearch from search to search, this information is thereafter always available to be accessed when needed.

6 Conclusions

The York–Toronto–Helsinki Parsed Corpus of Old English represents a midpoint in the programme of creating syntactically parsed corpora for the whole attested history of the English language. This programme, when complete, will comprise a resource for the study of the history of English unimaginable only twenty years ago. Such corpora eliminate the difficulties encountered in earlier empirical work in diachronic syntax, making it fast, efficient, flexible and accountable, and thereby increasing the amount and quality of work in the field. Although creating syntactically annotated corpora is a difficult and time-consuming task, the utility of the result makes it well worth the effort.

Notes

1. In the PPCME2, this structure is represented as in the second example. It was our experience with the difficulty of accessing such structures in the PPCME2 that led us to make this change.
2. At the time of going to press a new open-source version of CorpusSearch, CorpusSearch 2, had just been released (http://corpussearch.sourceforge.net). It differs slightly in detail from CorpusSearch 1.1, described in this chapter, but the concept is the same.

References

Bean, M. 1983. *The Development of Word Order Patterns in Old English*. London: Croom Helm.

Canale, W. M. 1978. 'Word order change in Old English: base reanalysis in generative grammar'. PhD dissertation, McGill University.

Collins, M. 1998. 'Head-driven statistical models for natural language parsing'. PhD dissertation, University of Pennsylvania.

Crisma, P. (forthcoming). 'Genitive constructions in the history of English'. *Typological Change in the Morphosyntax of the Indo-European Languages*, ed. by G. Banti, P. Di Giovine and P. Ramat. München: Lincom Europa.

Ellegård, A. 1953. *The Auxiliary* do*: The Establishment and Regulation of its Use in English*. Stockholm: Almqvist and Wiksell.

Haeberli, E. 2000. 'Adjuncts and the syntax of subjects in Old and Middle English'. *Diachronic Syntax, Models and Mechanisms: Proceedings of DIGS 5*, ed. by S. Pintzuk, G. Tsoulas, and A. Warner, pp. 109–31. Oxford: Oxford University Press.

Haeberli, E. 2002. 'Inflectional morphology and the loss of verb-second in English'. *Syntactic Effects of Morphological Change*, ed. by D. Lightfoot, pp. 88–106. Oxford: Oxford University Press.

Han, C. 1998. 'The structure and interpretation of imperatives: mood and force in universal grammar'. PhD dissertation, University of Pennsylvania.

Han, C. 2000. 'The evolution of Do-support in English imperatives'. *Diachronic Syntax, Models and Mechanisms: Proceedings of DIGS 5*, ed. by S. Pintzuk, G. Tsoulas, and A. Warner, pp. 275–95. Oxford: Oxford University Press.

Healey, Antonette diPaolo (ed.). 1986–. *Dictionary of Old English*: http://www.doe.utoronto.ca/index.html

Kohonen, V. 1978. *On the Development of English Word Order in Religious Prose Around 1000 and 1200 A.D.: A Quantitative Study of Word Order in Context*. Åbo: Åbo Akademi.

Kroch, A. 1989. 'Function and grammar in the history of English: periphrastic *do*'. *Language Variation and Change* (Current Issues in Linguistic Theory, 52), ed. by R. Fasold and D. Schiffrin, pp. 133–72. Philadelphia: Benjamins.

Kroch, A., B. Santorini and L. Delfs. 2005. Penn–Helsinki Parsed Corpus of Early Modern English: http://www.ling.upenn.edu/hist-corpora/PPCEME-RELEASE-1

Kroch, A. and A. Taylor. 2000. The Penn–Helsinki Parsed Corpus of Middle English, 2nd edn: http://www.ling.upenn.edu/hist-corpora/PPCME2-RELEASE-2

Kroch, A. and A. Taylor. 2000. 'Verb–object order in Early Middle English'. *Diachronic Syntax, Models and Mechanisms: Proceedings of DIGS 5*, ed. by S. Pintzuk, G. Tsoulas, and A. Warner, pp. 132–63. Oxford: Oxford University Press.

Kroch, A., A. Taylor and D. Ringe. 2000. 'The Middle English verb-second constraint: a case study in language contact and language change'. *Textual Parameters in Older Languages* (Current Issues in Linguistic Theory, 195) ed. by S. C. Herring, P. van Reenen and L. Schøsler, pp. 353–91. Philadelphia: Benjamins.

McFadden, T. 2002. 'The rise of the to dative in Middle English'. *Syntactic Effects of Morphological Change*, ed. by D. Lightfoot, pp. 107–23. Oxford: Oxford University Press.

Mitchell, B. 1985. *Old English Syntax*. Oxford: Clarendon.

Pintzuk, S. 1999. *Phrase Structures in Competition: Variation and Change in Old English Word Order*. New York & London: Garland.

Pintzuk S. and L. Plug. 2000. The York–Helsinki Parsed Corpus of Old English Poetry: http://www-users.york.ac.uk/~lang18/pcorpus.html

Pintzuk, S. and A. Taylor. (2006). 'The loss of OV order in the history of English'. *Blackwell Handbook of the History of English*, ed. by A. van Kemenade and B. Loss. Oxford: Blackwell.

Roberts, I. 1985. 'Agreement parameters and the development of the English modal auxiliaries'. *Natural Language and Linguistic Theory* 3:21–58.

Silverstone, M. S. 2004. 'An analysis of topicalisation in Old English'. MPhil dissertation, University of York.

Taylor, A. 1994. 'The change from SOV to SVO in Ancient Greek'. *Language Variation and Change* 6:1–37.

Taylor, A., A. Warner, S. Pintzuk and F. Beths. 2003. The York–Toronto–Helsinki Parsed Corpus of Old English Prose. Electronic texts and manuals available from the Oxford Text Archive: http://www.ota.ahds.ac.uk

van Kemenade, A. 1987. *Syntactic Case and Morphological Case in the History of English*. Dordrecht: Foris.

Visser, F. T. 1963–73. *An Historical Syntax of the English Language*. Leiden: Brill.

Williams, A. 2000. 'Null subjects in Middle English existentials'. *Diachronic Syntax, Models and Mechanisms: Proceedings of DIGS 5*, ed. by S. Pintzuk, G. Tsoulas, and A. Warner, pp. 164–87. Oxford: Oxford University Press.

Website

Oxford Text Archive: http://www.ota.ahds.ac.uk

10
A Corpus of Late Eighteenth-Century Prose

Linda van Bergen and David Denison

1 Introduction

The Corpus of Late Eighteenth-Century Prose is made up of unpublished letters transcribed from originals, about 300,000 words in all, and offered in plain text and HTML versions. The letters, held by the John Rylands University Library, date from the period 1761–90. The project was made possible by funding from the John Rylands Research Institute, which allowed Linda van Bergen and Joana Soliva to work part-time on the transcription of the material.

There is a great deal of hitherto unedited material in the John Rylands University Library of Manchester. From this, we selected the Legh of Lyme Muniments, an archive associated with the Legh family at Lyme Hall in Cheshire.[1] We subsequently homed in on letters written to Richard Orford, a steward of Peter Legh the Younger, as being of suitable date, suitably extensive, of varied and practical content, and having at least *some* connecting thread. An advantage of the material is that it is of interest to historians as much as to linguists (about half of the requests for access have come from historians), so that any future extension of the project might enlist support from either scholarly community. To some extent the corpus is opportunistic in origin, and we are modest in our aspirations for it, other than that it should be a useful resource.

The corpus was mainly intended to help fill the gap between the major diachronic corpora of English (the Helsinki Corpus, the Helsinki Corpus of Older Scots, and so on), most of which stop in the early eighteenth century at the latest, and modern multi-genre corpora, which start in the 1960s.[2] It was also specifically designed to illustrate non-literary English and English relatively uninfluenced by prescriptivist ideas, in the belief that it might help with research into change in (ordinary, spoken) language in the Late Modern English period. It would also be of interest to scholars working on dialectal English of the North-west (north Cheshire and south Lancashire in particular). It has become clear to us since the corpus was compiled that there has been a recent upsurge of interest in the study of non-standard documents within

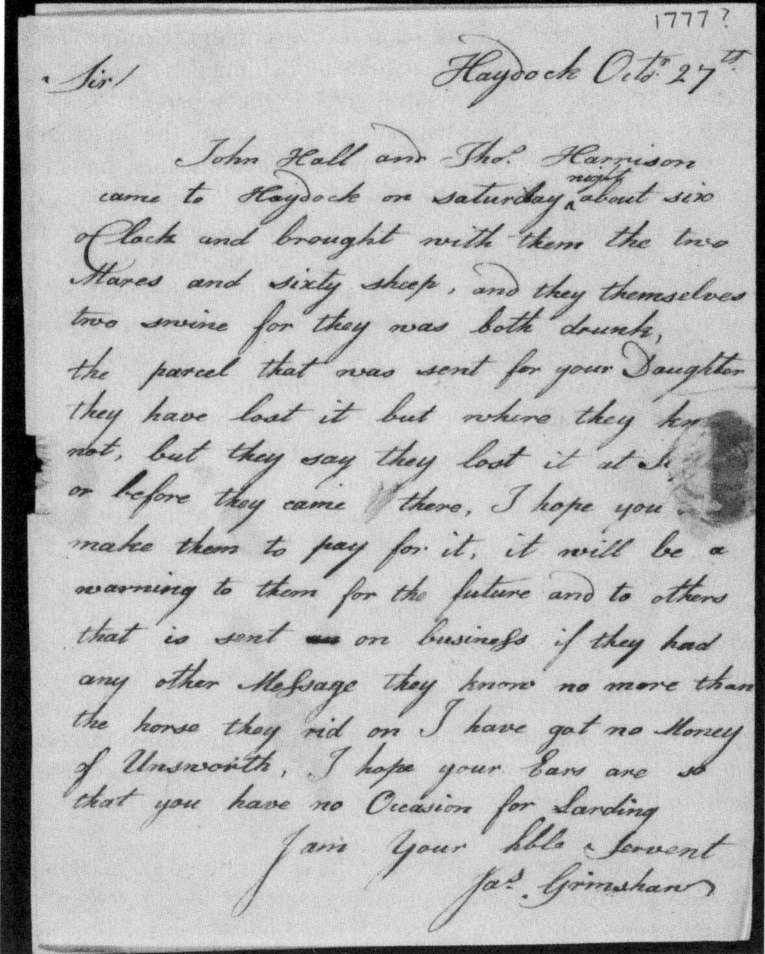

1777 ?

Sir / Haydock Octr 27th

John Hall and Thos Harrison came to Haydock on saturday night about six oClock and brought with them the two Mares and sixty sheep, and they themselves two swine for they was both drunk, the parcel that was sent for your Daughter they have lost it but where they kn[illegible] not, but they say they lost it at S[illegible] or before they came there, I hope you [illegible] make them to pay for it, it will be a warning to them for the future and to others that is sent on business if they had any other Message they know no more than the horse they rid on I have got no Money of Unsworth, I hope your Ears are so that you have no Occasion for Larding

I am Your Hble Servent
Jas. Grimshaw

Reproduced by courtesy of the University Librarian and Director, John Rylands University Library, University of Manchester.

Figure 10.1 A letter from James Grimshaw (original)

languages that have a standardized form; see, for example, in this connection Fairman (2000), Elspaß (2002, 2004) and Vandenbussche (2002), and the conference 'Language History from Below: Linguistic Variation in the Germanic Languages from 1700 to 2000' (Bristol, 2005).

The short letter shown in Figure 10.1 will serve to illustrate everyday subject matter in the corpus, and grammar that would not be standard in present-day English. First we show the original of the letter.

We quote the letter from the plain text version of the corpus (Figure 10.2), adding line numbers to facilitate a brief linguistic commentary; an explanation of coding symbols is given in the Appendix.

The spelling in this letter happens to be standard, the punctuation less so. Some other forms are odd by present-day standards, though not necessarily non-standard at the time of writing. Common nouns sporadically have initial capitals, something not infrequent in eighteenth-century spelling, and <I> and <J> can still be treated as variants of the same letter, hence <Iohn> (line 1) and <J> (17). Abbreviation was common to save time and postage costs, hence <Thos> for <Thomas> (1) and <Ja^{s}> for <James> (18), <hble> for <humble> in the closing formula (17). Past tense *rid* for *rode* is historically correct for the past plural and is actually recorded by *OED* as a variant for the past tense that was still current around 1909, when the fascicle containing *ride* (v.) was published (s.v., A.2(γ)). *Have got* (14) is not yet a mere synonym for *have* 'possess' and still means 'have obtained'. Causative *make* (10) is nowadays usually followed by a plain infinitive, except when passive, but here is construed with a *to*-infinitive even though itself active, as was still common at the time. *They was* (5) has remained widespread in dialect, and notice *is* with a plural subject in line 12. The syntax of *the parcel ... they have lost it* (6–7) is clumsy: the object noun phrase is topicalized (Denison, 1998, pp. 237–8) and then repeated in a resumptive pronoun that is strictly speaking unnecessary. (*Larding* (16) is probably a reference to the application of grease as ointment: in the next letter Grimshaw writes 'I am sorrey to here you are no better of your head'.)

To return to the general content of the corpus, there are no immediate plans to extend it. However, since we were not able to transcribe all the letters contained in this part of the archive within the time available, ideally we would like to include the remaining material as well, if and when resources can be found. We have transcribed about four-fifths of the letters sent to Richard Orford. Other sections of correspondence contained in the archive (especially those written to members of

<A GRIM SHAW JAMES>
<O?1777>

M=r=. Orford
Lyme
by Manchester
Cheshire

<P>

Haydock Octo=r=. 27=th=.

Sir

Iohn Hall and Tho=s=. Harrison
came to Haydock on saturday ^night^ about six
oClock and brought with them the two
Mares and sixty sheep, and they themselves
two swine for they was both drunk,
the parcel that was sent for your Daughter
they have lost it but where they kn{ow}
not, but they say they lost it at S{*...} [^seal^]
or before they came [^one or two letters rubbed out ^] there, I hope you {*...} [^seal^]
make them to pay for it, it will be a
warning to them for the future and to others
that is sent [^word crossed out^] on business if they had
any other Message they know no more than
the horse they rid on I have got no Money
of Unsworth, I hope your Ears are so
that you have no Occasion for Larding
J am Your hble Servent
Ja=s=. Grimshaw

Figure 10.2 A letter from James Grimshaw (plain text version)

the Legh family, containing material on eighteenth-century northern politics) are used comparatively frequently by historians, so expansion in that direction would certainly be useful for them, as well as of probable interest to linguists. Even as it stands, however, the corpus provides easy access to a substantial body of material that otherwise in all likelihood would rarely be used.

As already indicated, we always intended the corpus to be of use to others besides linguists. A number of requests for access have come from historians, mostly without further specification of their specialism, though one did mention a particular interest in mining and smelting.

2 Material included in the corpus

Given the nature of the material, the corpus is unbalanced and heterogeneous. We could have tried to make the corpus more balanced and/or homogeneous in various ways, and indeed our original intention had been to be more selective with respect to the letters included in the corpus. However, in addition to the practical difficulties involved in selection, we felt that, on balance, this would have had negative effects on the value of the corpus in view of the range of purposes we had in mind for it.

Selection of material (or more specifically, *exclusion* of letters) on the grounds of linguistic value soon turned out to be far from straightforward. The temptation would be to include letters more readily where there was any evidence of non-standard usage or anything else that caught our attention, which would have given a misleading impression of the language by making it look less standard and/or more unlike present-day usage than it actually was. From a more practical perspective, deciphering the letters could be at least as time-consuming as the actual transcription, especially where there was only a small amount of material available for a particular author so that there was little opportunity to become familiar with the handwriting. In other words, selection would have taken up a significant amount of time (without visible results where letters were excluded). Moreover, given that we hoped that the corpus would prove useful to non-linguists, using linguistically-based selection criteria might detract from its value for them. So in practice, the policy adopted was to include letters unless they were both very brief and highly formulaic, and thus unlikely to be of use to anyone.

Our own particular goals would have favoured the inclusion of personal letters, since they are the most likely to exhibit informal language. However, there were few letters which could be described as being of a (purely or even predominantly) personal nature. Most were of a 'business' nature, yet many of these seemed quite informal in tone, and they often did not conform completely to standard language norms. (Generally speaking, we found non-standard features to be more frequent and widespread than we had expected them to be in the late eighteenth century.) Moreover, the dividing line between business and personal letters turned out to be very fuzzy; in practice, it was easily and frequently crossed. Since the material seemed valuable for our purposes regardless of the precise nature of the letter, we made no attempt to select (or even distinguish) on this basis. This again had the added benefit that it was more likely to cater for the needs of any historians who might be interested in the corpus.

Figure 10.3 is a short letter illustrating the easy transition from business to personal matters and from formal to informal style, and presented in its HTML version (apart from colour coding; see the Appendix for coding conventions).

Again, for interest we show the original (Figure 10.4).

The corpus makes no attempt to achieve a balance between the contributions of different authors. We could have simply excluded authors with little material to their names, but such authors were more likely to fall into the category of relatively inexperienced writers exhibiting a higher degree of non-standard usage. Conversely, we also considered imposing an *upper* limit on the amount of material from any one author where a large set of letters was concerned, to avoid over-representation of the language of particular individuals. However, we felt that such cases were too valuable, and could usefully act as subsections of the corpus. They allow researchers interested in linguistic aspects to concentrate on individual usage. In addition, these letters would tend to be linked in terms of content, so including all of them gives historians access to as much material as is available in this part of the archive.

We also decided not to impose any restrictions on the provenance of the letters. Aside from the issue of whether doing so might have led to a misrepresentation of the range of Orford's dealings, there were practical problems involved. First, not all letters give an indication of where they were written. Second, and more importantly, the place where letters were written and/or where the author lived is not necessarily the same as that where they grew up. There are a number of cases where it is clear that an author who is not based in the North-west of England nevertheless has family living there and/or has previously lived in that area. Conversely, it is entirely possible that some of the people writing

author DICKENSON JOHN
1780
M^{r}. Orford
Lyme
new page
Taxal Thurs: 2^{d} Nov^{r}.
[different hand:] 1780

D^{r} %Sir!
An old Woman dyed Yesterday, who was
a Life in a Lease, and by whose Death an Estate descends
to me. Her Brother, (who is to be sure a very honest man)
took her to live with him a few Years ago, & then sold what
little property she had,wch. he did to prevent my having
an Harriot, whenever she dyed, as he knew J was entitled
to the best Good. Pray am J to be fobb'd off with
an old dirty Red Petty Coat, or am J to have Recourse
to the Tenant who occupys the Premises.? Her Brother
likewise intends to have the whole of this Years Rent, &
only leave me the winter Pasture.
J shall be much obliged to you for yor. friendly advice,
how J am to act in this Affair, — . J am, Sir
Your obed^{t} hble%Servt.
John Dickenson
My Son waites upon You $^{\text{^with this^}}$ pray
don't give him too' much Lyme Beer
& do you see that he does not bring
Johnson along with him.

(A *heroit* or *harriot* is a feudal payment due to a lord on the death of a tenant. LvB/DD)

Figure 10.3 A letter from John Dickenson (HTML version)

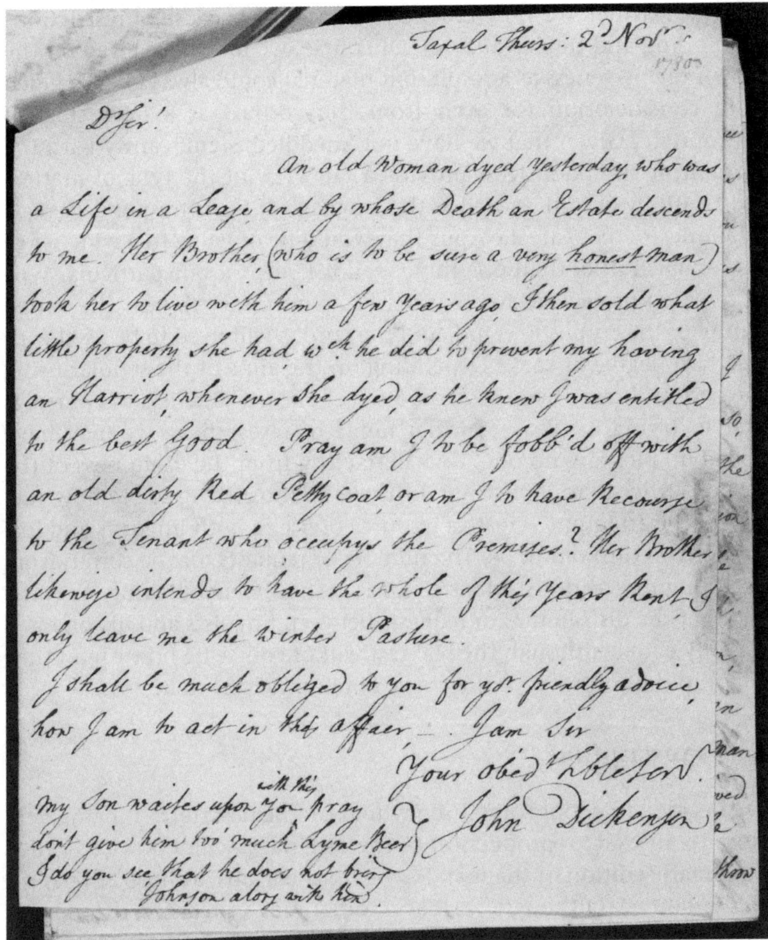

Taxal Thurs: 2d Novr:
1780

Dr Sir!

An old Woman dyed Yesterday who was a Life in a Lease and by whose Death an Estate descends to me. Her Brother (who is to be sure a very honest man) took her to live with him a few Years ago & then sold what little property she had wch he did to prevent my having an Harriot, whenever she dyed, as he knew I was entitled to the best Good. Pray am I to be fobb'd off with an old dirty Red Petty Coat, or am I to have Recourse to the Tenant who occupys the Premises? Her Brother likewise intends to have the whole of this Years Rent & only leave me the winter Pasture.

I shall be much obliged to you for yr. friendly advice how I am to act in this affair. I am Sir

Your obedt. Servt.

John Dickenson

My Son waites upon You with this pray don't give him too much Lyme Beer & do you see that he does not bring Johnson along with him.

Reproduced by courtesy of the University Librarian and Director, John Rylands University Library, University of Manchester.

Figure 10.4 A letter from John Dickenson (original)

from somewhere in the North-west were not actually from the area originally. Exclusion of letters written outside the area would have meant leaving out some valuable material, and it would not have dealt with the real issue. A coherent selection policy in this respect would have involved background research on individuals, which was impractical.

The result of this is that nearly all material present in this subsection of the archive has been included in the corpus (always excepting the final part, which we were unable to transcribe because of restrictions on funding and time available). Of course, we may have erred on the side of inclusiveness as a result, but material could always be excluded from consideration (or even from the corpus) at a later stage if appropriate. Given that we have not 'meddled' significantly with the content, it should at least provide a fair view of the type of matters dealt with by Orford, as well as the language of his correspondents.

Our desire to create a corpus that would be of value to a wide set of researchers rather than one that is tailor-made for one particular type of research project means that it will be necessary to bear the varied nature of the corpus in mind, and the corpus will need to be used with a certain degree of care.[3] Depending on the aims of the scholar using the corpus, it may be necessary to select part(s). The risk, of course, is that in trying to please a wider range of researchers, we may have ended up pleasing no one, thus detracting from the usefulness of the corpus rather than increasing it. It will be interesting to see how successful the attempt to create a resource of use to both linguists and historians will turn out to be. The number of requests for the corpus from both linguists and historians so far is certainly encouraging, as is the fact that the distribution of requests between linguists and historians is roughly equal, although the real test will of course be how useful they will find the corpus once they have obtained access to it.

3 Transcription

We decided to adopt something which can be described as being very close to an exact reproduction of the original documents: a so-called diplomatic edition of the text. For obvious reasons, as little as possible was modified (although we have sometimes opted for the nearest present-day equivalent of punctuation, for example, for practical reasons). Lineation has been preserved, mainly because it was very easy to do and would make it easy to find specific parts if anyone wishes to go back to the original text, and in the same spirit, page breaks were marked. However, words hyphenated across line breaks were silently recombined, and we made no attempt to reproduce any other aspect of layout faithfully, except that the web version goes some way towards representing the disposition of tabular material.

Since we were dealing with unedited material, the transcription process was far from straightforward. The documents could be difficult to read in places, some characters could be difficult to distinguish from one another in the handwriting of particular authors, capitalization (or lack of it) could be difficult to determine, and so on. We have dealt with such matters as best we could, including explicit marking of readings that we felt to be tentative where the identity of the letter-form was in doubt. One particular and frequent area of doubt was not so marked, however: where the only uncertainty was between upper- and lower-case forms of a letter. We decided that marking such readings as conjectural was potentially misleading and would have cluttered the text to little purpose; instead we have simply tried to be as consistent in our transcription practice as we could be. Proofreading after transcription was essential, of course. Inevitably, there will be some errors, but we have done our best to keep these to a minimum. Some inconsistency is likewise impossible to avoid altogether (especially between the two transcribers involved, but also for individual transcribers), although naturally we have tried to limit it as much as we could.

We have included in the corpus nearly all the information contained in the letters. The only things normally omitted were calculations and other scribbles that seemed unrelated to the content of the letter, and anything (for example, drawn plans) that could not be transcribed using text, although even then we generally note such omissions. Where possible, we marked in-text corrections and deletions and noted illegible material. The reasoning was that we could not be certain of what information individual researchers were going to need, and that it was easier and less time-consuming to include it now than have to go back to the originals at a later stage.

The lack of normalization of spelling and the inclusion of detailed information, especially the use of in-text comments, means that users of the corpus have a version of the text that allows them to reconstruct most properties of the original letters. While this has obvious advantages, the disadvantage is that it hampers text searches, since words may be spelled in various ways and phrases may be broken up by in-text comments. The latter problem could be solved by the user of the corpus if required: it should be relatively easy to produce a version of the corpus without comments, although it would need to be used side by side with the original version of the corpus to make sure that any comments set aside are in fact irrelevant to the data found. There is, however, no easy solution to the other problem: lemmatization or producing a parallel normalized version are the obvious possibilities, but either would be time-consuming. We have gone a small way towards facilitating normalization by transcribing what we call 'deviant word division', such as <a fore> for <afore>, as <a_fore>, and 'deviant word joining', such as in <Iam> for <I am>, as <I %am>.

4 Coding

The coding of the corpus (especially for the plain text version) is largely based on that used in the Helsinki Corpus, mainly for practical reasons. Almost anyone using historical corpora of English will be familiar with that particular corpus and its coding conventions (Kytö, 1993). It makes an ASCII version of the corpus possible (still required for certain types of text retrieval software, and compatible with virtually all types), while allowing additional information to be included. In a few cases we have adapted the codes or added new ones, such as a code for tentative readings. We also allowed the use of extended ASCII (the upper 128 symbols) where this was of use, for example for <½ ¼ £>, which the Helsinki compilers, working with DOS in the 1980s and 1990s, avoided.[4]

The extent of text-level coding was radically reduced from what the Helsinki Corpus contains. While it would be desirable to add more information at this level, it would have taken up a significant portion of the time available to do the necessary background research on the individual authors. In some cases information was obvious from the letters themselves, but where it was not, it would often have been difficult, if not impossible, to find out.

We decided to provide the corpus initially in two versions. One was as a single text file (approximately 1.6 MB), suitable for use in concor-

To A % Pair of Superfind 4 (*) d Hose / forgot the price given but think	3/6
To Attending Wm Frith and Servering with a written notice to Quit his Liverhood	6/8
To lames Miller and P Pott to Bear witness that the Said notice was Properly Served Tow Glassed Gim	0.0.3
To Wm Frith to heal his wounds Ginn	0 ½
& to writeing this Acctd	0 0
	£10:5 ½

Figure 10.5 Part of a letter from J. Hancock (HTML version)

dancing programs. The other is designed for ease of reading in a web browser, and uses the standard rendering of HTML to convey superscript, interlineations, underlining, strike-through and so on, with a larger font size to signal the author at the start of a letter. It also employs different colours as a quick visual clue to editorial decisions, following the general convention that red signifies conjectural, crossed-out or illegible text, while blue indicates editorial material. For some of the tabular material, HTML is an improvement over plain text. Figure 10.5 is part of a letter from J. Hancock in 1788 which throws interesting light on the expenses attendant on the serving of a writ by a 'Sherriffs offecer'.

Our attempt to preserve the tabular form may be compared with the original, displayed in Figure 10.6.

Another advantage of the HTML version is line length, since various in-line comments are obviated. (Remember that we are committed to preserving original manuscript lineation.) Compare what appears in the text version, all on one line, with its HTML equivalent. Figure 10.7 shows the original opening of a letter by Shaw Allanson in 1789.

For our edited illustration (Figure 10.8), hard line breaks in both files are represented by <¶>, and colours are removed from the HTML version.

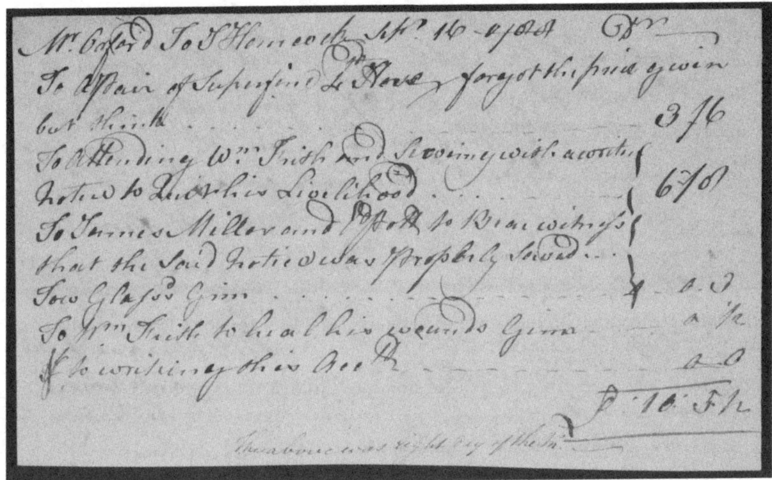

Mr Oxford To J Hancock Sepr 16 1788 Dr
To a Pair of Superfine Lr Hose forgot the price given
but think ... 3/6
To Attending Wm Frith and Serving with a writing
Notice to Quit his Livelihood ... 6/8
To James Miller and Assist to Bear witness
that the said Notice was properly served
Two Glasses Gin ... 0.3
To Wm Frith to heal his wounds Gin ... 0.1½
For writing this Acct ... [illegible]
£0.10.7½

Reproduced by courtesy of the University Librarian and Director, John Rylands University Library, University of Manchester.

Figure 10.6 Part of a letter from J. Hancock (original)

Sr
Yours I Recd yesterday and as such have
been with Mr Rigby this morng and has
given him 5£..5..6 which will make up he
thinks for Saturday next if that does not
Come from Grosppenhall this week its may
do something towards the reckoning following
he had of me last reckoning 10..10..0 as he
was short of paying the men about that
Sum, we have at Edgegreen Colliery
Coal & Coaks about 280 whs the Carts you
See going to their on your return was the
throngest day we have had of Carting as
the roads was not fit for carting till monday
before that; we have only a part of the Carts
as they sell their Coals at bottom of the green
at 2½ ℔ bast and will uphold them 9 score
each basket so they are sure to have sale
for all they can get; and they tell me their
Slag road will be finished down the green
in a few days so they will have a winter
road for there Coals, they hire all the Carts
they can to get its forward Golborn people
go very badly on with theirs, a great many
Golborn Carts assists Crouchley with his road
and lets their own Stand for want of Carts
Turn over

Figure 10.7 The opening of a letter by Shaw Allanson (original)

To avoid excessively long downloads, the HTML version comes as a sequence of three files (909, 883 and 804 KB), plus a synopsis of the coding conventions (6 KB) which is given here as an Appendix. The four files are notionally numbered as 1, 2, 3 and 0 (coding conven-

<u>Text version</u>

Yours I Rec'd yesterday [^"{day}" added above the line, and subsequently crossed out^] and as such have¶
been with M=r=Rigby this morn=g=and has¶
given him 34=£=..3=s=..6=d=

<u>HTML version</u>

Yours I Rec'd yesterday $^{\wedge day \wedge}$ andas such have¶
been with Mr Rigby this morn^{g} and has¶
given him 34$^{£}$..3^{s}..6^{d}

Figure 10.8 The opening of a letter by Shaw Allanson (plain text and HTML versions)

tions), with links at the head and foot of each web page to allow a reader to move easily back and forth through the set. Conversion was an extremely time-consuming business. Some of the decisions may not have been optimal. For example, a long dash is coded as the string <—> rather than simply as <—> or <–>, so that the HTML version would look unnecessarily opaque if loaded direct into a concordancer. On the other hand, the frequent changes of font colour, often within a word, make the HTML version unsuitable for searching anyway, unless the search engine can ignore HTML tags. (The simple search functions within commonly used browsers do indeed ignore attributes like font colour and superscript.)

Lou Burnard of the Oxford Text Archive has raised with us the possibility of a conversion to XML (Extensible Markup Language), which would allow a more structured and standardized coding of textual features. Indeed, at the workshop on which these volumes are based there was some discussion of the merits of TEI-conformant coding (Text Encoding Initiative), of which XML is an exemplar. We were not sufficiently convinced of the utility or practicality of XML to attempt it ourselves for the original release of the corpus, since XML-aware readers and editors are not yet sufficiently widely available: without such a reader, XML tags would intrude on the displayed text and interfere with searches. However, a conversion may follow eventually (see also note 4 on Unicode).

What is lacking altogether is grammatical coding, whether word-class tagging or sentence parsing. As linguists we would certainly have welcomed a corpus equipped with such tools, however problematic a particular analysis might have been, but our resources simply did not run to this.

5 Conclusion

We have not yet had much information on the purposes to which others are putting the corpus, apart from the pleasing discovery in it of the earliest known modern uses of the elliptical adverb or interjection *please* without following *to*-infinitive (Tieken-Boon van Ostade and Faya, 2004): 'You'l please return the apointment that I may destroy it' (I. Hodson, 23 June 1775); '(Please see over)' (James Hammond, 27 June 1778); and 'Please Remembar mee to my Ant and All my Cosins and My Uncall Iohn' (John Mercer, 12 April 1789). Not only do these examples antedate *OED* by over a century (s.v. *please* v. 6c), they may support a different syntactic origin from that proposed by *OED*. Since we ourselves had not at the time of writing used the corpus for linguistic investigation, our review of its utility and its limitations is necessarily provisional. A recurrent theme in this chapter, as in the team's discussions while we were working on the corpus, was the difficult choice between size of corpus and richness of annotation. Some of the desiderata of annotation or coding were not really consistent with each other, while others would have required a flow chart of stages, each a prerequisite for the next. For example, a version of the text with normalized spelling would certainly have been a helpful, though not perhaps an essential, preliminary to tagging, and certainly to production of parallel aligned texts. On balance, though, it seemed best to concentrate our efforts on the original text.

Appendix: coding conventions

The following material forms the 'zeroth' of the four pages which make up the web version of the corpus. The files are not publicly available online, as we ask interested scholars to submit an access request form before providing the information needed to access or download them. However, the file of coding conventions reproduced here in monochrome will gladly be emailed without formality to any interested scholar.

The English language of the north-west in the late Modern English period: A Corpus of late 18c Prose, coding conventions

For conditions of use see 'readme.txt'. If unavailable, please get and return access request form.

0 | *1* | *2* | *3*

The corpus is available as a single text file, **orford.txt** [1.6 MB] or as three linked HTML files, **orford1.htm, orford2.htm** and **orford3.htm** [approx. 800–910 KB each]. (An XML version may be on the way.) The text version is coded in a similar way to the Helsinki Corpus, whereas the HTML version aims for greater readability, following the general convention that red signifies conjectural, crossed-out or illegible text, while blue indicates editorial material.[5]

Coding conventions

meaning	**text version**	**HTML version**
writer's name	<A XXXX>	**author XXXX**
date (year)	<O nnnn>	**nnnn**
new page	<P>	*new page*
new page with indication to turn from foot of previous page	<P Turn over/turn/ Please to turn>	*new page* Turn over
new page with word repeated at foot of previous page	<P xxxx>	*new page* xxxx
underline	(_xxxx_)	XXXX
superscript	yy=xxxx=yy	yy^{XXXX}yy
subscript	yy=xxxx=yy (+ note indicating **sub**script)	yy$_{XXXX}$yy
interlineation	yy^xxxx^yy	yy$^{\wedge XXXX \wedge}$yy
deviant word division e.g. "a fore" for "afore"	a%fore	a_fore

meaning	**text version**	**HTML version**
deviant word joining e.g. "Iam" for "I am"	I %am	I %am
abbreviation indicated by author	~	~
conjectural reading	{xxxx}	xxxx
crossing out or rubbing out	[^ "XXXX" crossed/ rubbed out^]	~~XXXX~~
crossing out or rubbing out with some part uncertain	[^ "YYXXXXYY" crossed/ rubbed out?^] or [^ "YY{XXXX}YY" crossed/ rubbed out^]	~~YY{XXXX}YY~~ or ~~YYXXXXYY~~
illegible (number of asterisks indicates approx number of letters)	{**}	{**}
illegible (see below)	{*...}	{*...}
our comment	[^xxxx^]	[xxxx]

For illegible text the number of asterisks estimates number of letters where possible; otherwise {*...} is used. If there is a specific cause for the illegibility, this is specified in a comment.

The HTML version does not distinguish crossing out from rubbing out, and for readability it ignores any uncertainty in the words crossed or rubbed out. In such cases the text version preserves more detailed information. The comment [corrected] indicates a correction made in the original letter by the author. It is often difficult to determine whether a letter-form is upper or lower case though the letter itself is not in doubt: we have not marked such readings as tentative and have merely tried to be reasonably consistent. You will therefore need to consult the original documents if capitalization is of particular importance to you.

Hyphenation at the end of a line has not been preserved and the whole of the word has been put at the end of the first line, unless there is a reasonable chance that the hyphen belongs to the word form. Otherwise, lineation has been preserved, except in some cases where the text runs parallel. The remainder of the layout has largely been ignored.

Accounts or calculations — the terms are used interchangeably — are sometimes omitted, but if so, this is noted in the text. London postmarks are not generally noted.

0 | *1* | *2* | *3*

Notes

1. Lyme Hall is a fine, originally Tudor house, home to the Legh family for 600 years, now run by the National Trust (http://www.nationaltrust.org.uk/). The John Rylands University Library gives the following information on the Legh of Lyme Muniments on its Special Collections website (http://rylib web.man.ac.uk/data2/spcoll/legh/): 'Extensive family papers of the Leghs of Lyme Park, Cheshire. These comprise muniments of title, including large numbers of medieval deeds and charters, 17th- and 18th-century manorial court records, original architect's plans of Lyme Hall, surveys, wills, abstracts of title, estate correspondence, accounts and other papers. The muniments relate to the Lancashire estates (the manors of Newton and Golborne, and property in Newton-le-Willows, Golborne, Lowton, Haydock, Ashton-in-Makerfield, Ince-in-Makerfield, Warrington, Burtonwood, Poulton and Fearnhead, Bold, Pemberton and Dalton), and the Cheshire estates (with property in Lyme Handley, Disley, Pott Shrigley, Macclesfield, Grappenhall, Norbury, Marple, and Broomedge and Heatley in Lymm).

   There is an extensive and important selection of personal correspondence, dating from the 16th century onwards, including correspondence with members of the Gerard, Egerton and Chicheley families, with much material on 18th-century northern politics.'
2. Another filler of this gap is CONCE, the Corpus of Nineteenth-Century English (Kytö and Rissanen, 1999, p. 181). Since we conceived our corpus, other corpora of Late Modern English have been announced, including the Corpus of Late Modern English Texts (De Smet, in press) and Fitzmaurice (this volume).
3. Compare here the NECTE (http://www.ncl.ac.uk/NECTE: Allen *et al.*, this volume) and SCOTS (http://www.scottishcorpus.ac.uk/: Anderson *et al.*, volume 1) projects, which have also been compiled with a wide range of users in mind.
4. At the workshop at Sociolinguistics Symposium 15 on which the present volumes are based, Wolfgang Schmidle suggested the use of Unicode character encoding, although Ylva Berglund of the Oxford Text Archive felt that the time was not yet ripe. In principle, the universal, device-independent nature of Unicode and the wealth of characters available would both be of obvious advantage. On the other hand, plain text is more compact and (for the time being) more widely usable, and we chose the more conservative option in producing and releasing the corpus. The decision is not irrevocable, however.
5. Colours have of course been lost in this printout.

References

Anderson, Jean, Dave Beavan and Christian Kay. 2006. 'SCOTS: Scottish Corpus of Texts and Speech'. *Creating and Digitizing Language Corpora: Synchronic Databases (Volume 1)*, ed. by Joan C. Beal, Karen P. Corrigan and Hermann Moisl, pp. 17–34. Basingstoke: Palgrave Macmillan.

Denison, D. 1998. 'Syntax'. *The Cambridge History of the English Language*, 4, 1776–1997, ed. by S. Romaine, pp. 92–329. Cambridge: Cambridge University Press.

De Smet, H. (in press). 'A corpus of late Modern English texts'. *ICAME*.

Elspaß, S. 2002. 'Standard German in the 19th century? (Counter-) evidence from the private correspondence of "ordinary people"'. *Standardization: Studies from the Germanic Languages* (Current Issues in Linguistic Theory, 235), ed. by A. R. Linn and N. McLelland, pp. 43–65. Amsterdam and Philadelphia: John Benjamins.

Elspaß, S. 2004. 'A view "from below": historical sociolinguistics and the study of present-day language change'. Paper due to be presented at Sociolinguistics Symposium 15, Newcastle upon Tyne, April 2004.

Fairman, T. 2000. 'English pauper letters 1800–34, and the English language'. *Letter Writing as a Social Practice*, ed. by D. Barton, and N. Hall, pp. 63–82. Amsterdam and Philadelphia: John Benjamins.

Kytö, M. 1993. *Manual to the Diachronic Part of the Helsinki Corpus of English Texts: Coding Conventions and Lists of Source Texts*, 2nd edn. Helsinki: Helsinki University Press for Department of English, University of Helsinki.

Kytö, M. and M. Rissanen. 1999. 'English historical corpora: report on developments in 1998'. *ICAME*, 23:175–88.

Tieken-Boon van Ostade, I. and F. Faya. 2004. 'Saying "Please!" in eighteenth and nineteenth-century English'. Paper presented at Second International Conference on the English Language in the Late Modern Period 1700–1900, Vigo, November 2004.

Vandenbussche, W. 2002. 'Dutch orthography in lower, middle and upper class documents in 19th-century Flanders'. *Standardization: Studies from the Germanic Languages* (Current Issues in Linguistic Theory, 235), ed. by A. R. Linn and N. McLelland, pp. 27–42. Amsterdam and Philadelphia: John Benjamins.

Websites

John Rylands University Library: Legh of Lyme Muniments: Special Collections website: http://rylibweb.man.ac.uk/data2/spcoll/legh/

National Trust: http://www.nationaltrust.org.uk/

NECTE: http://www.ncl.ac.uk/NECTE

OED Online: http://dictionary.oed.com/

SCOTS Project: http://www.scottishcorpus.ac.uk/

Index